101 ARENA EXERCISES

A RINGSIDE GUIDE FOR HORSE & RIDER

★

CHERRY HILL

STOREY
BOOKS

W9-CCJ-071

*The mission of Storey Communications is to serve our customers by publishing practical information
that encourages personal independence in harmony with the environment.
We seek to do this in a positive atmosphere that promotes editorial quality, team spirit, and profitability.*

Edited by Amanda R. Haar and Elizabeth McHale
Cover design by Cindy McFarland and Eugenie Seidenberg Delaney
Cover illustration and line drawings designed by Cherry Hill and drawn by Peggy Judy
Text design and production by Eugenie Seidenberg Delaney

Copyright © 1995 Cherry Hill

All rights reserved. No part of this book may be reproduced withoutwritten permission from the publisher, except
by a reviewer who may quote brief passages or reproduce illustrations in a review with appropriate credits;
nor may any part of this book be reproduced, stored in a retrieval system, or transmitted in any form or by any
means — electronic, mechanical, photocopying, recording, or other — without written permission from the publisher.

The information in this book is true and complete to the best of our knowledge. All recommendations are made
without guarantee on the part of the author or Storey Books. The author and publisher disclaim any liability in
connection with the use of this information. For additional information please contact
Storey Books, Schoolhouse Road, Pownal, Vermont 05261.

Storey Books are available for special premium and promotional uses and for customized editions.
For further information, please call Storey's Custom Publishing Department at 1-800-793-9396.

Printed in Canada by Transcontinental Printing
15 14 13 12 11 10

Library of Congress Cataloging-in-Publication Data

Hill, Cherry, 1947–
      101 arena exercises : a ringside guide for horse & rider / Cherry Hill.
              p.   cm.

      ISBN 0-88266-316-X (pb - comb binding)
        1. Horsemanship — Study and teaching. 2. Horsemanship. I. Title.
SF310.5.H55 1995
798.2'3'076 — dc20   95-12930
                            CIP

101 Exercises List

Section 3: CIRCLES

Section 5: MINI-PATTERNS

SUGGESTED READING

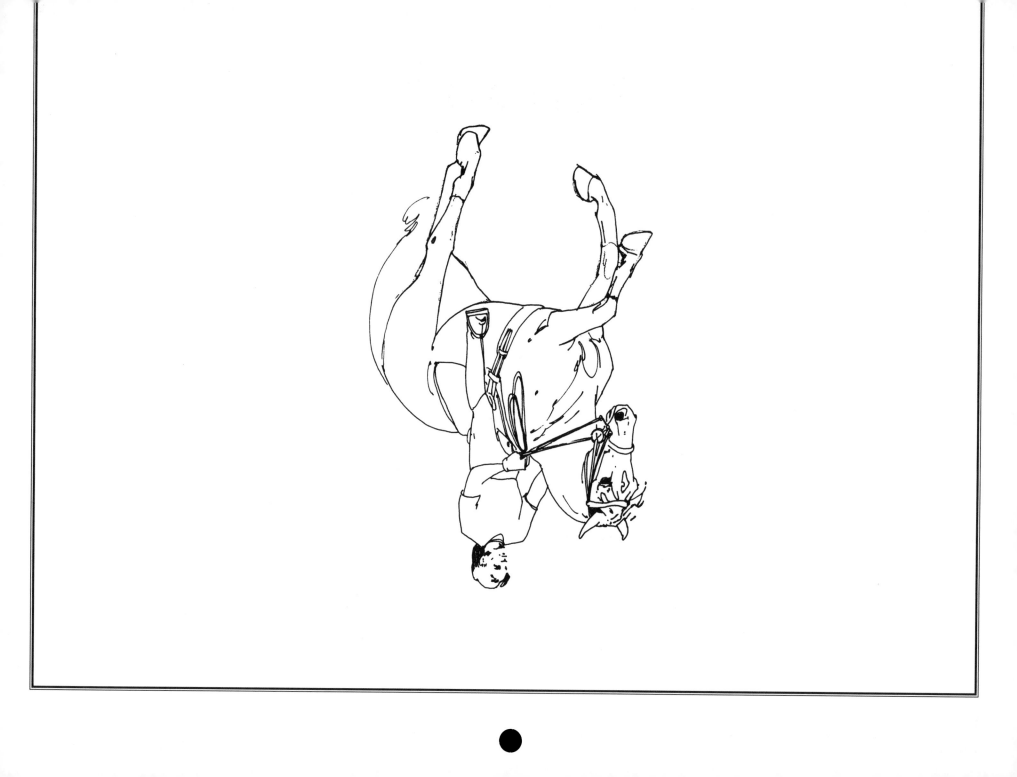

Foreword

As an instructor, trainer, and coach of amateur and youth riders, I am always looking for helpful materials. Thank you, Cherry Hill, for your background as an instructor, as well as for your experience as a horsewoman!

Good knowledge of horse training is very hard to find. Cherry Hill demonstrates both the understanding and experience needed to produce a book with in-depth, correct procedures.

For riding instructors, this book is a dream come true. Instructors will find these exercises will make day-to-day lesson plans a breeze.

The Western rider and trainer will find wonderful suppling exercises as well as preparatory work for turns and lead changes.

The dressage rider will find a training program already set up. The progression is continuous and thoughtful.

For the horse trainer, this book is ideal. It contains a useful system to follow, from basic to complicated maneuvers. The illustrations are very well done and correct. Cherry Hill's style is enjoyable, and she explains each exercise thoroughly.

A good horseman is a good horseman whether performing Western riding, reining, Western or English equitation, dressage, or hunt seat. All will benefit from this book, which ties together many "loose ends" for all riding disciplines.

This book is perfect for anyone who is seeking to improve their riding skills or their horse's performance. Enjoy . . .

Carla Wennberg

Carla Wennberg is an American Quarter Horse Association (AQHA) World Championship rider and international AQHA and National Reining Horse Association judge. She was a college equine science program instructor for ten years and has trained and coached amateur and youth riders in state and national competitions. Carla is the Director of Reining for the United States Equestrian Team.

Introduction

Arena exercises are a cross between gymnastics, meditation, and geometry. They are essential keys for discovering many important principles about training and riding.

The exercises in this book are organized by groups and presented in their approximate order of difficulty. However, depending on your horse's level and style of training and his natural abilities and inherent problems, you might find some of the elementary exercises challenging and some of the advanced exercises easy.

*Remember: The **quality** of the performance is **much more important** than just getting through the exercise!*

I cannot stress this enough. Take your time and do the simple things well before you tackle more complex maneuvers and patterns. First, study the exercises in your favorite chair and ride them in your mind before you head out to the arena. That way you will reap the great benefits of pre-performance visualization. Read a good book on riding to be sure you are riding correctly. Refer to the appendix for some suggestions.

HOW CAN YOU TELL IF THE WORK IS CORRECT?

1. Work regularly with a qualified instructor. (See the appendix for books on how to select and work with an instructor.)

Can I tell when my horse is performing a four-beat lope or canter?

Can I tell when my horse is walking in front and trotting behind?

Can I tell when my horse is performing a pacey walk?

In a few of the early exercises, I have diagrammed the exercises in both directions. Be sure that you eventually perform *every* exercise in *both* directions.

Whenever possible, ride off the rail so your horse is being held in position by your aids, not by the rail. The true test of your training will come when you perform these exercises in an unenclosed flat spot in your pasture!

Although it might seem like some exercises are more appropriate for a reining horse and others for an upper level dressage horse, *all* horses can benefit from *all* of the exercises. The dressage horse that is "bound up" can be loosened up by some of the traditional Western-style exercises. And the Western horse that is a bit of a runaway can benefit from the proper form and collection inherent in dressage exercises. So, I invite you to experiment and improvise.

How many times should you repeat an exercise? This can vary from once or twice to infinity! With lead changes, backing, pirouettes, and so on, repetition often causes boredom and invites problems. Such maneuvers are best saved for the end of your arena ride when the horse is thoroughly

2. Ask a qualified person to stand on the ground, observe your exercises, and report to you what he or she sees. For example, where the right hind was during a particular movement.

3. Have someone record your exercises on videotape. Then watch the tape carefully using slow motion and freeze frame.

4. As you ride, watch yourself and your horse in large mirrors on the wall.

5. Without moving your head, glance down at your horse's shoulders, neck, poll, and eye during different maneuvers to determine if he is correct up front.

6. Ultimately, the key is to develop a *feel* for when things are going right and when they are going wrong by utilizing all of the above feedback techniques. Answer the following by feeling, not looking:

   Is there appropriate left to right balance on my seat bones? Can I feel them both?

   Can I feel even contact on both reins?

   Is the front to rear balance acceptable or is the horse heavy on the forehand, croup up, back hollow?

   Is the rhythm regular or does the horse speed up, slow down, or break gait?

   Is my horse relaxed or is his back tense?

   Is he on the bit or above or behind it?

   Am I posting on the correct diagonal?

   Is my horse cantering on the correct lead?

   Can I tell when his inside hind leg is about to land?

warmed up and prepared. Then you can ask for a few repetitions of these more advanced maneuvers. Transitions, circles, and shoulder in, however, are the mainstay of your horse's arena program and should be repeated often.

WHAT DO YOU DO WHEN THINGS GO WRONG?

1. Review each component of an exercise.

2. You might need to return to some very basic exercises to establish forward movement, acceptance of contact, or response to sideways driving aids. Returning to simple circle work will often improve straightness and subsequently improve lateral work and collection.

3. Ride an exercise that the horse does very well, such as the walk-trot-walk transition. Work on purity and form. Don't think you are wasting your time. I have seen $150-an-hour instructors work on walk-trot transitions with Grand Prix riders!

4. Perform a simpler version of the exercise. If it is a canter exercise, try it at a walk or trot first. In some cases, I have offered variations, but you will be able to create many of your own.

5. Perform the exercise in the opposite direction. Sometimes, because of an inherent stiffness or crookedness in a horse, you will have difficulty with an exercise to the left but no problems to the right! Capitalize on this by refining your skills and the application of your aids in the "good" direction and then return to the "hard" direction with a renewed sense of what needs to be done. I often find that doing work to the right improves work to the left.

TERMS USED IN RIDING IN AN ARENA

Short end or *far end:* end of the arena across from the gate or across from the starting point of most exercises.

Gate end: the short end of the arena with the gate, or the end used as the starting point for most of the exercises.

Up the long side: from the gate end to the far short end.

Down the long side: from the far short end to the gate end.

(Up or down the) Center line: from the midpoint of one short end of the arena to the midpoint of the other short end.

(Up or down the) Quarter line: from one short end to the other on a line halfway between the rail and the center line.

Across the arena or *across the school:* from the midpoint of one long side to the midpoint of the other long side.

Across the long diagonal: (see Exercise #32).

Across the short diagonal: (see Exercise #33).

Track right: ride along the rail, making right turns. This can be confusing in a show or lesson when you're told to come in the gate and track right and you have to turn left to do so (as in the arena pictured in this book).

Track left: ride along the rail, making left turns.

Stride: one complete revolution of the horse's legs in the footfall pattern of the gait in which he is performing (see Gaits).

Step: one beat in a gait. There are several steps in each stride. A step may involve more than one leg (see Gaits).

Inside: generally refers to the inside of the bend of the horse's body, which is also usually the inside of the arena. For example, when tracking to the right with normal bend, the inside is the right — the side toward the inside of the arena. However, when a horse is counter-bent or performing a counter-canter, the inside aids might be on the outside of the arena. For example, if tracking right on the left lead performing a counter-canter, the inside aids would be the left aids, yet they would be located on the outside (rail) of the arena.

Outside: generally refers to the outside of the bend of the horse's body, which is also usually the outside of the arena. See above.

SUGGESTIONS FOR MEASURING YOUR FIGURES

★ Begin by measuring your arena.

★ If you are a dressage rider, setting up a small or large dressage ring with properly positioned letters will help you determine the size of figures.

★ For nondressage arenas, make a mark or use ribbon or flagging tape on the arena rail every ten feet to help you gauge the size of your figures. Your starting point can be one end of a rail or the middle of that rail.

★ Walk in a normal stride and measure your own stride. Two steps usually equal five feet. Use this when placing cones as markers for circles or other maneuvers.

★ Use hydrated lime sprinkled on the ground for a temporary marker.

DIMENSIONS USED IN PREPARING ARENA MAPS

The arena used in the maps is 200 feet by 120 feet.

FIGURE	CIRCUMFERENCE IN FEET	DIAMETER IN METERS	DIAMETER IN FEET
Circle, large	207	20	66
Circle, med.	104	10	33
Circle, small	63	6	20

	LENGTH IN METERS	LENGTH IN FEET
Long side	60	200
Short end	36	120
Long Diagonal	56	180

STRIDE NOTES

It takes 26 strides to trot a 20-meter circle;
13 strides to trot a 10-meter circle.

To ride 100 feet down the long side, it takes:

★ 18 strides at a working walk.

★ 12–13 strides at a working trot.

★ 10 strides at an extended trot.

★ 12–13 strides at a working canter.

Horses in the arena maps in this book are not necessarily drawn to scale for all exercises. In some cases they were made larger or smaller for clarity.

METRIC EQUIVALENTS

METERS	FEET
6	20
8	26.5
10	33
20	66
40	132
60	198

AVERAGE LENGTH OF STRIDE AT VARIOUS GAITS

Note: Horses vary greatly in their stride lengths. Use the following information as a guideline.

GAIT	LENGTH OF STRIDE IN FEET
Working walk	5.5
Collected walk	5.0
Extended walk	6.0
Working trot	8.0 +
Collected trot	7.0
Extended trot	10.0
Working canter	10.0
Collected canter	8.0
Extended canter	12.0

ARENA MAP INFORMATION

working walk . . . .

collected walk ....

extended walk . . . .

working trot - - - - - - - - - - - -

collected trot - - - - - - - - - - - - - -

extended trot ____ _____ ____ ____

canter _____

back ∿∿∿∿∿

halt **X**

half halt ∞

transition within a gait _____ | _____

● Start

Half halts should be used before, during, and after every transition; before, during, and after every corner; periodically throughout any movement to re-balance the horse. Half halts are not indicated on the arena maps everywhere they should be used.

In order for the exercises to produce positive results, a horse must be ridden "on contact," "on the bit," "on the aids," "bridled up," or whatever term you are accustomed to hearing and using. In essence, these various ways of describing the communication between rider and horse mean that the horse moves forward from leg aids and accepts and responds willingly to pressures on his mouth via the bit and bridle. Refer to the books recommended in the appendix for a more thorough discussion of these principles.

SECTION 1

Gaits

A gait is any of the footfall patterns of a horse, such as a walk, trot, canter, or gallop. A gait is like a simple musical piece written in its own specific time. Every horse expresses each gait in his own particular tempo and style. Some horses have one or two gaits that do not have an even, precise rhythm. It is the goal of riding exercises to develop a regular rhythm in each gait and therefore to develop the purity of the gait.

A *working gait* is the ordinary gait of an average horse that is moving in balance and with a regular rhythm and average impulsion.

A *collected gait* is performed at the same tempo as the working gait but has a shorter, more elevated stride with a longer support phase, and therefore it covers less ground than a working gait.

An *extended gait* is performed at the same tempo as the working gait but has a longer stride with more reach and an increased period of suspension, and therefore it covers more ground than a working gait. A *lengthening* is a stage on the way to an extended gait.

At the Halt

HOW TO EVALUATE YOUR POSITION AT THE HALT

Note: In each question, the desirable is mentioned first.

★ Is your breathing deep and regular, or are you holding your breath?

★ Is there equal weight on both seat bones, or is it difficult to feel one of them? Are your seat bones in the deepest part of the saddle, or are you braced against the cantle?

★ Are your hip bones directly over your seat bones, or are they behind your seat bones in the "Cadillac" position?

★ Is your lower back relaxed, or is it braced and tense?

★ Is your upper body above your hips, or is it leaning extremely forward or backward?

★ Is there a straight line from your shoulder through your hip to your heel, or are your legs way in front of your body? Are you slumped forward or leaning back?

★ Are your shoulders back, or are they rounded forward?

★ Is your sternum lifted upward, or is it collapsed inward?

★ Are your shoulders level, or is one higher than the other?

★ Are your head and neck straight, or are they tilted to one side or rolling forward?

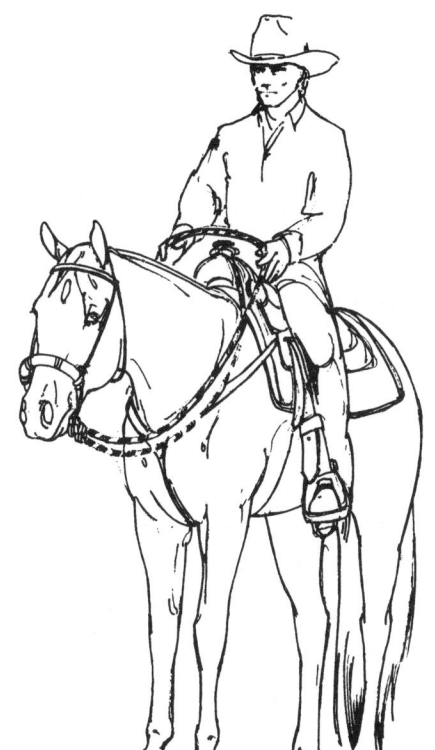

★ Are your eyes looking straight ahead, or are they looking down?

★ Are your thighs relaxed, or are they gripping or forcibly stretching?

★ Do you have appropriate lower leg contact, or are you holding your lower legs away from your horse?

★ Can you see just the toe of your boot when you glance down at your foot, or is most of your foot and part of your lower leg visible?

★ Is there equal weight in each of your stirrups?

★ Are your hands at an even, appropriate level? Is there a direct line from the bit to your elbows?

★ Is there even contact on the reins?

★ If your horse suddenly disappeared out from under you, would you topple over when you landed on the ground, or would you stand?

A horse stands square at the halt when he is allowed to position his legs comfortably underneath himself in accordance with his conformation.

DESCRIPTION

The halt should be square and balanced with the horse's legs under his body. The halt is a perfect time to check your position before you begin moving your horse.

It is a privilege to ride. It is a responsibility to ride correctly. Close your eyes. Do you feel balanced?

USE

The halt is necessary for training-level dressage and all Western competitions.

If your horse halts square, he will tend to move forward in balance.

CAUTION

A young horse might find it difficult to stand square and still under your weight and might move around trying to find a comfortable way to support your weight on his still undeveloped back. Sit quietly balanced, and gradually extend the period of time you require the young horse to stand square and still.

NOTE

Develop your own personal mental checklist so that when you first mount, you can evaluate and correct your basic position. Only then will you be able to proceed correctly with the exercises in this book.

Working Walk

DESCRIPTION

The walk is a four-beat gait that should have a clear, even rhythm as the feet land and take off in the following sequence: left hind, left front, right hind, right front. The walk has alternating lateral and triangular bases of support. At one moment, the horse's weight is borne by two left legs, then the right hind is added, forming a triangle of support. Later in the cycle, all weight is borne by two right legs. That's why the walk creates a side-to-side and front-to-back motion in the saddle. A Western horse that really walks out with good forward energy is said to have a "rein-swinging" walk. A dressage horse should walk with head and neck unconstrained and lightly on the bit. The speed of the average walk is about four miles per hour. The hind footprints should at least touch or land partially on top of the front prints, but ideally the hind prints should be in front of the imprints of the forefeet.

How to Ride the Walk

To get in tune with a horse's normal walk:

★ Sit with a relaxed seat and legs.

★ Let your body sway to the movement of the horse's back and hind legs.

★ Note that at one moment your right leg will swing against the horse's barrel and your left leg will swing away from it. In the next instant, the opposite will occur.

★ Allow yourself to sway from side to side freely.

Use

The working walk is used in training-level dressage and all Western performances.

Caution

A horse that is rushing at the walk might either jig or prance —impure gaits comprised of half walking, half trotting. He might also develop a pacey walk. The pace is a two-beat lateral gait where the two right limbs rise and land alternately with the two left limbs. Although the pace is a natural gait for some Standardbred horses and other breeds, a pacey walk is considered an impure gait for most riding horses because the even four-beat pattern of the walk has been broken and the walk becomes almost a two-beat gait. This is a difficult habit to change and so must be prevented.

A horse that is walking too slowly often lacks the energy (impulsion) to properly flex his joints. As a result, he drags his toes and might stumble.

A walk can easily be spoiled by bad riding.

This Western horse would improve his walk if his face were 5 to 10 degrees in front of the vertical and he were reaching forward with his head and neck and legs more energetically. His right hind is dragging upon landing and his right front is dragging after breakover, so he needs to be ridden with less constraint and more energy.

For more information about a good walk, see drawings in Exercises #34 and #81.

Signs of a good walk:

★ a relaxed back

★ a raised and swinging tail

★ a slight head nod and swing, side to side as well as up and down

Extended Walk

HOW TO RIDE THE EXTENDED WALK

★ Establish the swaying rhythm of the working walk (or your horse's *lazy* walk, as the case may be).

★ As your horse's right front leg is moving back, ready to break over, your right leg should make contact with his barrel. At that moment sit on your right seat bone, press with your right calf and knee, or, if he is really lazy, give his side a little bump with your heel.

★ Instantly release the right seat and leg aids.

★ As his left front moves back, sit on your left seat bone and give a squeeze or bump with your left leg.

★ Repeat this rhythmically in time with the horse's natural movement to increase the activity of each of his hind legs, causing him to push off more energetically and take longer strides underneath himself.

This definitely shows a difference from the previous drawing of a Western working walk. The horse shows more reach with the head, neck, and legs. For some horses this would be the working walk.

DESCRIPTION

An extended walk is a lengthening but not a quickening of the walk stride. The horse's hindquarters, head and neck, and forelegs all reach forward. Contact with the bit is maintained.

If you examine the hoofprints, each hind foot should reach beyond the print of its corresponding forefoot.

USE

The extended walk is used in third-level dressage and trail riding.

CAUTION

Take care not to throw away bit contact (surrender the reins completely) or your horse may fall on his forehand (let all of his weight fall on his front legs) or begin jogging.

Collected Walk

HOW TO RIDE THE COLLECTED WALK

★ Keep your weight light but even.

★ Keep your upper body vertical.

★ Drive with both legs into a feel of the horse's mouth in your hand.

★ Maintain light contact with both hands.

This rider appears to be trying to pull the horse into a collected walk, causing stiffness in the front end. Although the stride is shorter, the shortening occurs in the hind steps. This causes the croup to come up and the back to hollow somewhat. With proper driving and a lighter, lifting hand, the gait should attain a light, springy engagement.

DESCRIPTION

A collected walk has shorter steps and covers less ground than the working walk, but has the same four-beat rhythm. The collected walk has a crisp cadence similar to marching. Because of the shorter stride, there is no over-step of the hind prints on the frontprints. The hinds touch slightly behind the front imprints. The joint angles are more acute and the action more springy.

NOTE

The walk is so easily damaged that the collected walk is the last collected gait to work on, not the first one. If it becomes stilted or ambling, immediately move into a more forward gait such as an extended trot or canter to improve the horse's desire to go forward, or use lateral movements to correct by increasing the drive of the hind legs.

USE

The collected walk is used in second-level dressage and trail obstacles.

Free Walk

HOW TO RIDE A FREE WALK

★ From a working walk, gradually let the reins slide through your hands until you can no longer feel contact with the horse's mouth.

★ Sit balanced and quiet with passive aids.

★ Note and assess your horse's behavior.

NOTE

The previous work was correct if:

★ The horse lowers his head and neck and reaches for the ground, stretching the muscles on the top of his neck.

★ The horse exhales and blows through his nose.

★ The horse softly mouths the bit.

★ The horse's back swings.

The previous work was incorrect if:

★ The horse raises his head and neck using the muscles on the underside of his neck.

★ The horse holds his breath.

★ The horse clamps rigidly on the bit or chews it nervously.

★ The horse's back is rigid and his free walk is tense.

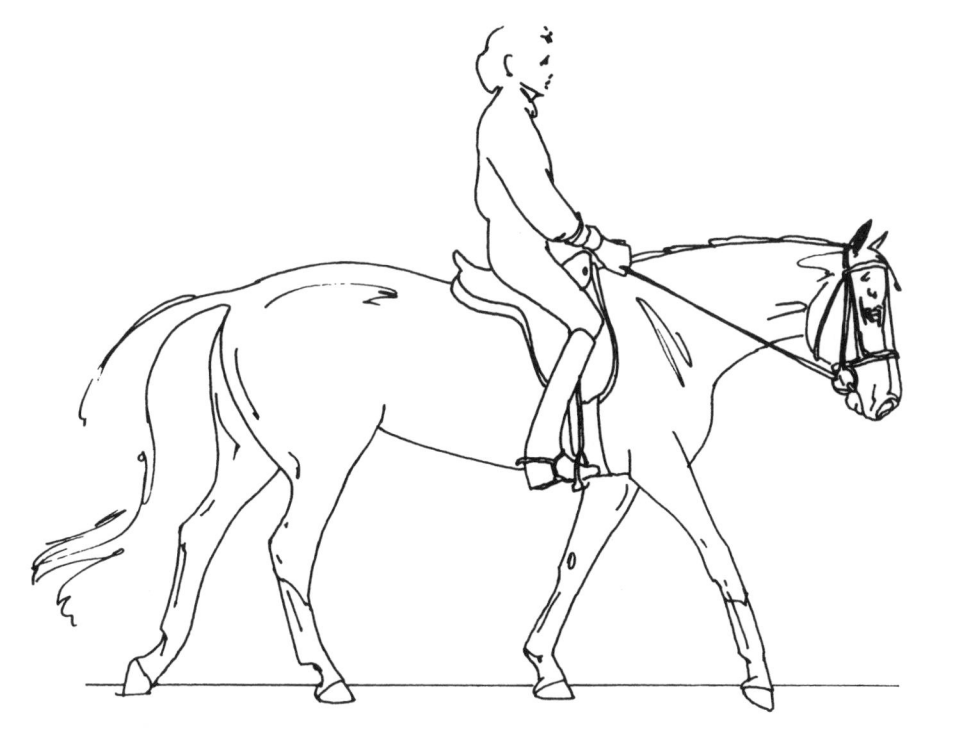

Here is the beginning of a free walk. The rider is letting the horse reach downward with his neck and forward with his nose. See the drawing in Exercise #28 for the end stage of this lowering.

DESCRIPTION

A free walk is characterized by long strides, a relaxed back, and a lowered head and neck. This can be ridden on a *loose* rein, which means no contact. It is sometimes referred to as "on the buckle" because the rider has let the reins out fully and is holding only the buckle. The free walk can also be ridden on a *long* rein, which means there is very light contact. In either case, the horse should be allowed to carry his head and neck as low as he'd like.

The free walk is a good way to check and see if the previous work has been correct.

USE

The free walk is used in training-level dressage and to reward a horse during a rest break for good work.

Working Trot (Posting Trot)

HOW TO POST THE TROT

★ Rise and sit with the corresponding movement of the horse's outside diagonal (inside hind leg and outside foreleg). *Inside* customarily refers to the inside of a circle or turn, which is often also the inside of the arena. *Outside* refers to the side of the horse nearest the arena rail. When tracking to the left in an arena, the outside diagonal is the right diagonal.

★ As the horse's left hind and right front legs are landing underneath you and accepting weight, you should be sitting. As those legs push off and are in the air (swinging forward), you should be rising.

★ Learn to feel the action of the inside hind leg by having a ground person tell you each time it has landed.

★ If you must work alone, you can check to see if you are on the correct diagonal by carefully glancing down at the horse's outside shoulder. When the outside shoulder is farthest forward, you should be at the peak of your rising.

★ When rising, balance over the center of your foot. Do not allow your foot to swing backward or forward as you rise, which will greatly reduce your stability.

★ Rise using your thigh muscles and pivot at your knees. Be careful not to grip with your knees. Although your weight should be deep in your heels during posting, you should not post by pushing yourself up from your stirrups.

A

B

To what diagonal is the rider posting and in what direction would she be traveling? See also drawing in Exercise #32.

The horse in this sequence shows more knee action than would be desired for most working trots.

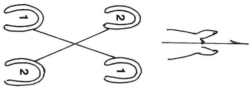

★ When you sit, land in the saddle softly.

★ If you find you are on the incorrect diagonal, simply sit two beats and resume your normal posting rhythm.

DESCRIPTION

The trot is a two-beat diagonal gait where the right front and left hind legs (called the right diagonal) rise and fall together and the left front and right hind legs (called the left diagonal) rise and fall together. Between the landings of the diagonal pairs, there is a moment of suspension that results in a springy gait. The working trot is an active, ground-covering trot. Posting allows you to ride an actively trotting horse more smoothly, and the horse can support a rider's weight better in turns if the rider sits with the inside hind. The average speed of a working trot is 6–8 miles per hour. The hind feet should step into the tracks of the front feet.

NOTE

★ See Exercise #7 for comments on sitting the trot. Note, though, that in English riding, the sitting trot is performed at a working trot pace.

★ A good working trot is the basis for a good canter.

★ You should be able to post without stirrups.

USE

The working trot is used in training-level dressage and hunter under saddle.

CAUTION

Never lean over to check if you are on the correct diagonal. Use only your eyes, because even if you tilt your head down, you will throw your upper body off balance.

Jog (Sitting Trot)

How to Sit the Trot

★ Regulate your breathing.

★ Position your seat bones so they are directly underneath you, not rolled in front of you or squashed out behind you.

★ Check to see that your upper body is directly over your seat bones and that your shoulders are over your hips.

★ Keep your lower back straight, not hollow, and support it with muscle strength from your abdominal muscles.

★ Periodically open your thighs so that they fall vertically along the horse's sides and let your seat bones drop even more deeply on the saddle.

★ Lightly embrace your horse's ribs with your lower legs if appropriate for your style of riding.

A well–balanced jog. See drawings in Exercises #22 and #33.

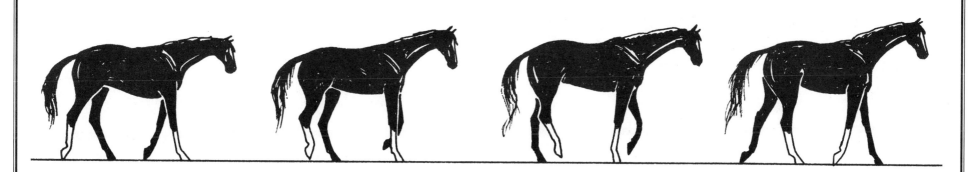

DESCRIPTION

Trot refers to the gait as performed under English tack with a greater length of stride and impulsion than the *Western jog*, which has a shorter stride and minimal suspension. The jog is usually performed on a loose rein with a great deal of relaxation.

Since the jog and sitting trot are usually the most steady, stable, and rhythmic of a horse's gaits, they are useful for developing the rider's seat. They are also cornerstones of many exercises for the horse's training.

USE

The jog is required for all Western performances, and the sitting trot is required in training-level dressage.

CAUTION

★ Do not grip with your thighs or knees because the resulting tension will lift you right out of the saddle.

★ Don't be tempted to lean your upper body backward at an extreme angle because this will roll your seat bones too far forward and cause your legs to swing out ahead of you, causing you to lose stability.

★ When first learning to sit the trot, avoid developing tension and over-riding with the bridle. Otherwise the horse may develop a hollow back and high head.

★ If jogging, take care not to go too slow or the horse's gait might become impure when the diagonal pairs of legs "break" and no longer land and take off at the same time. When the foreleg lands before its diagonal hind leg, the horse has lost suspension entirely and he is walking in front and trotting behind.

Extended Trot

HOW TO RIDE THE EXTENDED TROT/POSTING

★ Jog/Sitting trot (Exercise #7).

★ Working trot/Posting trot (Exercise #6).

★ Drive with your seat each time you prepare to rise.

★ Squeeze with your legs each time you prepare to rise.

★ Keep your hands low, especially your outside hand, to encourage your horse to reach long and low.

★ Eventually learn to ride the extended trot sitting.

A balanced and energetic extended trot.

See drawings in Exercises #24 and #88.

DESCRIPTION

At the same tempo as the working trot, the horse has longer strides, pushing and driving with the hindquarters with great impulsion, really reaching with the front legs. This trot has the longest moment of suspension and therefore covers the most ground possible as the horse glides through the air. The hind hoofprints should over-step the front prints by a considerable distance. There is a distinct lengthening of the frame, with the nose stretching forward and somewhat down.

NOTE...RELATED TROTS:

★ A *lengthened* trot is the very beginning stage of learning extension.

★ A *medium* trot is a middle stage of learning extension — a prelude to the extended trot.

USE

The extended trot is used in third-level dressage.

CAUTION

★ Don't let your horse get too low (deep) in front because he will lose impulsion from behind, which is necessary to create the extra push for extension.

★ Don't over-ride the bridle because it could result in false extension, where the front limbs reach out farther than the hindquarters are driving under.

Collected Trot

HOW TO RIDE THE COLLECTED TROT

★ Ride the working trot, sitting.

★ Perform the half halt (Exercise #14).

- Close your lower legs on the horse's sides, and keep your knees down.

- Tighten your abdominals.

- Deepen your seat bones.

- Hold your shoulders back slightly.

- Squeeze reins with both hands.

- Let horse's front end come up a bit.

- Keep driving with your lower legs.

★ Repeat this for a few strides (collected trot).

★ Resume the working trot.

In many ways, this is a positive example of the collected trot as long as the rider is not pulling to "hold" the horse in collection. See the poor example in drawing in Exercise #66.

DESCRIPTION

The collected trot is performed at the same tempo as the working trot but with shorter steps, more marked cadence, more joint flexion, a rounded back, and well-engaged hindquarters, which result in a naturally (not forced) elevated neck and more vertical flexion in the poll. This is an energetic trot with the balance shifted rearward, allowing free shoulder movement. This trot has the shortest moment of suspension and therefore covers the least ground. The hind feet usually do not reach the imprints of the front feet.

NOTE

★ The best way to *teach* a horse what you want is to show him a very distinct difference between a working trot and a collected trot for a few strides.

★ The best way to develop collected gaits is to perform a large number of upward and downward transitions.

★ Practice the collected trot on straight lines first. Tight turns and small circles can cause a loss of rhythm and position.

USE

The collected trot is used in second-level dressage.

Working Canter and Lope

HOW TO RIDE THE CANTER, RIGHT LEAD

Keep your horse on the correct lead. Ride every step to keep him in balance and in the correct position.

★ Keep your right seat bone forward, and your left seat bone in normal position.

★ Hold your upper body erect.

★ Hold your shoulders even unless you are turning.

★ Keep your right leg on the girth, actively, creating right bend and keeping the horse up on left rein.

★ Keep your left leg behind the girth, actively, keeping the horse's hindquarters from swinging to the left and maintaining impulsion.

★ Apply right direct rein to create the appropriate amount of bend and flexion.

★ Maintain left supporting rein or neck rein if appropriate.

DESCRIPTION

The canter (lope) is a three-beat gait with the following footfall pattern:

1. Initiating hind leg (outside hind)

2. The diagonal pair (inside hind and outside foreleg)

In this quiet lope left lead, the horse is getting ready to reach his leading foreleg (left) forward and land on it while starting to lift his initiating hind (right hind).

DESCRIPTION (CONTINUED)

The canter has an alternating rolling and floating feeling to it. The energy rolls from rear to front, then during a moment of suspension the horse gathers his legs up underneath himself to get organized for the next set of leg movements. The rider seems to glide for a moment until the initiating hind lands and begins the cycle again.

A lope is a relaxed version of the canter with less rein contact and a lower overall body carriage.

3. Leading foreleg (inside foreleg)

4. Regrouping of legs (a moment of suspension)

If the initiating hind leg is the left, the diagonal pair will consist of the right hind and the left front. The leading foreleg will be the right front and the horse will be on the right lead. When observing a horse on the right lead from the side, his right legs will reach farther forward than his left legs. The right hind will reach under his belly farther than the left hind; the right front will reach out in front of his body farther than the left front. When turning to the right, normally the horse should be on the right lead.

NOTE

The trot-canter transition develops a good forward working canter.

USE

The working canter and lope is used in all Western performances and training-level dressage.

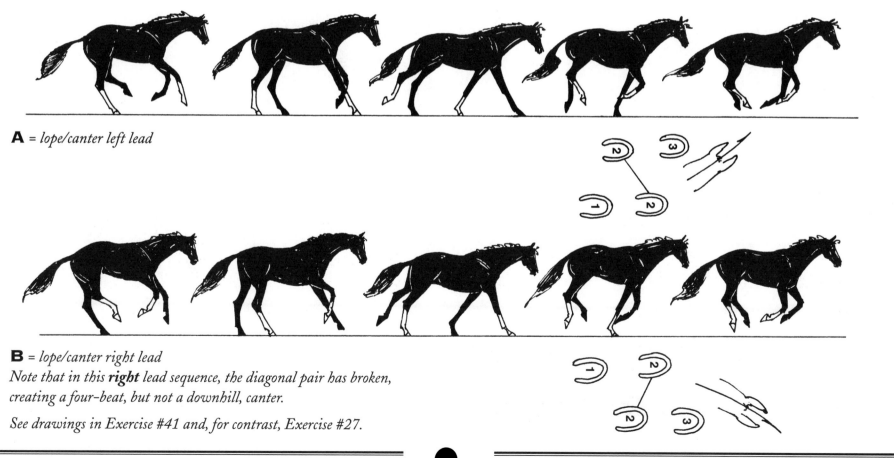

A = *lope/canter left lead*

B = *lope/canter right lead*
*Note that in this **right** lead sequence, the diagonal pair has broken, creating a four-beat, but not a downhill, canter.*

See drawings in Exercise #41 and, for contrast, Exercise #27.

Extended Canter

HOW TO RIDE THE EXTENDED CANTER

★ Sit as for a normal canter or lope.

★ Don't lean the upper body forward.

★ Keep a light driving seat.

★ Move the reining hand(s) forward to allow the horse to stretch his neck forward.

NOTE

★ There should be no increase in speed from a working canter to an extended canter. If you close your eyes, the sound of the hoofbeats would be the same for the working canter and the extended canter.

★ There should not be a shift into the gallop, which is a maximally extended four-beat racing gait.

★ The term *hand gallop* is often called for in the hunter show ring. In many cases what is really desired is an extended canter.

This is a fairly good example of an energetic, extended lope (right lead) for a Western horse; however, it appears as if the leading foreleg (right front) is out of sync and will need to hurry to catch up.

See also drawings in Exercises #25 and #40.

DESCRIPTION

This extended canter (right lead) has a long, strong stride, with the horse's head and neck reaching forward. This canter is horizontal in contrast to the vertical nature of the collected canter. The extended canter has maximum ground coverage per stride while retaining the tempo of the working canter.

Related terms

★ *Disunited* is when a horse is on one lead in front and another behind (also called cross-leaded). This is very rough to ride.

★ *Counter-cantering* is cantering on the "outside" lead on purpose as a means of developing obedience, strength, balance, and suppleness. If counter-cantering on a circle to the right, the horse would be on the left lead and he would be flexed left.

USE

The extended canter is used in reining, working cow horse, and third-level dressage.

CAUTION

Restraining the horse too much with the bridle will limit the reach with his leading foreleg.

Collected Canter

HOW TO RIDE THE COLLECTED CANTER

★ Use the aids as for the working canter.

★ Ride the horse "in position."

★ Increase forward driving aids along with light but effective half halts (Exercise #14).

NOTE

Be careful to maintain the pure three-beat canter. If a horse is slowed down too much, collected too early (before he has developed sufficient strength), or ridden too strongly with the bridle, the purity of the canter suffers. The diagonal pair breaks and the inside hind lands before its diagonal foreleg.

In this collected canter right lead, the initiating hind (left) has landed, the diagonal pair (right hind and left front) will land next, and the leading foreleg (right) will pass the left front and land as the final beat of the gait. See drawings in Exercises #29, #79, and #80.

DESCRIPTION

In this collected canter (right lead) the strides are shorter, the legs move higher, and there is more joint folding (flexion) than the working canter. The head and neck are up and flexed, and the hindquarters are well under the horse's body. The collected canter is almost always ridden "in position" — that is, with an inward flexion (see "Circles") even on straight lines. "In position" refers to the inward flexion of the horse's head at the poll and throat latch, while the rest of the body remains straight. The horse's frame creates the impression that he is cantering uphill.

USE

The collected canter is used in second-level dressage and circles in reining.

CAUTION (FOR ALL CANTERS)

★ Don't force a horse to carry his head too low or he will be unable to round his topline and bring his hind legs underneath himself. He will subsequently travel downhill, heavy on the forehand.

★ Don't slow a horse down too much at the canter because the diagonal pair of legs can "break" (front landing before its diagonal hind), giving rise to a four-beat gait where the horse appears to be loping in front and jogging behind.

★ Be sure the horse is moving straight ahead, not doing a crab-like canter with his body held at an angle.

Back

HOW TO RIDE THE BACK OR REIN BACK

★ Always start on a straight line from a good square halt.

★ Keep even weight on both seat bones, but don't sit real deep. Bear some weight on your thighs without leaning forward.

★ Flex your gluteal muscles and abdominals to tilt your pelvis and bring your seat bones forward.

★ Straighten your lower back to help your seat bones come forward.

★ Apply equal pressure with both legs at the girth.

★ As the horse arrives at the bit, maintain non-allowing equal direct rein pressure to encourage the horse to let his impulsion out backwards.

★ Once the horse has yielded at jaw, poll, and loin, and has begun moving backward, lighten rein aids but maintain contact and continue seat and leg aids.

★ To discontinue backing, release rein aid but continue seat and leg aids momentarily to drive the horse up to a halt or a forward gait.

A Western horse rounding his topline as he begins to settle weight on one diagonal pair (right front and left hind) and gets ready to pick up the other diagonal pair.

DESCRIPTION

The back, or rein back, is a "man-made" diagonal, two-beat gait in reverse. In nature, horses rarely back up for more than a step or two.

When backing promptly, the left hind and right front are lifted distinctly, moved backward, and placed down together. They alternate with the right hind and left front in a precise synchronization. When backing more slowly, the diagonal pairs break on landing, the front landing ahead of its diagonal hind.

The back is best ridden when thought of as a "forward" gait because the horse must first be ridden up into contact as if he were going to walk.

USE

★ Riding the back is valuable for suppleness, obedience, and developing strength of back and hindquarters of any horse.

★ Riding the back is used in all Western performances and second-level dressage.

NOTE

★ If your horse "gets stuck" or "freezes," use squeeze and release, vibrations, or light alternating reins to untrack him. Never try to *pull* a horse backward.

★ If a horse backs too slowly or unwillingly, the back becomes a labored, four-beat gait, and often the horse drags his feet backward rather than lift his legs.

★ If a horse backs crookedly, apply the leg on the side to which he is angling his hindquarters. If he is swinging his hindquarters to the right, first be sure you are not causing it with your left leg or left rein. If they are OK, apply your right leg behind the girth or cinch to straighten him.

CAUTION

★ Never start the back with the reins.

★ Backing can be overdone and can cause anticipation, a dangerous rapid rushing backward, *or* the horse learns to use backing as an avoidance behavior.

★ A horse needs to become gradually accustomed to the concept of backing, and he must be allowed to build up his coordination and strength before he is asked to back for long distances.

Transitions

A *transition* is a shifting of gears. Good transitions are prompt yet not sudden. A horse *must* be prepared for every transition. No transition is correct without the proper use of half halts or checks (Exercise #14).

Transitions should be a smooth balance between your driving aids and your restraining aids. Although the driving and restraining aids should approach being equal, it is a good idea to use slightly more driving energy so the transitions are forward.

Most commonly, an *upward* transition indicates a change from a standstill or a slower gait to a gait that is more ground-covering. Examples of upward transitions are halt to walk, walk to trot, trot to canter, and walk to canter. In addition, an upward transition can indicate a change in the movement within a gait. For example, a trot can be regular (often called "working"), extended, or collected. The change from a working trot or a collected trot to an extended trot would be considered an upward transition.

A *downward* transition is a change from a gait that is more ground-covering or faster to one that is less so. Examples are canter to trot, canter to walk, trot to walk, and walk to halt. Downward transitions can also indicate decreases within a gait, such as extended canter to collected canter.

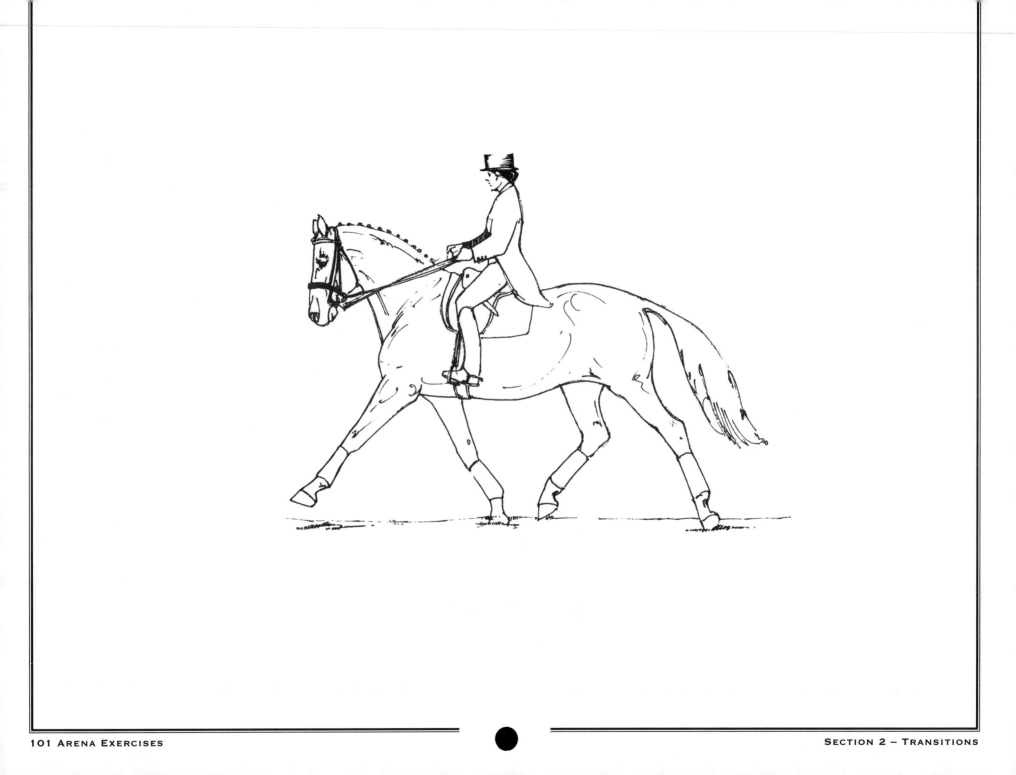

Half Halt or Check

HOW TO RIDE THE EXERCISE

★ Trot (Exercise #6)

★ Corner (Exercise #31)

★ Halt (Exercise #19)

★ Trot (Exercise #19)

★ Halt

★ Trot

★ Half halt

★ Trot

★ Half halt

★ Trot

A half halt is a preparatory set of aids that simultaneously drives and checks the horse. In essence you are "capturing" your horse momentarily between the aids. A half halt is a way of calling your horse to attention and getting organized before all transitions and during all movements. It is a means of momentarily re-balancing the horse, elevating the forehand, increasing hindquarter engagement, evening an erratic rhythm, slowing a pace, and reminding the horse not to lean on the bit or rush. A half halt is a *momentary* holding (a non-allowing in contrast to a pulling or taking), immediately followed by a *yielding* (within one stride or a split second). This results in a moment of energized suspension with a listening and light horse. Once a horse has learned to respect half halts, they serve as a reminder that encourages self-carriage.

BENEFITS

Improves balance, collection, an essential piece of the riding puzzle.

How to Apply a Half Halt

Think. Apply seat, leg, and hand aids. Yield. Half halt is an almost simultaneous application of the following with an emphasis on the seat and legs, and a de-emphasis on the hands:

★ Keep upper body straight or slightly back with elevated sternum.

★ Maintain deep, still contact of seat bones on saddle from flexed abdominals and a flattened lower back, bringing seat bones forward.

★ Keep both lower legs on horse's side at the girth or cinch. Tap with the whip or spurs if necessary, depending on the horse's level and response.

★ Use an appropriate intensity with both hands. The following is a list in increasing intensity:
  • Close fingers.
  • Squeeze reins.
  • Roll hands inward.
  • Move arm backward from shoulder.
  • Lean upper body back.

Yield aids without throwing away what you have gained. Apply the half halt a second or two ahead of the maneuver to allow the horse to respond, but not prolonged enough to result in tension. Occasionally a strong half halt is necessary to be sure it "goes through." After using a major half halt, confidently use light ones to maintain their effectiveness.

The All-Important Yield

The timing of the yield is often more important than the driving and non-allowing.

Did you feel a positive response...even a hint of compliance?
If you wait so long that you can feel the *full* effects of the half halt, it is way past time to yield. The yield is what encourages self-carriage. No yield leads to stiffness and tension.

Should you use more than one half halt at a time?
Sometimes it takes a series, one each stride, to re-balance.

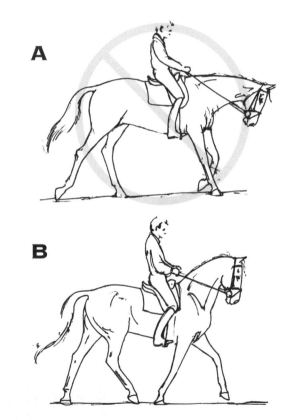

In **A** *the horse has fallen on his forehand, is strung out, and moving lazily. The use of half halts helps the horse to be balanced and organized (* **B** *).*

Halt–Walk–Halt

HOW TO RIDE THE EXERCISE

★ Check your position at the halt (Exercise #1).

★ With contact, apply the aids for walk:

   • Tighten abdominals and deepen seat.

   • Keep upper body straight.

   • Close both calves on horse's side.

   • Maintain rein contact, but yield slightly.

   • Relax seat and calves.

   • Repeat application of entire sequence if horse is sluggish.

   • If response is still slow or sluggish, use a light but brisk tap with the whip immediately after the application of the aids.

   • Follow movement at walk.

★ Ride corner (Exercise #31).

★ Ride straight (Exercise #30).

★ Halt.

   • Keep a still seat.

   • Position shoulders over hips.

   • Close calves on horse's sides.

   • Fix hands, then yield.

★ Pause for three seconds.

★ Walk.

★ Halt three seconds.

★ Walk.

★ Halt.

★ Repeat in opposite direction.

NOTE

Compare the results of the exercise to the left and to the right, and you will know what you need to work on in subsequent lessons.

When going to the right, did your horse tend to hold his head higher and did he bend more stiffly around the corner?

When going to the left, did he tend to drop his head to the inside and want to fall on his inside shoulder? Did he bend too willingly to the left?

For a horse with a long back, use your legs well behind the cinch or girth to get a more engaged halt.

BENEFITS

Use this to determine your tendencies: Do you ride straight or crooked? Straighten *yourself* before you look to correct your horse.

Does your horse have a tendency to drift one way or the other with his hindquarters upon halting?

A good example of the release after a square halt.

CAUTION

★ Use intermittent leg aids. Don't hold your legs on. Get a reaction.

★ Be sure you offer the "reward" of the yielding of your aids when your horse begins to comply by moving forward.

★ Be ready to correct a crooked response. If the hindquarters swing right, use your right leg at or behind the girth. If the head veers to the left, straighten with right rein.

Walk—Posting Trot—Walk

HOW TO RIDE THE EXERCISE

★ Walk (Exercise #15).

★ Walk the corner (Exercise #31).

★ When horse is straight (Exercise #30), apply aids for sitting trot. (See Exercise #15 and increase intensity.)

★ Sitting trot 2 strides (Exercise #7).

★ Post 4 strides (Exercise #6).

★ Sitting trot 2 strides.

★ Walk (Exercise #15).

★ Walk 1½ strides.

★ Sitting trot 2 strides.

★ Posting trot 4 strides.

★ Sitting trot 2 strides.

★ Walk 1½ strides.

★ Sitting trot 2 strides.

★ Posting trot 4 strides.

★ Corner at posting trot.

★ When horse is straight, ride the sitting trot 2 strides.

★ Walk.

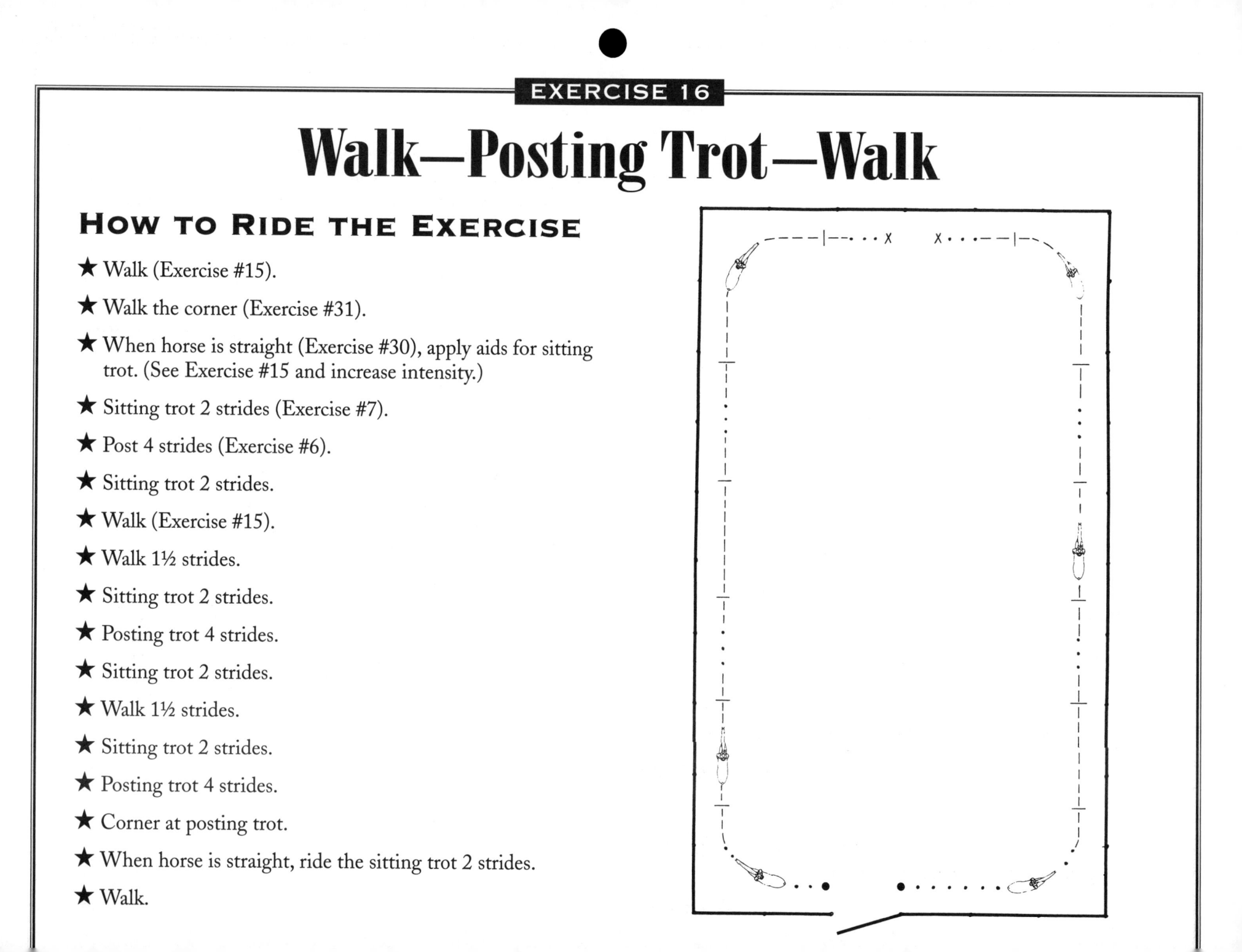

★ Halt.

★ Perform exercise in opposite direction.

This drawing has both positive and negative aspects.

When you first ask for a trot from the walk, sit a beat or two before you begin posting. Depending on the timing of your aids and how well the horse was stepping under himself during the walk, when the horse breaks into a trot, you will either get a hind leg action that pushes up or one that pushes backward (as shown in this drawing). An upward push results in a more springy, engaged trot than a backward push, which, for the first stride of the trot at least, gives you the feeling that the horse is strung out behind.

NOTE

At first, just do one set of transitions on a long side and gradually work up to two sets.

BENEFITS

With each downward transition, the horse collects more. You should be able to feel him sitting down more behind and coming into your hand. His neck and poll should rise.

With each upward transition, you should feel the horse's springiness increase, and as a result he should begin lifting his back with a slight arch.

This exercise gives you a chance to work on the timing of the application of your aids.

CAUTION

If you do not have a solid, sensitive, following seat at the trot, the few strides of sitting trot in this exercise might cause discomfort to your horse's back. He may hollow his back and perform rough transitions. Perfect your work at a posting trot before trying any sitting trot exercises.

Walk—Sitting Trot—Walk

HOW TO RIDE THE EXERCISE

★ Walk from halt (Exercise #15).

★ Walk corner (Exercise #31).

★ Walk straight (Exercise #30).

★ Sitting trot (Exercises #7 and #16) 25 feet.

★ Walk 1–2 strides.

★ Sitting trot 25 feet.

★ Walk 1–2 strides.

★ Sitting trot.

★ Sitting trot around the corner, letting the horse rise into the outside rein.

★ When straight, walk.

★ Halt.

★ Repeat in opposite direction.

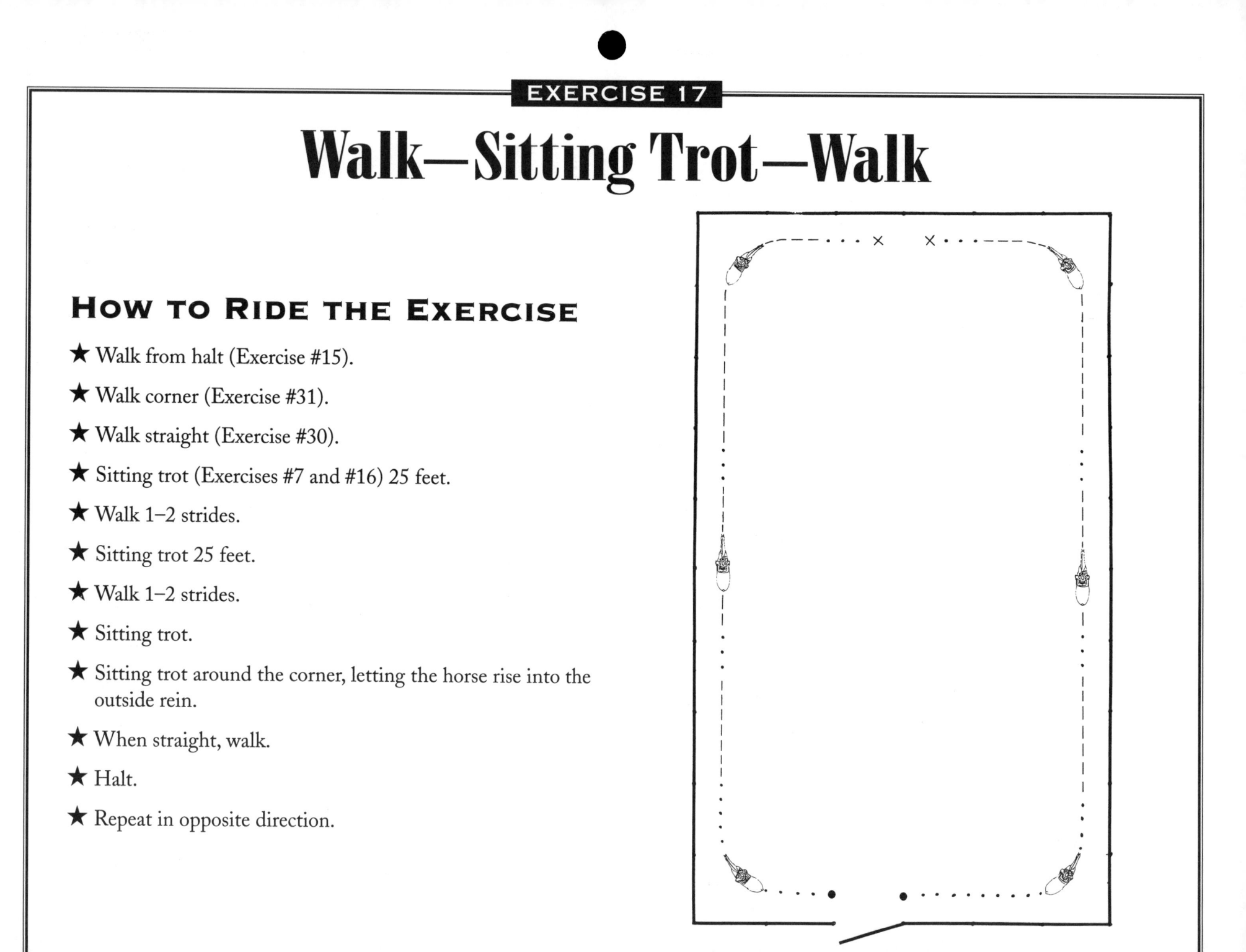

The fine solid line depicts the frame at the beginning of the exercise, the dotted line an interim stage, and the heavy solid line, the goal: elementary engagement and collection as shown by hind legs stepping farther under the horse's belly, a dropped croup, and an automatic rise of the head and neck.

NOTE

At first, perform only one set of transitions per long side, then increase to two and three.

BENEFITS

★ This is the simplest and best exercise for elementary collection. You will feel the horse come up in front and start to lift his back.

★ This type of exercise tends to increase joint flexion, which may be desirable in training-level dressage and some English show horses, but it is undesirable in Western pleasure show horses and show ring hunters.

★ With this exercise, you will be able to assess and develop straightness because you will be applying bilateral aids: seat, legs, and rein.

★ Most horses begin to flex at the lower jaw and poll, work the bit, and slather.

CAUTION

Beware of doing this exercise before a horse has learned how to move actively forward. A horse must know how to reach well underneath himself with his hind legs *before* he is collected. If a horse starts to get bunched-up or antsy from this type of exercise, immediately move into a forward posting trot.

Beware of using too much hand because a horse can easily get behind the bit.

Trot-Canter-Trot

HOW TO RIDE THE EXERCISE

★ At **A**, ride the working trot in a large circle to the right (Exercises #16 and #17).

★ At **A**, canter right lead:

• Half halt (Exercise #14).

• Right leg at the girth causing horse's right hind to reach further forward, creating right bend and keeping horse up on left rein.

• Add more with right rein to produce right flexion at poll.

• Maintain left rein contact to control the degree of right flexion and limit the reach of the left foreleg.

• Left leg behind the girth to control the hindquarters and prevent the left hind from stepping to the left.

• Push right seat bone forward with weight in right stirrup (lower your knee and heel) to keep from collapsing your right side while weighting your right seat bone.

• Apply pressure with both legs: right at the girth and left behind the girth.

• Apply forward pressure with both seat bones, rolling forward from the left to the right, but don't lean forward or you lose your left seat bone. And don't pump your upper body as this tends to hollow the horse's back.

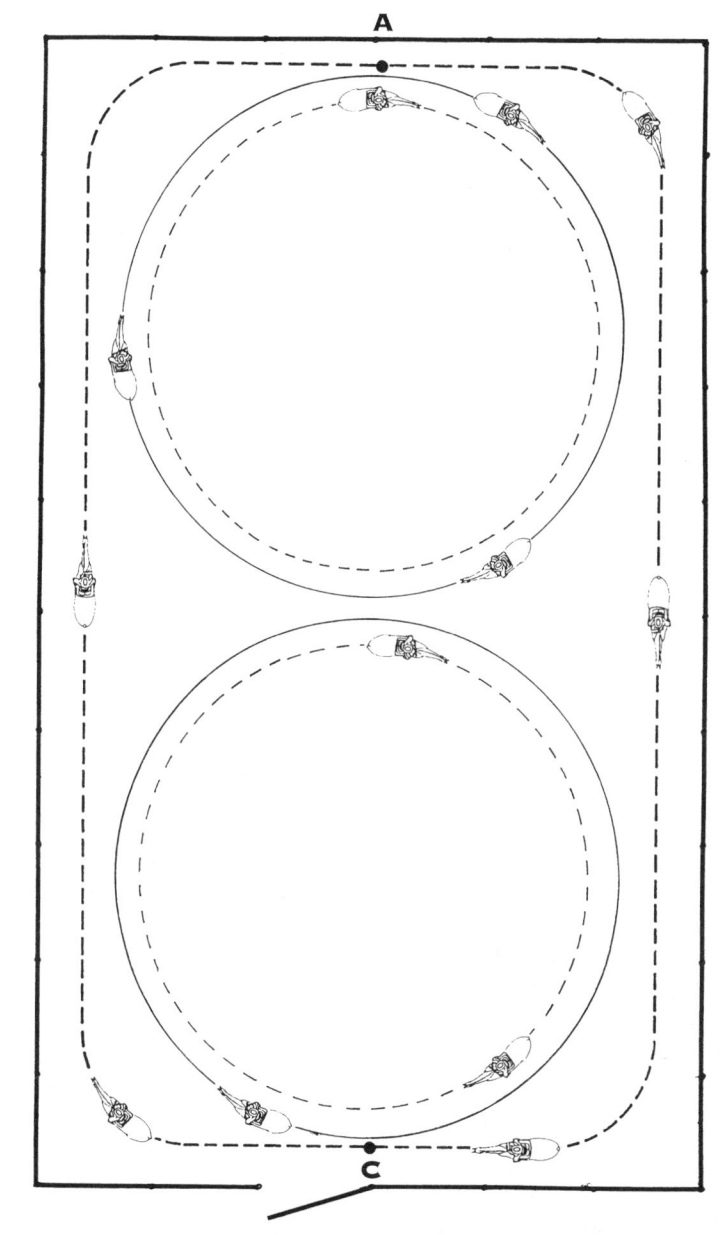

- Follow canter movement with a vertical upper body and inside (right) hip forward.
- Don't let your left shoulder fall behind and don't let your outside leg come off the horse.
- Continue with half halts (Exercise #14) to keep canter from flattening.

★ At **A**, trot large circle:

- Half halt(s).
- Move left leg to girth.
- Maintain a still seat.
- Flex abdominals.
- Re-balance seat slightly to outside.
- Close hands on reins, slightly more on left.

★ As soon as horse trots, yield with both hands to re-establish softness.

★ Change seat to a following trot seat (Exercise #7).

★ Check (Exercise #14) every stride for a few strides to regain desired rhythm and balance.

★ Trot arena at large from **A** to **C**.

★ At **C**, working trot (Exercise #6) in large circle to right.

★ At **C**, canter right lead.

★ At **C**, working trot large circle to right.

★ At **C**, working trot to **A**.

★ Reverse and ride in the opposite direction.

This horse is trotting with very little impulsion and is above the bit, with a hollow back and inverted neck. The rider needs to lower her hand, get her lower leg under her seat, and apply effective half halts before asking for a canter. This exercise, if properly ridden without pulling or bracing, will improve this horse's forward motion and topline roundness.

BENEFIT

Large circles and long lines encourages free, forward movement.

CAUTION

★ It may be necessary to trot or canter more than one circle at first to be sure your horse has proper contact, rhythm, and balance. However, because transitions are really more beneficial than continuous trot or canter work, aim for one circle at each gait.

★ You may need to use a series of half halts to prepare your horse for both the upward and downward transitions.

Trot-Halt-Trot

HOW TO RIDE THE EXERCISE

★ Trot, sitting (Exercise #7).

★ Trot the corner to the right (Exercise #31).

★ When the horse is straight (Exercise #30), ride a series of half halts (Exercise #14).

★ Halt for 3 seconds.

★ Soften but hold your driving aids slightly to maintain contact and form up in front so you can strike off at any gait at any moment.

★ Trot, thinking "spring into action" (a stronger more exaggerated version of aids in Exercise #17).

★ Hug the horse's abdominals with your lower legs to cause him to "get light" and lift himself up.

★ Intermittent lower leg in a strong quiver rather than heavy, steady pressure.

★ Trot 30 feet.

★ Halt 3 seconds.

★ Trot 30 feet.

★ Halt 3 seconds.

★ Trot.

★ Trot the corner.

★ When straight, halt.

★ Reverse.

NOTE

In dressage, a halt is a series of half halts followed by a yield. In the case of a stock horse, a halt is often taught as an immediate response to one cue.

BENEFITS

★ Develops discipline and collection.

★ Quickens and lightens your horse's response to the aids.

★ Improves training-level dressage.

CAUTION

★ Don't surprise your horse with aids that have not been preceded by a preparatory cue.

★ Only practice the transitions on straight lines.

★ Ease without losing contact when you feel that your horse has "started to stop."

★ Don't let your horse get behind the bit or get antsy. If he does, immediately ride forward in an active posting trot.

Can't you just predict that the halt following this trot will end in a nose-dive? The rider is "curled up": rounded back and shoulders, head down, forearms and hands rolling inward. Although her horse is moving forward with nice impulsion, it looks like his nose will go down and his croup will come up when he halts. Proper use of a series of half halts is necessary to re-balance this horse before *the halt. See drawing in Exercise #32 for comparison.*

Canter–Walk–Canter

HOW TO RIDE THE EXERCISE

★ Trot (Exercise #6).

★ Canter (Exercises #10 and #18).

★ Canter large circle (Exercise #35).

★ Three strides before rail, do a series of half halts (Exercise #14).

★ Canter straight one stride (Exercise #30).

★ Walk, keeping weight on both seat bones and shoulders over hips.

★ Walk 1–2 strides.

★ Make a slight bend right.

★ Use a strong inside leg to outside rein.

★ Bend to the inside.

★ Hold outside leg.

★ Canter right lead in a large circle.

★ Continue the sequence.

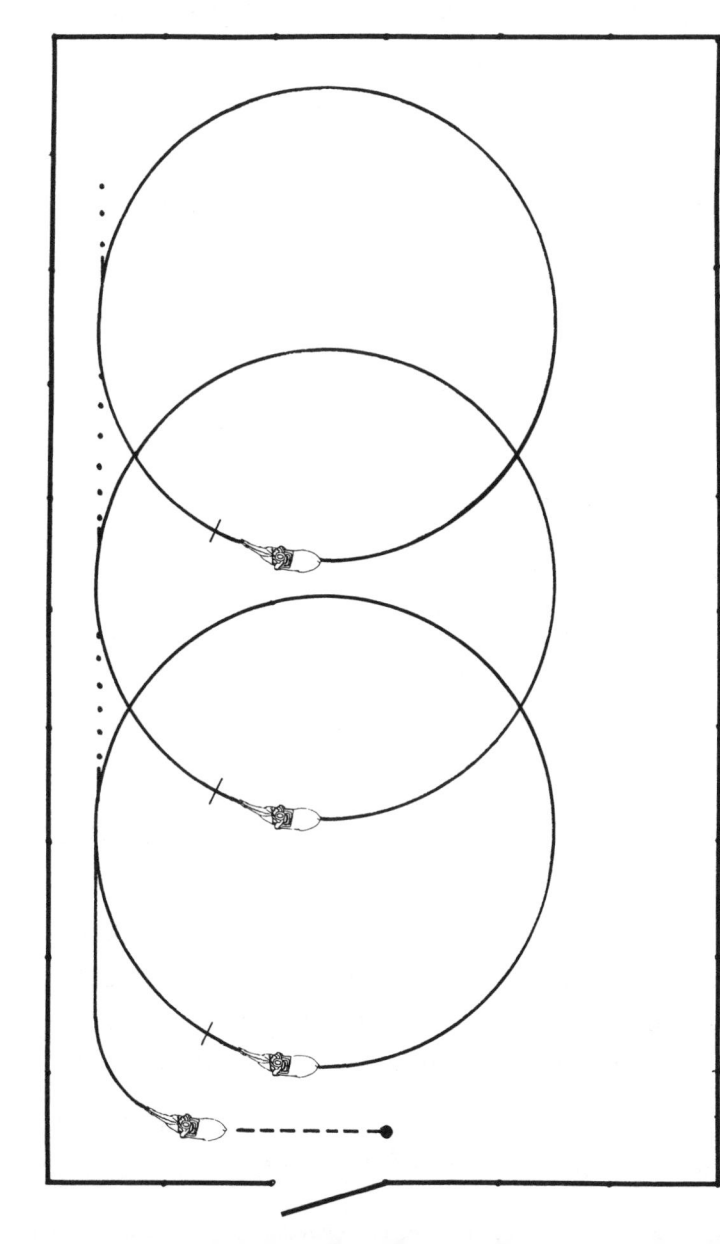

This canter-to-walk transition is far too abrupt, causing the horse to stiffen his jaw, neck, back, and front legs. Downward transitions must be forward and round, and initially they should take several strides to accomplish. The rider has made some of the most serious riding errors: she is stiff and not at all with her horse; she has lost her seat; she has no weight in her heels; her knees have come forward; she is pulling downward and stiffly on the horse's mouth.

BENEFITS

★ This helps to develop left-right balance in the horse and rider.

★ You get a more collected canter with a walk-canter transition than a trot-canter transition.

★ You can align your horse's body more correctly with a walk-canter transition than a trot-canter transition.

★ It is easier to teach the walk-canter depart after you have been cantering.

★ At first, the canter-walk transition might require a few steps of trot. Gradually, you and your horse will develop the balance and coordination to go directly from a canter to a walk.

CAUTION

★ Don't lean forward on the upward transition. This would hinder the horse by weighting his forehand.

★ Your horse must be on the aids and able to canter in balance before you attempt the walk-canter transition.

★ Don't sacrifice the forwardness of the canter. If the horse is getting behind the bit or taking mincing steps before the canter depart, trot actively forward, then half halt, walk, and canter.

★ If your horse throws his head or inverts his neck, he has had improper preparation and balance.

★ If you use the inside rein too strongly, it could cause the horse to take the incorrect lead. If the horse is already cantering, using the inside rein too strongly could cause him to circle tightly to the inside and break into a trot.

★ If your horse breaks into a trot, go back to the walk. Don't be tempted to push him into the canter from a fast trot.

★ Keep your horse up on the outside rein so he won't drop to the inside and become heavy on his leading foreleg. You want him to be light!

★ Initially, anticipation can work for you to show your horse what you want!

Listen Up

How to Ride the Exercise

★ Sitting trot (Exercise #7).

★ Half halt (Exercise #14), corner (Exercise #31).

★ Walk 1–2 strides (Exercise #17).

★ Sitting trot about 4 strides.

★ Walk 1–2 strides.

★ Sitting trot about 4 strides.

★ Halt.

★ Sitting trot.

★ Half halts where necessary; corners.

★ Walk.

★ Sitting trot.

★ Halt.

★ Sitting trot.

★ Half halt.

★ Sitting trot.

★ Half halt.

★ Collected trot (Exercise #9) both corners.

★ After straight, lengthen the trot (Exercise #8 and #24), posting.

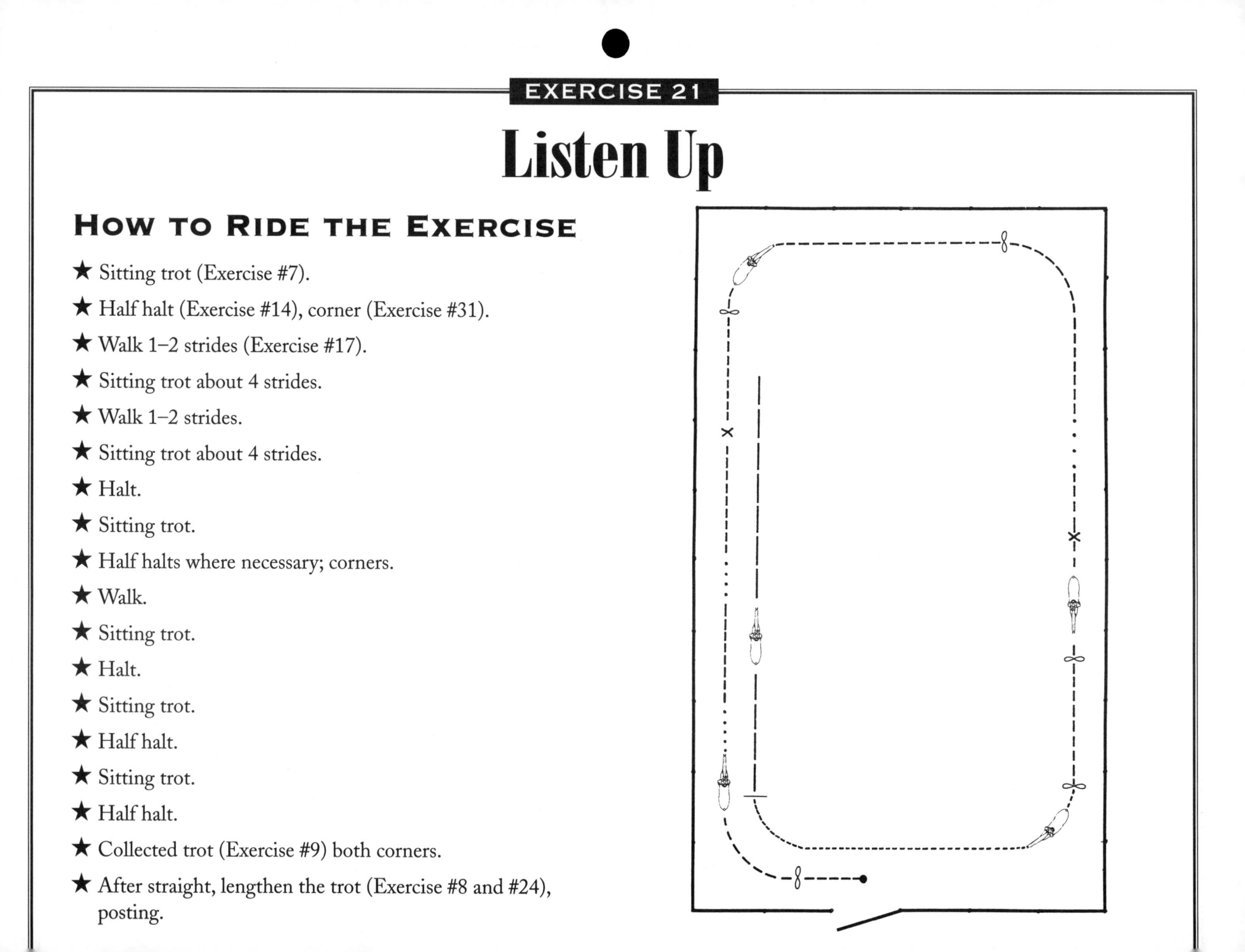

Here is a horse that is a prime candidate for this exercise. He really needs to "listen up!" He is strung out, above the bit, and is not using his back or hindquarters. The rider has a loose seat and is leaning forward as if she is trying to help the horse move with more energy. Compare with drawing in Exercise #17.

BENEFITS

★ Teaches collection.

★ Teaches the horse to differentiate between the subtle differences in aids for related upward and downward transitions.

★ Builds up energy and corrects balance and goes into the posting trot to develop some reach.

★ The idea is to ride the horse in a progressively more organized and collected frame and then allow him to release and reach! If the exercise were ridden in reverse — posting trot into sitting trot and downward transitions — the result can be pulling and resistance.

CAUTION

So much concentrated work can cause a horse to "bunch up" if done excessively or incorrectly.

Trot-Halt-Back-Walk

HOW TO RIDE THE EXERCISE

★ Trot (Exercise #7).

★ Trot corner (Exercise #31).

★ When straight, walk (Exercise #17).

★ Walk 1–2 strides.

★ Trot 4–6 strides.

★ Halt.

★ Trot 4–6 strides.

★ Halt, making sure horse yields at the jaw and poll during the transition.

★ Back 2 strides (Exercise #13).

★ Walk.

This young horse is in an ideal position to halt from the trot: he is softly on the aids with a rounded topline, adequate engagement for the jog, and a soft-looking jaw and poll. When the rider starts picking him up to prepare for the halt, it looks like the horse will be able to step under himself to halt.

NOTE

The suppleness and position of your horse's jaw, poll, and back at the final halt are key to getting fluid back steps without tenseness or resistance.

The entire exercise is to be ridden along the rail. The arena map is "exploded" sideways to show the components that occur on top of each other.

BENEFITS

★ Increases engagement of hind legs.

★ Is a barometer of how supple the horse is through the jaw, poll, and back.

CAUTION

Take your time. If you are abrupt with the halts or back, your horse will likely lose form.

Trot-Halt-Back-Trot

HOW TO RIDE THE EXERCISE

★ Trot (sitting) (Exercise #7).

★ Trot the corner (Exercise #31).

★ When straight (Exercise #30), walk 1–2 strides.

★ Trot 1–2 strides.

★ Halt (Exercise #19).

★ Trot 1–2 strides.

★ Halt.

★ Back 2 strides (Exercise #13).

★ Walk 1 stride.

★ Trot 1–2 strides.

★ Halt.

★ Back 2 strides.

★ Trot forward and around both corners of the short end.

★ When straight, halt.

★ Back 2 strides.

★ Trot 2–3 strides.

★ Halt.

★ Back 2 strides.

★ Trot forward.

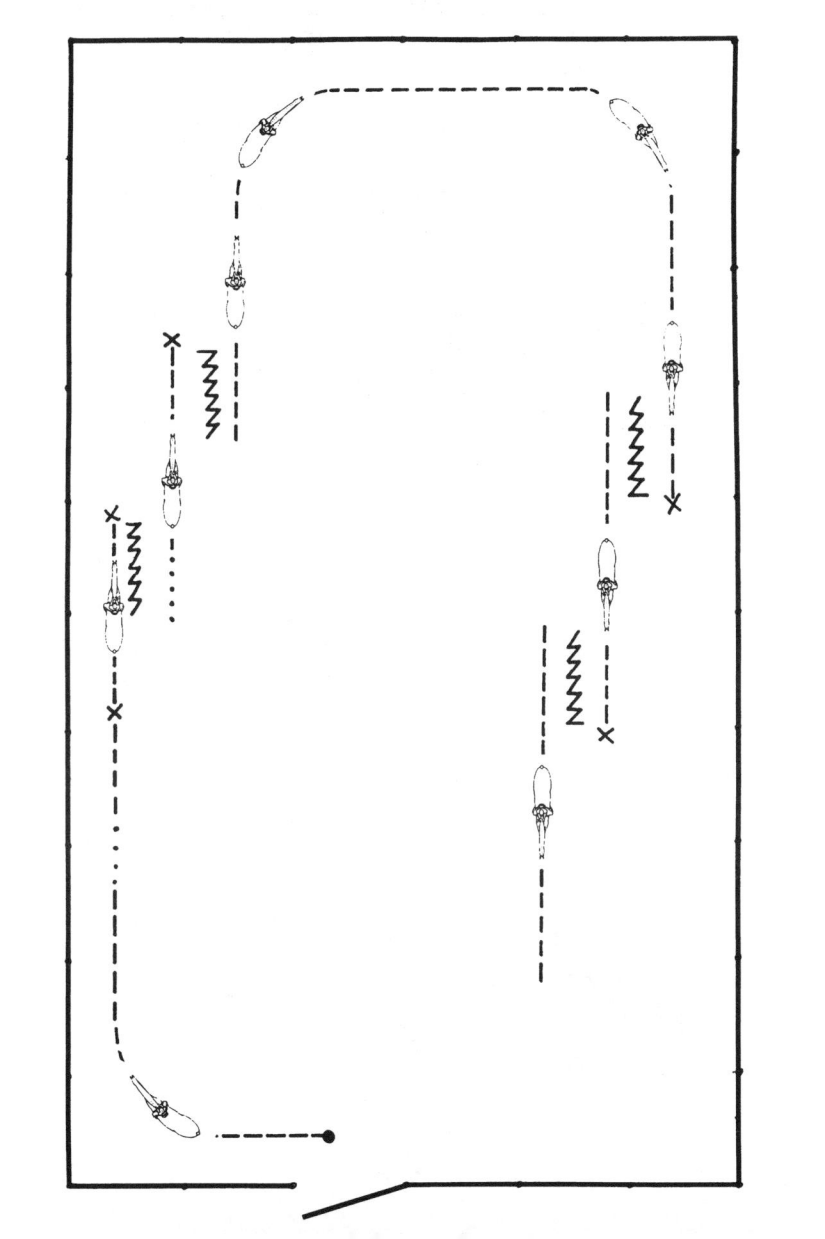

Note

This is a transition from a diagonal gait in reverse to a diagonal gait forward, so it should be very fluid and energetic. The horse's weight should *just settle* on the last rearward step and instantly be translated to the first forward trot step. If you fumble or get imbalanced in the middle of the transition or the horse locks up, you have lost the benefit of the exercise.

Benefits

★ Develops springiness to the trot depart.

★ Engages hindquarters and brings a roundness to the topline.

Caution

★ Backing can be overdone. It can also be used as an evasion by the horse. Be on the lookout for signs of anticipation or reluctance to move forward into the contact.

★ Don't lean back when backing up or you will cause the horse to hollow his back and place his hind legs way behind his body rather than up under his barrel. The hind legs need to be well under the horse for a prompt trot depart.

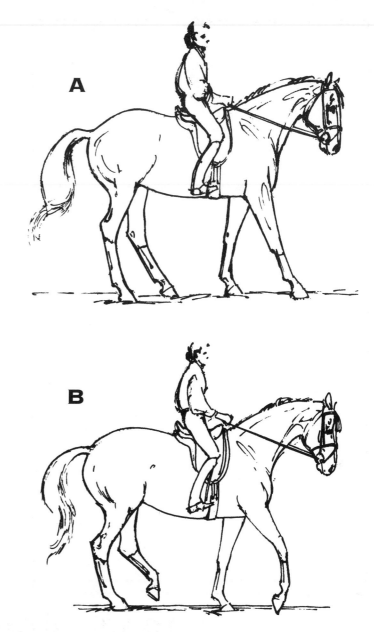

*As this horse takes his last step backward, his topline is round and his hind legs are well under his body (drawing **A**). When the rider drives him forward (drawing **B**), he springs up and out of the back into the trot.*

Lengthen Trot

How to Ride the Exercise

★ Posting trot (Exercise #6).

★ Trot around the corner (Exercise #31).

★ Trot down the long side.

★ Trot around the corner.

★ Sitting trot down the short end (Exercise #7).

★ In the second corner of the short end, ride a 40-foot circle (Exercise #36) in active sitting trot with strong right leg and right seat bone.

★ As you finish the circle, head across the long diagonal (Exercise #32).

★ After one stride straight, you should feel even contact in both of your hands.

★ Half halt (Exercise #14).

★ Lengthen (Exercise #8) across the diagonal, posting trot (Exercise #6).

★ Use exaggerated driving aids with each sitting beat.

★ Allow the horse to fill up a new frame with his increased impulsion and reach by letting both of your hands move forward.

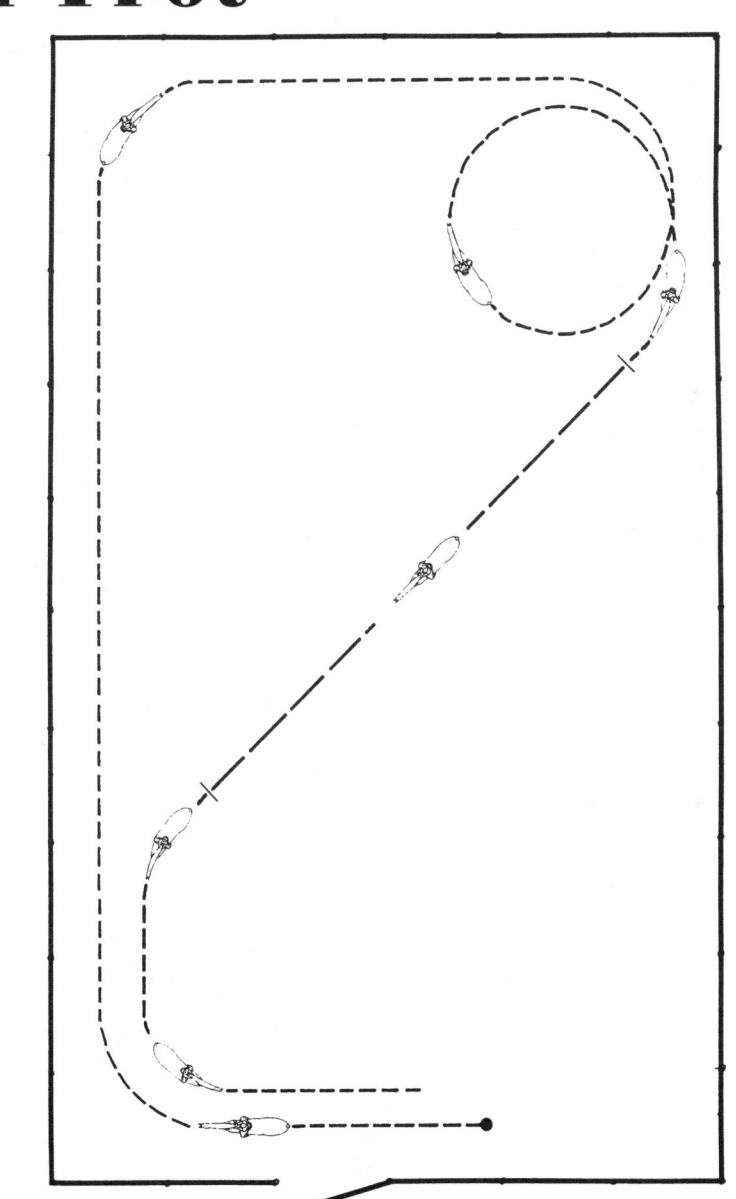

★ Ride the lengthening as many strides as the horse is capable of while staying in balance, from just a few strides to the entire diagonal.

★ Half halt as you end the lengthening.

★ Sitting trot straight and around the corner to the left.

BENEFITS

★ Teaches a horse to cover ground: hunter, endurance, cross country, trail riding.

★ Is essential for the training of a dressage horse.

★ Helps to "free up" an overcollected or "bunched up" Western horse.

★ Develops strength of back, loin, and hindquarter of any horse.

CAUTION

★ At first, just ask for a few strides. Over time, ask for the entire diagonal. A horse must develop the strength to lengthen.

★ Don't let things get too wild. Stay organized and don't let the horse speed up instead of reaching out farther. A lengthening is a longer reach and a lower frame, but in the same rhythm as the working trot.

★ The first steps of an extension are a fraction slower and more collected than the working trot: the horse is "setting back" and reaching under his belly with his hind legs.

This balanced, extended trot may be beyond your present capabilities for a lengthening, but it gives you a good idea of the direction you should be heading. Note that the horse steps well under his belly with his hind leg while reaching energetically with the diagonal foreleg. The rider is keeping this horse's impulsion appropriately balanced with contact on the bridle. Note that the nose is slightly in front of the vertical, which is good.

★ If you haven't developed an effective seat, the sitting trot on the circle may do more harm than good. Instead of preparing your horse, it may cause him to become tense and hollow his back.

★ A small balanced circle sets the horse up to drive with his inside hind leg for the lengthening.

★ Don't overflex with the reins because if the horse's nose gets too low or behind the vertical, it will limit his ability to reach with his forelegs.

Extended Canter

HOW TO RIDE THE EXERCISE

★ Canter right lead (Exercises #10 and #18).

★ Canter right corner (Exercise #31).

★ Canter down the long side.

★ Canter right corner.

★ In the middle of the short end, half halt (Exercise #14).

★ Canter 40-foot circle to the right (Exercise #36).

★ Canter the balance of the short end.

★ Canter the corner to the right.

★ When straight, extend as many strides as appropriate (Exercise #11).

★ Before the corner, half halt.

★ Working canter.

★ In the corner, canter a 40-foot circle to the right.

★ Come out of the corner and canter straight.

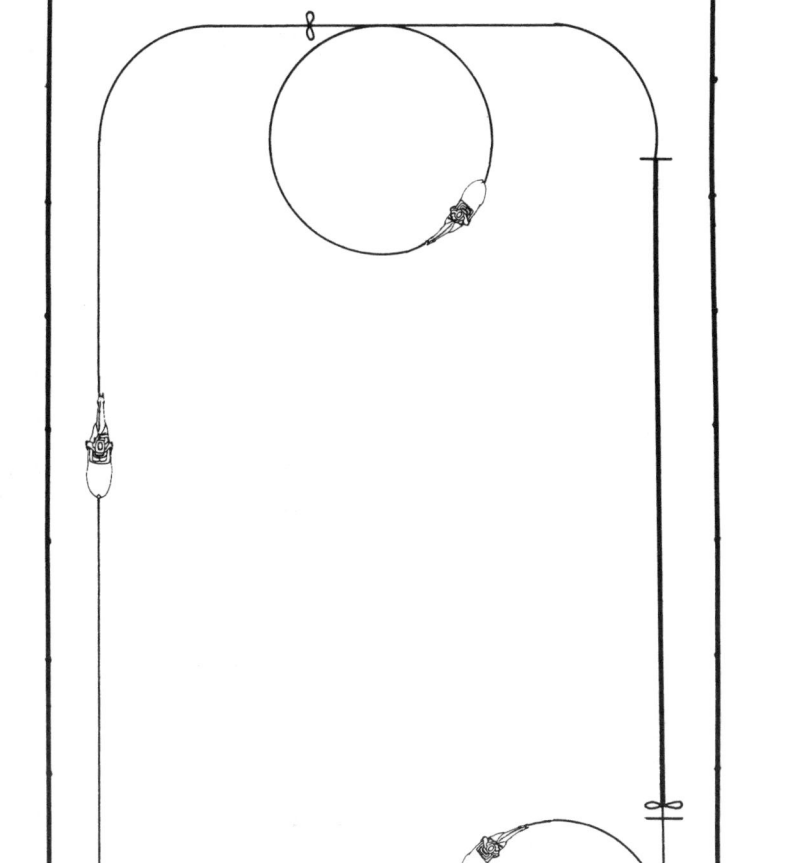

NOTE

The rhythm of the extended canter should sound the same as the regular canter.

BENEFITS

Introduces the concept of speed control or rating for hunting, jumping, cross-country, reining, dressage, and working cow horse.

CAUTION

★ Don't get loose, with your seat out of the saddle and flapping elbows. The extension should be a balanced driving.

★ The increase should not be asked for with a sudden spurring. The horse begins extending and gains momentum with each lengthened stride. The decrease is somewhat gradual as well.

A nicely balanced extended canter (right lead). Note the rider has not leaned forward or lost her seat. The horse reaches energetically forward yet stays up in front and balanced.

Collected Canter

HOW TO RIDE THE EXERCISE

★ Working canter right lead (Exercise #20).

★ Canter the right corner (Exercise #31).

★ Straight (Exercise #30) 2–3 strides with half halts each stride.

★ Collected canter 35-foot circle (Exercise #12).

★ Keep yourself and your horse very straight in the circle. Think "up" with your upper body and "deep" with your seat. Your mind and body language elicit the collection.

★ Apply half halts (Exercise #14) in rhythm with every canter stride just as the horse comes up in front.

★ Ride "in position" (see Section 4: Lateral Work), but ease with your inside rein so the stride can go forward; otherwise the horse may trot.

★ Ride straight 2–3 strides at working canter.

★ Half halt.

★ Collected canter 35-foot circle.

★ Straight 2–3 strides at working canter.

★ Half halt.

★ Collected canter 35-foot circle.

★ Retain collected canter and ride the short end.

★ After the second corner of the short end, regular canter straight ahead.

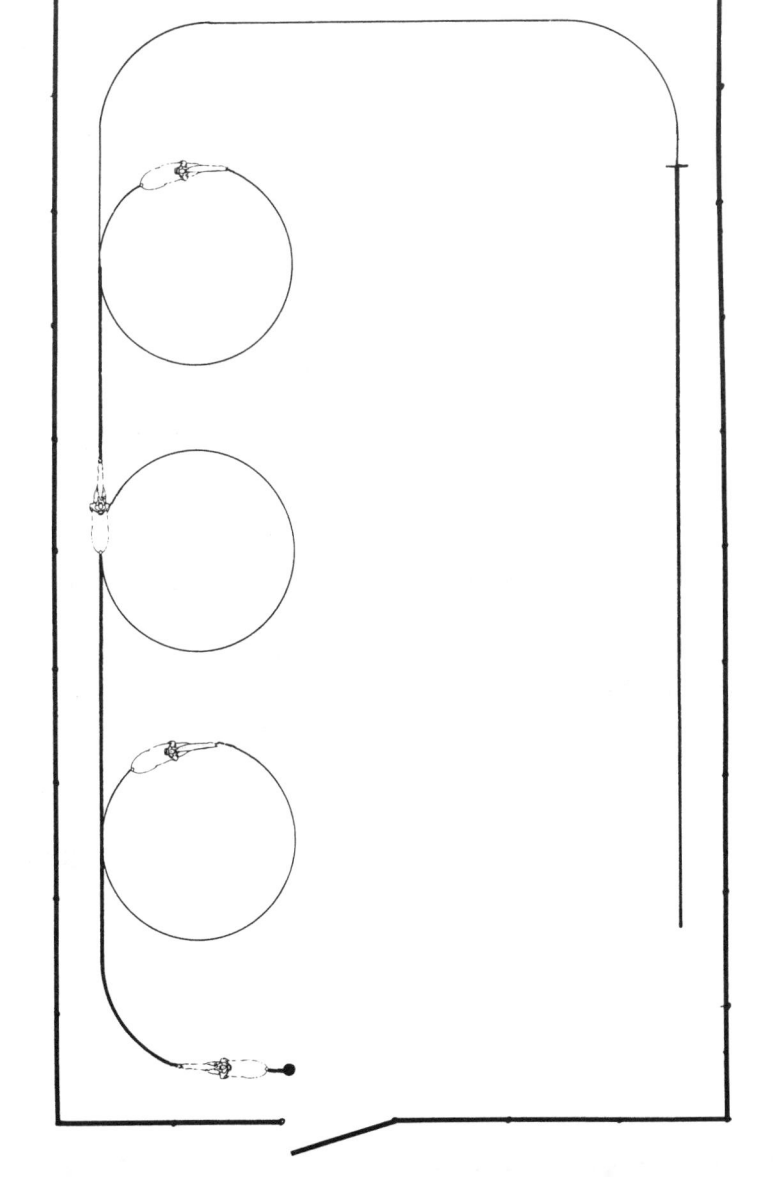

This is an example of what happens when a rider tries to pull a horse into a shorter stride length. The topline gets shorter and concave (hollow), and the underline gets longer and convex (bulges). This is the opposite of the goal, which is a long, rounded topline and a short, contracted underline. Contrast to drawings in Exercises #12, #29, and #80.

NOTE

★ The collected canter is the only gait where the horse is ridden in a slightly inward flexion (position in) even on straight lines.

★ The collected canter, properly performed, can be the ultimate in elegance and lyrical lightness, and is an example of the horse and rider in balance.

USE

★ The collected canter is used in third-level dressage.

★ The collected canter develops balance and roundness, improves rhythm, and increases strength and carrying capacity of the inside hind leg.

★ The circles test if the horse really stays up on the outside rein.

BENEFIT

Reining patterns call for large, fast circles followed by slow, small circles.

CAUTION

★ Take your time and develop the collected canter gradually.

★ Don't lean in or you could cause your horse's shoulder to drop into the circle and the outside hind to swing out of the circle.

★ If you try to hold the stride length down with the reins, you will likely cause the horse to trot or perform a four-beat canter.

Change of Lead through Trot

HOW TO RIDE THE EXERCISE

★ Lope right lead (Exercises #10 and #20).

★ Lope the right corner (Exercise #31).

★ Lope the long side.

★ Lope the right corner.

★ In the second corner of the short end, lope a 40-foot circle (Exercise #36).

★ As you finish the circle, head across the long diagonal (Exercise #32).

★ After loping straight a stride or two, half halt (Exercise #14), sit deep, and trot (Exercise #7).

★ Move your hands forward to allow the horse to fill up the trot frame.

★ As you trot, change your aids so the horse is ready to work to the left.

★ Apply aids for lope left lead.

★ Lope the corner to the left.

★ Lope straight ahead.

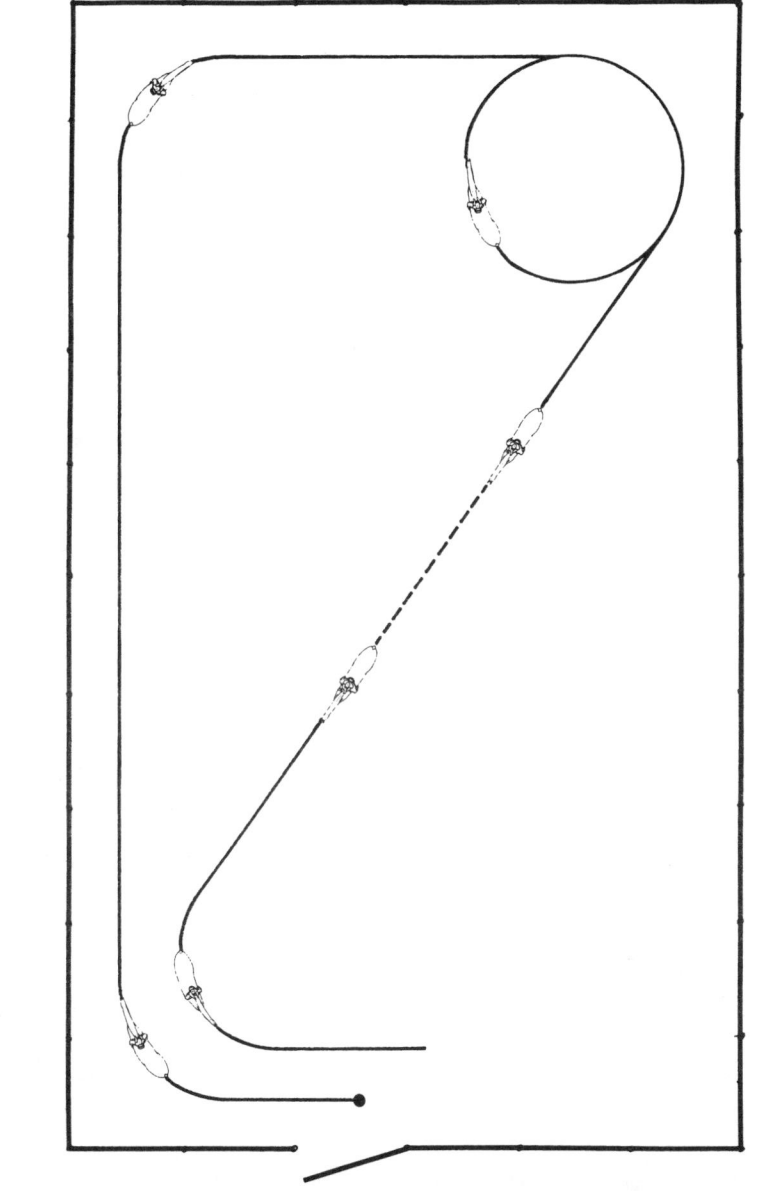

This horse looks like it has been jogging too long and too slow. Now his diagonal pair has broken, and he is essentially walking in front. With such little impulsion and a heavily weighted forehand, it will be difficult for him to muster up the energy for a balanced lope left lead. The rider has nice position, but she needs to be more effective with her seat and lower legs in conjunction with the bridle. See drawings in Exercises #10 and #41 for contrast.

NOTE

★ At first it may take several *strides* of trot for you to get organized. Eventually, you should lope on the new lead after three steps of trot.

★ Take advantage of the impulsion from the previous lope to give you a good, forward lope in the new direction by not trotting too long (see drawing).

BENEFITS

★ Changing to lead through trot is used in first-level dressage, as well as some Western horsemanship and hunter equitation patterns.

★ Allows you to change leads when you change direction on a young horse.

★ Allows you to focus on the departs to solidify timing.

CAUTION

Don't pull backward on the reins as this creates a backward, hollow transition, with the horse jamming his forehand stiffly on the ground. You need a forward, up-in-front transition to trot so you can readily lope off on the new lead.

Long and Low

How to Ride the Exercise

★ Working trot sitting (Exercise #7).

★ Half halt (Exercise #14).

★ In first corner, collected trot 30-foot circle (Exercise #36).

★ Working trot, posting down long side (Exercise #6).

★ Before corner, working trot sitting.

★ Working trot sitting around corner (Exercise #31), short end, and corner.

★ In second corner of the short end, collected trot 30-foot circle.

★ As you come out of the circle, working trot sitting.

★ Maintain working trot rhythm and impulsion all down the long side.

★ Gradually let the reins slip through your hands as you trot the long side.

★ Gradually regain contact before the corner.

★ Working trot, sitting around the corner.

I can just feel this horse's back swinging freely as he stretches down and forward. You can tell by his legs that he has maintained a good degree of impulsion.

Contrast to drawings in Exercises #18 and #21.

NOTE

This is a barometer of the correctness of your previous work. If, as you let the reins slip through your hands, your horse speeds up, raises his head, hollows his back, or chews the bit nervously, the previous work has been incorrect. If, instead, the horse stretches his neck forward and down, exhales softly through his nostrils (blows), and softly mouths the bit, your previous work was likely correct!

This exercise can be done at any gait. It is particularly rewarding at the canter.

BENEFITS

★ Allows the horse to stretch his topline. As his head and neck go down and forward, his back comes up.

★ Provides a great brief relaxer after more demanding (collected) work.

Quality Control Check (Self-Carriage Test)

HOW TO RIDE THE EXERCISE

★ Canter right lead (Exercise #20).

★ Canter the corner right (Exercise #31).

★ Canter straight 30 feet (Exercise #30).

★ Half halt (Exercise #14).

★ Canter 30-foot circle (Exercise #36).

★ Canter straight 10 – 20 feet.

★ Half halt.

★ Surrender the reins by moving both of your hands forward, but do not change your upper body, seat, or leg aids.

★ Allow the horse to canter on "the honor system" and evaluate.

★ Regain normal contact and canter on.

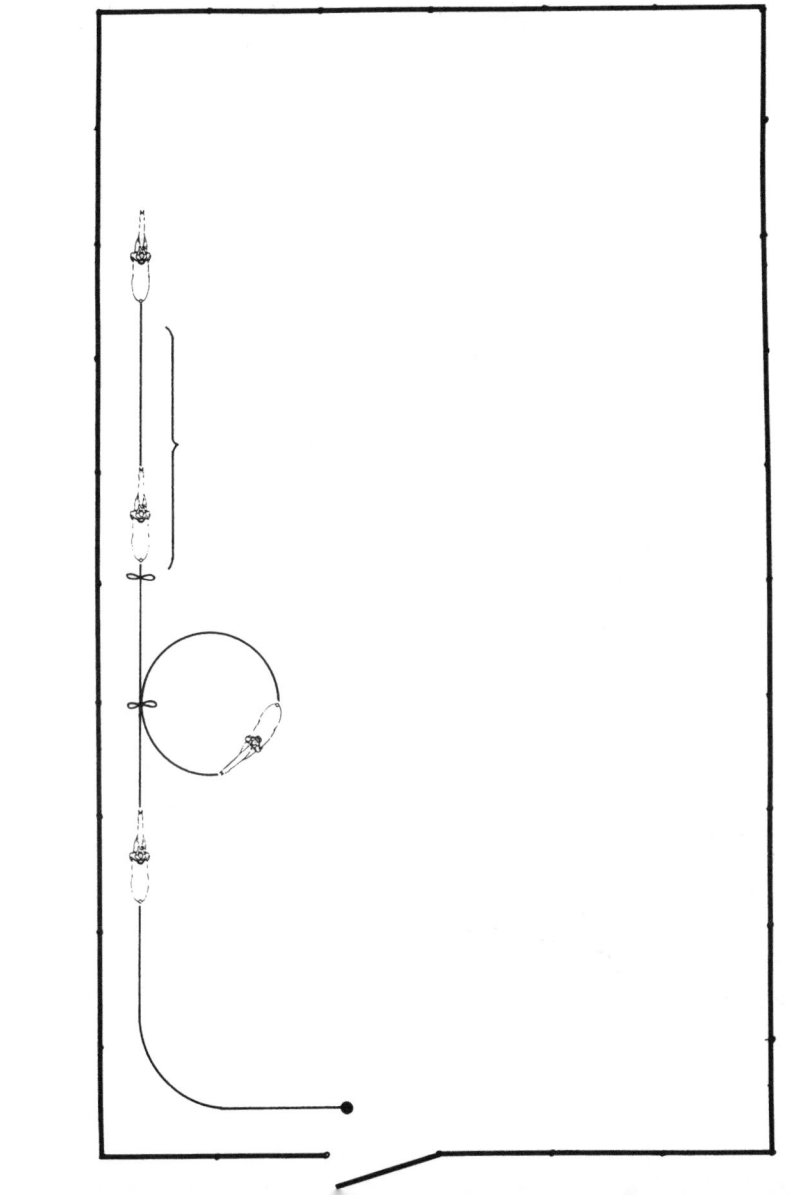

NOTE

This exercise can be performed at any gait.

Be sure the horse is moving in a consistent frame with the appropriate bend, rhythm, and balance *before* you surrender the reins.

When released, did your horse fall on his forehand, rush forward, toss his head, or bulge the underside of his neck? Or did he continue in the same balance, rhythm, and flexion as he had with rein contact?

When you regained contact, did your horse resist by poking his nose forward, flipping his head, bracing his jaw, poll, or back, or by shortening his stride? Or did he continue in the same balanced fashion as he did without rein contact?

This exercise is also useful for checking honesty of contact on one rein at a time.

★ To check inside bend, maintain contact on outside rein and release contact on inside rein. Did the horse retain inside bend or did he counter-flex?

★ To check if the horse is really up on the outside rein, maintain inside rein and release outside rein. Did the horse hold himself up on the outside or did he fall to the inside?

The rider has surrendered the contact on the reins but has maintained position, and the horse continues to canter in balance and rhythm.

BENEFIT

This is a means to evaluate a horse's balance and the thoroughness of his self-carriage development. The horse's reaction will reveal whether he is being held in position by the rider or if he has developed the strength, consistency, and integrity to move in balance when the rein aids are removed.

SECTION 3

Circles

Circles and circular figures require turning. The turn can involve an almost imperceptible arcing of the horse's spine on a very large circle or an extreme inward curving for a sharp, collected movement such as a quarter turn. Turning requires proper lateral flexion and lateral bending.

Lateral flexion is a turn of the horse's head to one side or the other. The movement takes place at the joint of the axis vertebrae, the junction of the neck and the head, more commonly referred to as the *poll* or *throat latch* area. When a horse is described as flexed, his head is "in position," but his spine (from the poll to the tail) is straight. Lateral flexion is created with rein aids only; the rider is otherwise evenly balanced. It is possible to have lateral flexion without lateral bend such as in the case of leg yielding (see Section 4: Lateral Work). Most times, however, a horse that is flexed is also bent.

Lateral bend is the arcing of the horse's entire body around the rider's inside leg. When circling right, the horse will be bent around the rider's right leg. Correct lateral bend requires lateral flexion. The bend must be uniform from poll to tail. The horse's neck is more flexible than the back, so the tendency is for a rider to overbend the front of the horse. This must be avoided.

For clarification, *vertical flexion* (a characteristic of collection) refers to the upward arching of the horse's topline and the increased flexion of the limb joints (most noticeably, the knees and hocks).

When a horse is ridden in a circular figure, he must be ridden "straight" on that figure; that is, his entire body must be bent according to the line he is working on, but his hind legs must follow in the tracks of his front legs. This is in contrast to the goals of the various lateral movements (see next section).

When a horse is ridden in a circle, his inside hind leg carries more weight than the outside one.

When performing circular maneuvers, be careful that you do not collapse one side of your body or the other. A collapsed side is one where the rib cage has sunken in, the shoulder has dropped down, and the hip has hiked up. To prevent this, you must learn to weight a seat bone and heel without collapsing your body on that side.

The term *change of rein* means changing the direction of travel and usually the bend. When a horse is tracking to the right, he is said to be on the left rein because that is the rein that essentially holds him up on the figure line. See Exercises #27, #32, and #33 for examples of change of rein.

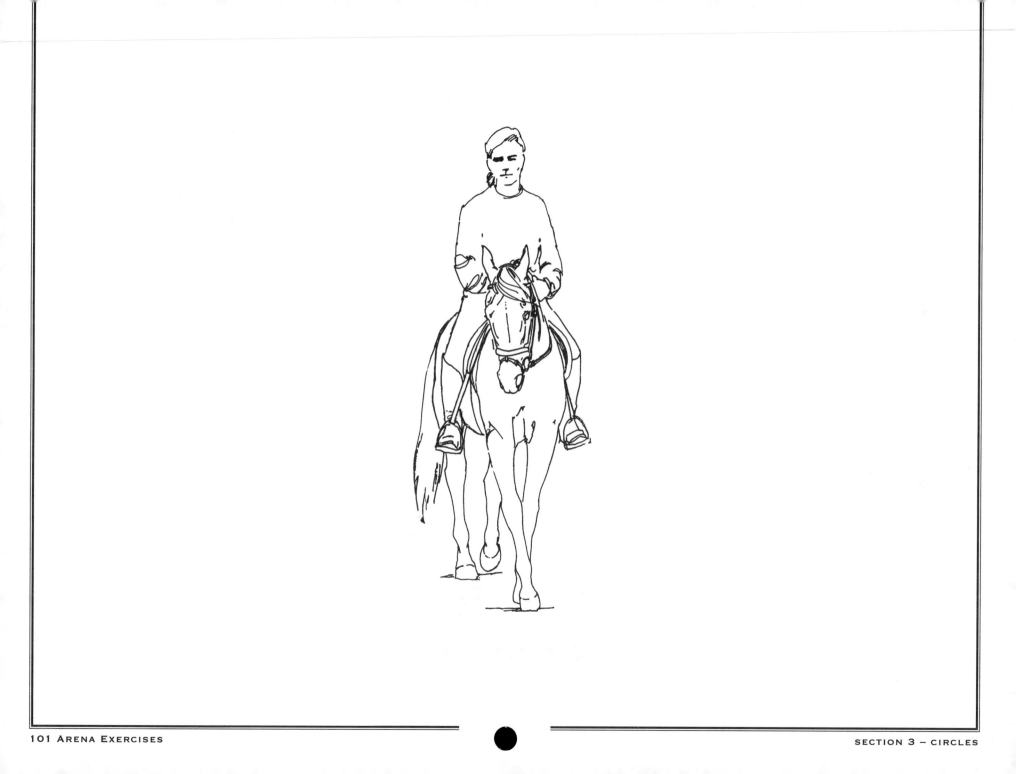

Straight

How to Ride the Exercise

★ Check your own straightness (Exercise #1).

★ Working trot, sitting (Exercises #6 and #7).

★ Corner (Exercise #31).

★ Straighten by bringing the forehand in front of the hindquarters. When tracking right, if the horse is counter-flexed left and the right hind is inside the track:

  • Place right leg behind the girth to prevent any more sideways deviation of right hind leg.

  • Right rein in a lifting motion to bring right front shoulder in front of right hind leg.

  • Keep left leg at the girth to keep the left hind moving forward.

  • Keep left rein low and supporting.

★ Ride the corner.

★ Ride straight about 20–40 feet.

★ Turn down the centerline.

★ Ride straight without the assistance of the arena wall or rail.

The straighter the rider sits and the more evenly the aids are applied, the straighter the horse will go. You might notice that this rider's right ear is slightly lower than her left; that her right shoulder and elbow are slightly lower than her left; and that her right knee is slightly higher than her left. All of this adds up to her rib cage being more contracted on the right and more stretched on the left. Here, the imbalance is very subtle and is in part due to the horse's right shoulder being behind the left in this phase of the trot. See also drawing in Exercise #38.

NOTE: CROOKEDNESS

The majority of horses move "crooked" naturally because it requires less effort than moving straight. Most training strives for *ordinary straightness* where the spine (midline) is in a straight line. Because a horse's hips are wider than his shoulders, the hind feet do not step directly in the tracks of the fronts when the horse is straight by ordinary standards. However, to be straight, the horse's hind feet should follow the lines of travel of his front feet.

Dressage strives for relative straightness where the inside hind follows in the exact track of the inside front.

Most horses (80–90 percent) travel crooked naturally in the following fashion: the right hind travels in a track that is offset to the right of the right front and therefore sends more weight diagonally to the left shoulder, causing the horse's forehand to fall to the left. The left hind leg carries more weight than the right hind. The position of the right hind continues to imbalance the body to the left. This results in the left side becoming stronger than the right side.

So, when going to the left, the horse overbends to the left, weights the left shoulder, and swings the hindquarters off the track to the right. The correction is to counter-flex (Exercise #51) to the right when going left.

When going to the right, the horse's neck almost counter-flexes to the left (counter-bends with a straight stiffness) and the hindquarters swing to the right. The correction is "in position" to the right (see Section 4: Lateral Work), shoulder fore (Exercise #61), or shoulder in (Exercise #62).

About 10–20 percent of horses travel crooked in the opposite way.

BENEFIT

Only through straightening can a horse be taught to be ridden in balance, which is necessary for every horse performance.

Corner

HOW TO RIDE THE EXERCISE

Riding the correct normal corner to the right:

★ Trot (Exercise #6).

★ When you are 20 feet from the rail, half halt (Exercise #14).

★ Transfer your weight to your inside seat bone (right) and forward.

★ Deepen your right knee (heel down) to prevent your right side from collapsing.

★ Flex the horse to the inside with the inside (right) rein.

★ Use the inside (right) leg at the girth to cause the horse's inside (right) hind to reach forward and give the horse's body a point to bend around.

★ Let the outside (left) rein yield enough to allow the flexion required.

★ Maintain enough contact with the outside (left) rein to keep the horse from bulging his outside shoulder to the left.

★ Use the outside (left) leg slightly behind the girth to prevent the hindquarters from stepping to the left.

★ Use the outside leg to bend the horse around your inside (right) leg.

A deep corner is a more advanced maneuver ridden in collected gaits.

★ Keep your inside hand from crossing the mane or you will cause the left shoulder to bulge outward.

★ Be sure to maintain the same rhythm through the corner.

NOTE

If a horse tries to cut the corner with no lateral bend, you must react instantly and decisively with a strong inside leg, seat, and rein.

BENEFIT

By riding each corner as if it were a specific maneuver (which it is!), you will reach your goal of developing a balanced and supple horse much, much quicker!

Arena key from starting dot:

★ Correct normal corner for working gaits

★ Cutting the corner, flat with no lateral bend

★ Incorrect deep corner with too much neck bend from too strong an inside rein; shoulder bulges outward

★ Correct deep corner for collected gaits

In a soft, balanced bend to the right, this horse's body creates an even arc from head to tail. His poll is up, not avoiding contact by dipping down. His expression is pleasant. See drawings in Exercises #34, #36, and #43. For contrast, see drawings in Exercises #50 and #90.

Change of Rein on Long Diagonal

HOW TO RIDE THE EXERCISE

★ Posting trot to the left, sitting when the right front and left hind legs land, and rising when they rise (Exercise #6).

★ Ride the short end.

★ Ride the second corner of the short end with a normal left corner (Exercise #31).

★ After the corner, ride straight (Exercise #30) 1–2 strides.

★ Turn left and head diagonally across the arena, aiming at a point on the opposite long side about two strides from the opposite corner.

★ Somewhere in the vicinity of the middle of the diagonal line, change the diagonal to which you are posting by sitting two beats instead of one. This will put you on the new diagonal.

★ As you approach the corner, change to right bend.

★ When you reach the end of the diagonal, turn right.

★ Ride straight 1–2 strides.

★ Ride a right corner.

★ Proceed ahead in the new direction.

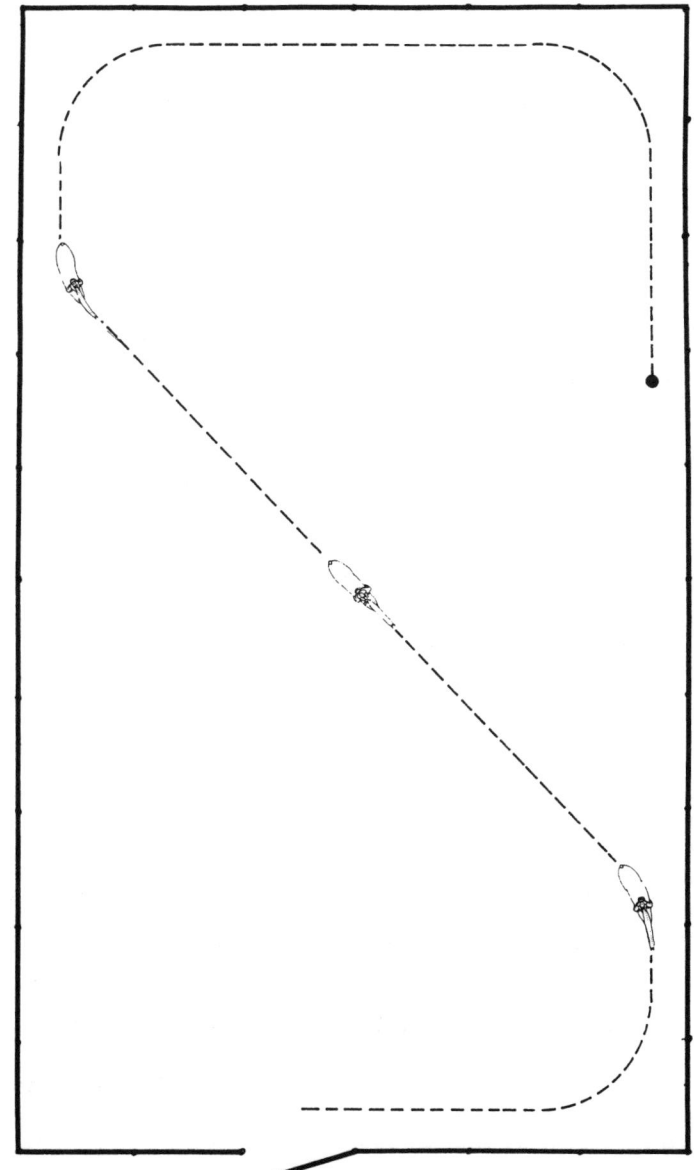

This horse is moving forward energetically at the posting trot. Assuming the rider is posting correctly on the rail, which way would she be tracking around the arena? Because she is sitting when the left hind and right front are landing, she would be tracking to the left.

NOTE

A change of rein occurs when you change direction. If you are tracking to the left, you are making left turns around the arena. If you want to track right, there are many ways to change the direction of your travel, and this is one of the simplest.

Properly executed, the rhythm and frame of the horse are consistent through the entire exercise.

BENEFIT

The change of rein on a long diagonal is a roomy way to change direction and bend. You have plenty of time to get organized for changing your seat, leg, and rein aids for the new bend. It encourages a horse to reach out rather than "suck back" when changing direction.

CAUTION

★ If your horse throws his head up, rushes forward, shortens his stride, or bobs his head down during the change, you need to improve the coordination of your aids.

★ Be careful not to pull back on the reins when you change your posting because this will cause your horse to lose his balance or shorten his stride.

★ Do not make your diagonal line directly from one corner to another because you will have to make very sharp turns that will be difficult for your horse to do without interrupting his balance and rhythm.

★ Do not try to change rein on a diagonal from the *first* corner of the short side because this will force you to make very sharp turns, defeating the purpose of this exercise.

Change of Rein on Short Diagonal

HOW TO RIDE THE EXERCISE

★ Jog (Exercise #7).

★ Right corner (Exercise #31).

★ Straight up the long side (Exercise #30).

★ First corner of short end normal (Exercise #31).

★ Short end.

★ Ride the beginning of a 30-foot circle (Exercise #36) in the second corner.

★ Head toward the opposite long side, aiming more for the middle.

★ Turn left.

VARIATION

The following "variation" is really more the standard:

★ Ride the second corner of the short side normally.

★ Ride the horse straight 1–2 strides.

★ Turn right.

★ Head to the middle of the long side.

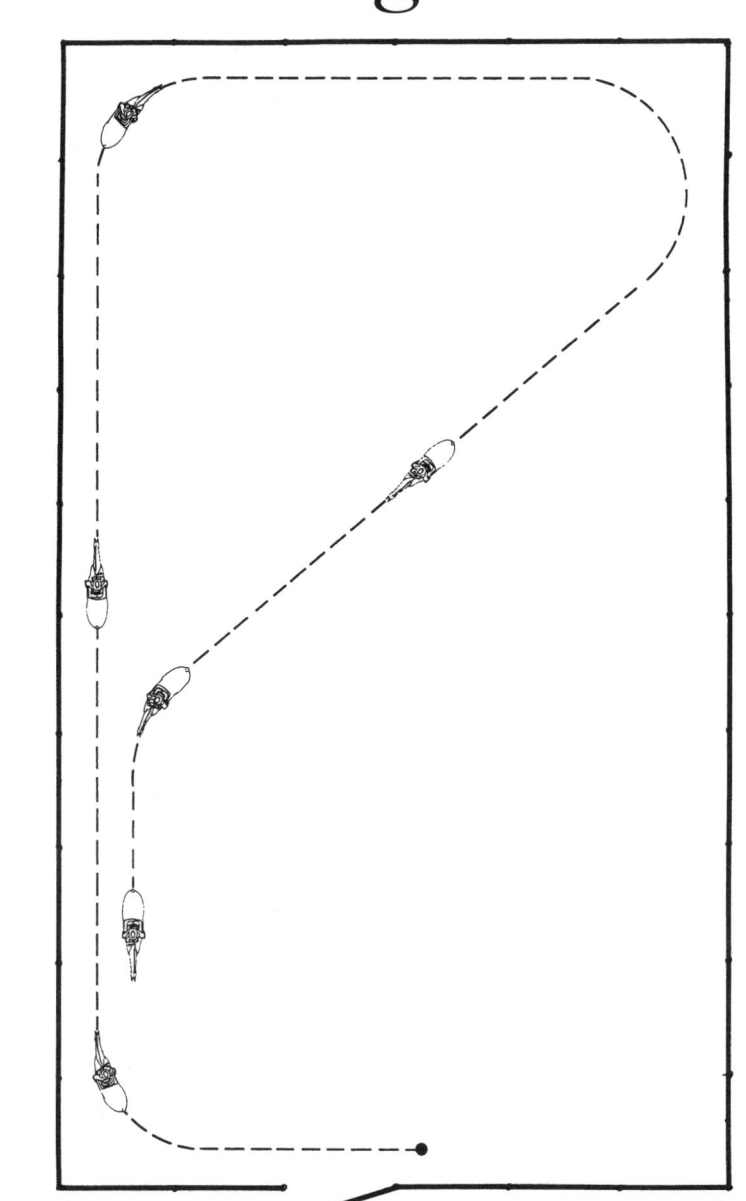

A picture-pretty jog. The horse is nicely on the aids with light rein contact. The rider sits in balance, not interfering with the horse's movement, but allowing him to work underneath her.

NOTE

The arena map shows the elementary version of this exercise used with beginning horses. The variation listed above is more appropriate for intermediate to advanced horses.

BENEFIT

This exercise pattern will come in handy when riding in more collected gaits and working on such things as flying changes.

Extra Large Circle

HOW TO RIDE THE EXERCISE

★ Set out some cones to define a 60–100 foot diameter circle.

★ Start on the inside of the cones, and walk (Exercises #2 and #15) a large circle to the right.

★ When you are circling right, the cones are to your left. Imagine that you want a point on the middle of your horse's barrel and your left leg to just brush the cones.

★ Slip to the outside of the cones, and trot (Exercises #6 and #17) a circle around the cones.

★ When you circle right and the cones are to your right, imagine you want your horse to curl around the cones, coming as close as possible, but never touching the cones.

★ Slip to the inside, and trot a circle.

★ Slip to the outside, and walk a circle.

★ Reverse, and ride the entire pattern to the left.

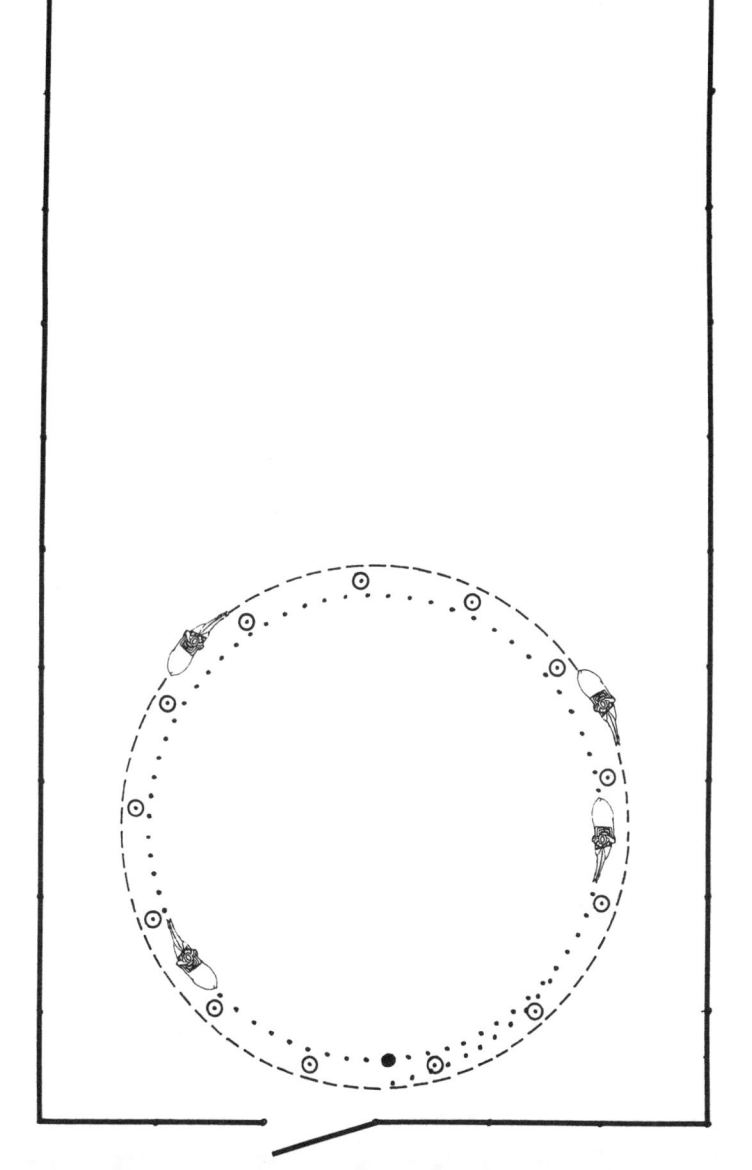

At the beginning, a rider might use a leading (opening) rein to teach a horse to bend softly into a circular maneuver. Note that the outside rein limits the bend.

NOTE

When riding a circle:

★ Guide and control the hindquarters with your legs.

Use your inside leg at the girth

- to activate inside hind leg,

- to create and maintain lateral bend to the inside,

- to prevent the horse from falling into the circle.

Use your outside leg behind the girth

- to maintain bend by holding the hindquarters,

- to cause the outside hind leg to step forward.

Move your outside leg forward

- to assist the outside rein in straightening a bulging shoulder.

★ Guide and control the forehand with your reins.

Use your inside rein

- sometimes a little higher than the outside rein,

- sometimes in a lifting or vibrating manner,

- to initiate inside flexion and bend.

Use your outside rein

- low and steady,

- to limit inside bend,

- to prevent outside shoulder from bulging.

BENEFIT

Circles are the foundation of any horse's training, making him equally supple on both sides of his body so he develops proper body alignment. A horse that performs circles properly in both directions won't lean on your aids when asked to perform other maneuvers.

CAUTION

Don't confuse circle work with lateral work. When you ride a horse on a circle, you should ride him *straight*. Riding "straight" on a circle means you must be sure the horse's hind feet follow his front feet and that the horse is bent uniformly from his head to his tail according to the size of the circle and the degree of bend it requires.

Large (20-Meter) Circle

HOW TO RIDE THE EXERCISE

★ Working trot, sitting (Exercise #7).

★ Ride the corner (Exercise #31).

★ Ride straight (Exercise #30).

★ At the midpoint of the long side, ride a 20-meter (66-foot) circle to the right (Exercise #34).

★ Return to the same point on the rail where you started the circle.

★ Ride straight ahead.

VARIATION

Ride the 20-meter circle at all gaits.

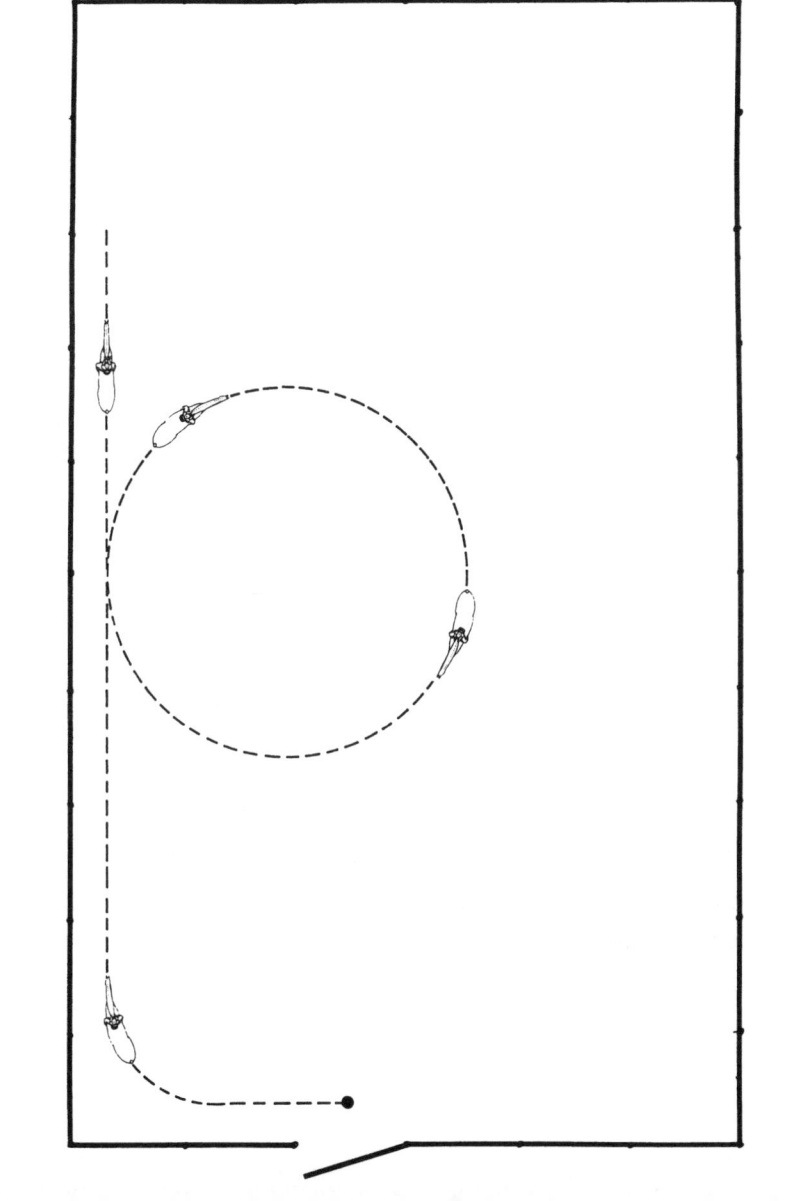

This rider has over-flexed the horse to the right with too strong a right rein. She has collapsed the right side of her body so that her left heel has come up. The horse is stepping under his body with his right hind leg in a lateral maneuver, rather than traveling "straight" (see Exercise #34) on the circle. To fix, the rider should use less right rein and right leg. She should sit evenly on both seat bones and then slightly weight the inside seat bone without letting the left side of her body "float." The left rein could be carried away from the horse's neck a bit to straighten him and keep him "up" on his left shoulder. Contrast to drawings in Exercises #31, #34, #36, #45, and #49.

NOTE

You need to be able to gauge whether your circles are the correct size and a uniform shape. Use cones, marks on the rails, lime spots on the ground, a knowledgeable ground person, or an instructor.

BENEFITS

For general benefits, see Exercise #34.

Large circles are a requirement for training-level dressage.

CAUTION

Be sure you aim for appropriate bend and rhythm. Riding circles in poor form can be very counterproductive.

Medium (10–Meter) Circle

HOW TO RIDE THE EXERCISE

★ Working trot, sitting (Exercise #7).

★ Half halt (Exercise #14).

★ Collected trot (Exercise #9).

★ Medium circle in first corner.

　• Inside rein, leg, eye in direction of movement.

　• Half halt on the outside rein.

　• Turn upper body so outside shoulder comes forward.

★ As you come out of the circle, drive forward into working trot sitting (Exercise #7).

★ Ride straight (Exercise #30) up the long side.

★ Before the corner, half halt and collected trot.

★ Medium circle.

★ Continue.

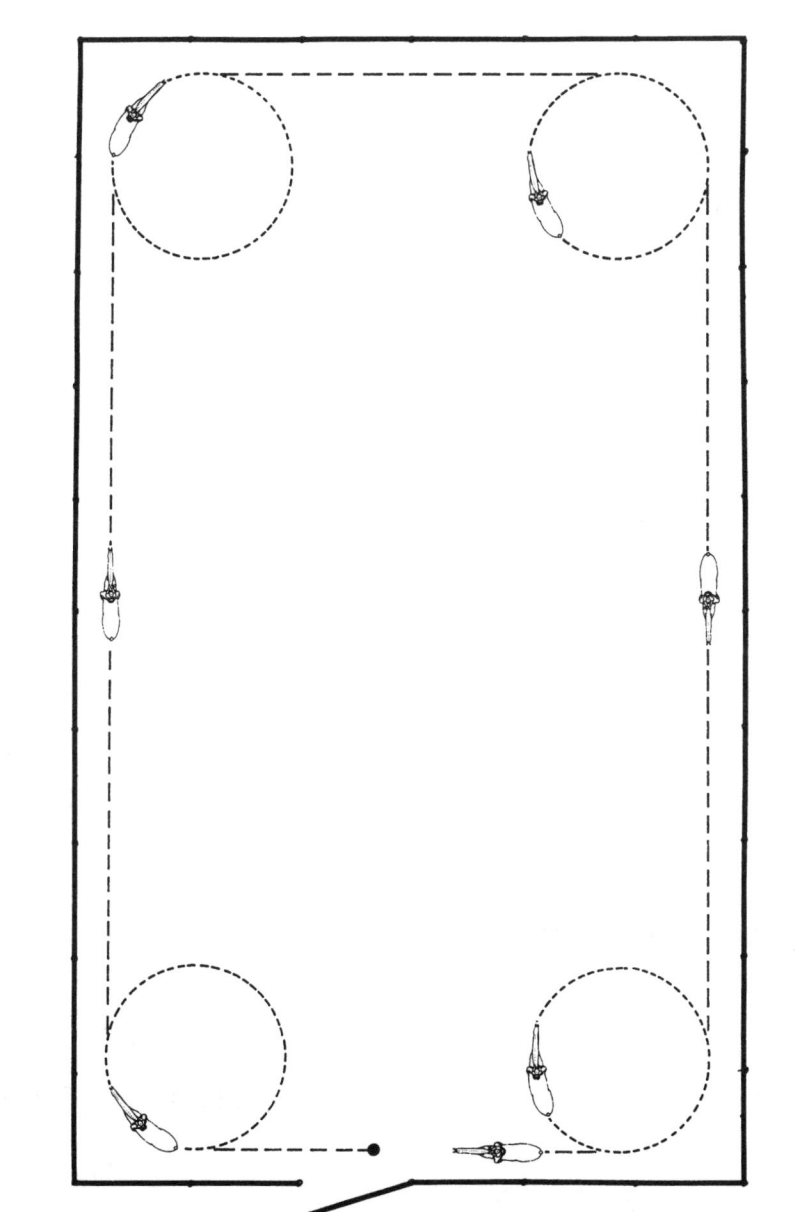

Here the medium circle is "test-ridden" at a walk so the rider can get a feel for the amount of bend necessary. To "straighten" her horse on the circle (to decrease the inside flexion), the rider moves the left rein away from the horse's neck just for an instant to keep him up on his left shoulder. Remember that too much inside bend causes the outside shoulder to bulge, a most hideous configuration! Note that as the right hind swings in and forward, it appears that it will land in the track of the front foot. This is desirable.

VARIATION

★ Try the exercise at a walk to determine the amount of bend necessary.

★ Use this exercise for canter work to develop speed control.

BENEFITS

★ Improves balance, enhances the engagement of the hindquarters, develops a more active inside hind leg and hock flexion, introduces the elements of collection.

★ Enhances first-level dressage.

★ Since most horses have a stronger left hind leg (see Exercise #30), performing this exercise to the right with a conditioning effect in mind will strengthen the right hind leg and increase its capacity to drive and carry weight. Such an exercise will help you straighten your horse because it will strengthen his weaknesses. When first introducing small circles (see also Exercise #37), do not repeat them too many times or you might end up straining your horse and making him temporarily weaker.

Small (6–Meter) Circle: Volte

How to Ride the Exercise

★ Collected trot (Exercise #9).

★ Ride the corner (Exercise #31).

★ Ride straight (Exercise #30) 20 feet.

★ Prepare for right volte.

  • Right rein to flex horse vertically at poll and inside to the right.

  • Weight inside heel so horse can balance your weight.

  • Maintain outside rein to prevent overbending.

  • With your right leg, ask for maximum lateral bend while keeping the horse's hind legs following the fronts.

★ Ride a small circle (volte) that is 6 meters (20 feet).

★ Ride straight 60 feet or so.

★ Right flexion.

★ Ride a volte to the right.

★ Ride straight.

In this example of right flexion, the horse is just being set up to begin a volte to the right. He is flexed to the right and is traveling in a collected frame (walk). His right bend is minimized as the rider is securing the base of his neck with the left rein. There could be a little more contact with the left rein if necessary. She is holding his body on the figure line with her left leg. See drawing in Exercise #85.

NOTE

Only use this exercise in true collected gaits because it requires the most acute lateral bend possible while keeping the horse aligned.

BENEFITS

★ Develops collection and increases strength of hindquarters.

★ Improves Prix St. George dressage.

VARIATION

★ Ride at collected walk or collected canter.

★ Ride 2–3 voltes in the same place.

CAUTION

★ Don't sacrifice rhythm for the extreme bend required for this very small circle. If you find the horse starts prancing (moving with mincing steps) or getting behind the bit, practice with larger circles and work your way down over a period of weeks.

★ Don't overuse the inside rein in an attempt to make a sharp bend — you will throw your horse off balance, and he will begin falling apart.

★ Never attempt a circle smaller than 20 feet in diameter because a horse cannot bend and stay aligned in a smaller figure than that. His hindquarters would fall out of the circle and his rhythm would become irregular.

Figure 8

HOW TO RIDE THE EXERCISE

★ Begin at the center of the arena with your horse facing one of the long sides of the arena. Focus on a fence post or cone that serves as the center marker.

★ Look straight ahead and ride straight forward (Exercise #30) at a jog (Exercise #7).

★ After 1–2 strides, begin circling your horse to the right (Exercises #34–36).

★ Make a large circle that is uniformly round by keeping your aids consistent.

★ When approaching the close of the circle, prepare to change your aids to straight (Exercise #30).

★ Ride straight ahead 1–4 strides, depending on the size of the circle.

★ Change the bend from right to left.

★ Begin circling your horse to the left. Be ready to catch the hindquarters with your right leg if they try to swing out of the new circle.

★ Make a large circle to the left that is uniformly round.

★ When approaching the close of the second circle, prepare to track straight ahead.

★ Walk ahead 1–2 strides (Exercise #17).

★ Halt (Exercise #19).

VARIATION

★ Ride at the walk to establish the pattern.

★ When you ride at the lope, you will have to perform either a simple lead change (Exercise #84), a flying lead change (Exercise #95), or the second circle in counter-canter (Exercises #52–54).

★ Vary the size of the circles from 100 to 40 feet, depending on the gait and the degree of collection.

★ Ride more than one circle to the right (or left) before changing direction.

NOTE

The line between the two circles should be parallel to the short ends of the arena. It should not be a diagonal line that makes an X in the middle of the pattern. An X configuration is a lazy way to change direction in a figure 8 and "eats up" part of each circle. The flat line in the center is more correct and more difficult because it requires you to keep your horse in balance.

Your ultimate goal is to ride only one stride straight in the center so that the circles are just "kissing."

When you ride the flat line between the two circles, keep your weight balanced equally and project straight ahead. See drawing in Exercise #30.

BENEFIT

The figure 8 is a simple exercise that combines straight and circular movements and allows you to practice a change of bend and a halt with plenty of preparation time. This exercise can help you develop good habits and coordination for the more advanced work that is to come. It is often a part of horsemanship, equitation, and reining patterns.

Large Circle — Small Circle

HOW TO RIDE THE EXERCISE

★ Lope right lead (Exercise #10).

★ Lope the corner (Exercise #31).

★ Lope straight about 50 feet (Exercise #30).

★ Large circle to the right (Exercise #35).

★ As you return to the point where you left the rail, check your horse.

★ Collect the lope.

★ Lope a small circle (Exercise #37).

★ When you return to the rail, resume a normal lope and lope straight.

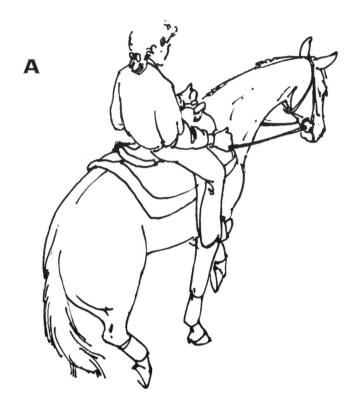

A

B

*In drawing **A**, the rider is trotting the exercise and using a leading rein to begin the small circle. Note that even though asking for bend, she keeps the horse's body in alignment.*

*In drawing **B**, in a later stage, tracking left at the trot, the rider asks for a more collected bend by using the direct rein.*

VARIATION

Try this at a walk or trot first (see drawings).

Repeat the exercises several times in other parts of the arena and note the tremendous improvement by the third set of circles.

BENEFITS

★ These circle exercises are a great means of developing speed control, collection, and balance.

★ Large circle — small circle is good preparation for Western reining.

Canter Springs

HOW TO RIDE THE EXERCISE

★ Active working lope right lead (Exercise #10).

★ Ride the corner (Exercise #31).

★ Ride straight one stride (Exercise #30).

★ Flex right, and ride large circle (Exercise #35).

★ Last stride of circle, check (Exercise #14).

★ Return to point of departure on the rail.

★ Ride straight one stride.

★ Flex right, and ride a large circle.

★ Continue the exercise until there is no room left in the arena.

VARIATION

This is also a good pattern for walk-lope transitions. Walk as you approach the rail, walk straight one stride, lope right lead.

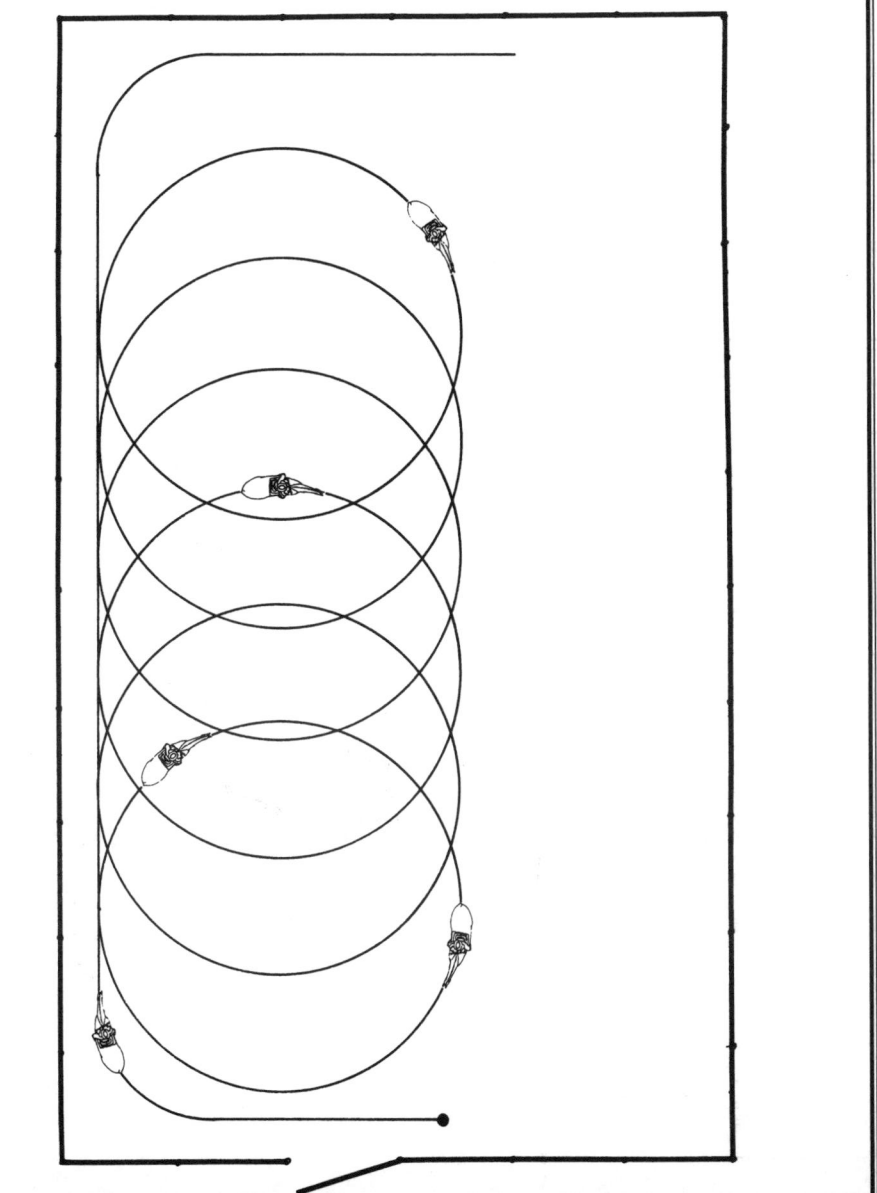

A nice forward lope with good body straightness. What lead is this horse on? Because the initiating hind is the left hind, the horse is on the right lead. Therefore, the horse could be flexed right a little more. See drawing in Exercise #11.

BENEFITS

★ Good for balancing and straightening the horse.

★ Helps with forward movement and developing speed control.

★ Prevents the boredom associated with loping a circle over and over again in the same spot.

CAUTION

★ Be sure to pay attention to the exact spot you leave the rail so you can return to it and receive maximum benefit from the exercise.

★ Take care that the shape of the circles does not become sloppy.

★ If a horse begins to anticipate the sequence after two or three springs, either ride forward and continue the exercise elsewhere in the arena or repeat the circle in the same spot.

Spiral

HOW TO RIDE THE EXERCISE

★ Trot (Exercise #7) a large circle (Exercise #35) to the right.

★ Begin spiraling in.

★ Maintain right bend using inside leg and rein if horse loses bend or slows down.

★ Use outside leg to keep the hindquarters aligned.

★ Inside shoulder back and outside shoulder forward.

★ Weight inside seat bone.

★ Use a slight opening rein on the inside and a neck rein on the outside (or just a neck rein if you are using a curb bit).

★ Push with your outside leg at the cinch.

★ Only go as far in as the horse is able to stay relaxed, in balance, and trotting in a proper rhythm.

★ Then spiral out, maintaining the bend of the circle but applying the opposite aids.

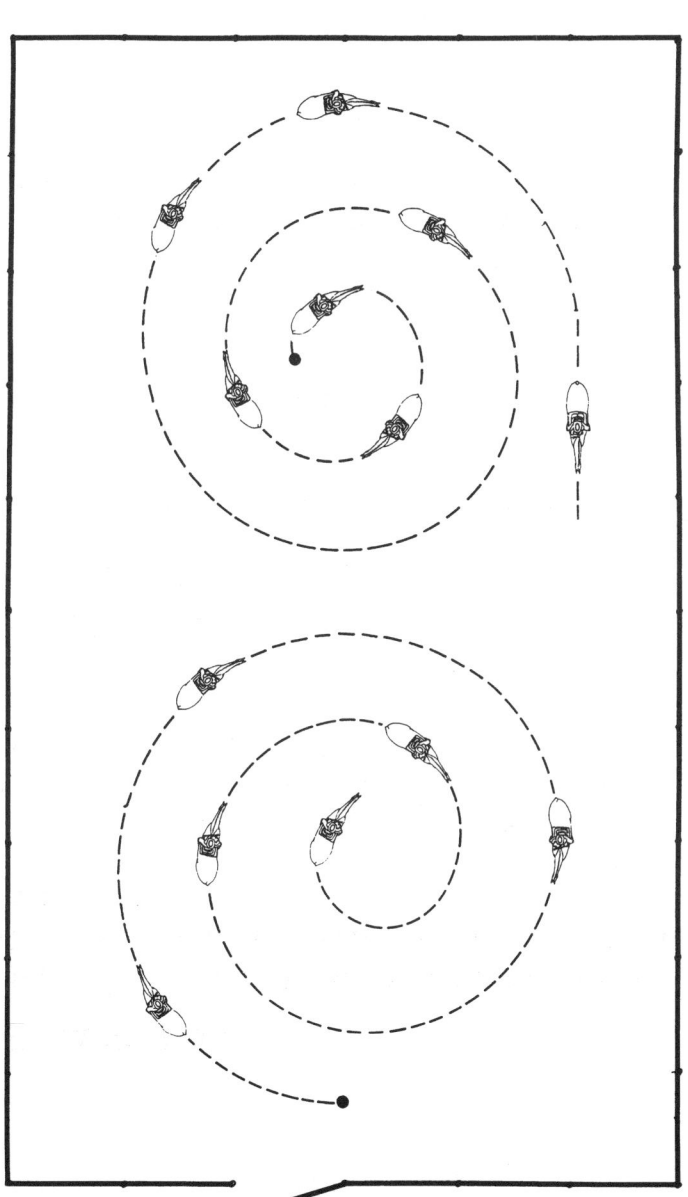

This picture-perfect example of the end of a spiral in to the right at a lope shows great impulsion, balance, rider finesse, and wonderful bend.

VARIATION

★ First practice at the walk, but be careful to keep the horse's body aligned — no leg yield or turn on the hindquarters steps here.

★ At the lope/canter, this exercise is very beneficial for developing the pirouette and conditioning the Western horse to lope small circles in balance.

BENEFITS

★ Gets the horse listening to your aids on a circle.

★ Begins collection by working in smaller figures for a short time.

★ Can be used as part of a warm-up or a warm-down.

CAUTION

★ Don't lean your upper body into the spiral as if on a motorcycle because you will throw your horse off balance.

★ Don't let your horse slow down as you decrease the circle size.

Loosen Up

HOW TO RIDE THE EXERCISE

★ Posting trot (Exercise #6).

★ Large circle to the right (Exercise #35).

★ Finish the circle and ride straight 2–3 strides (Exercise #30).

★ Right corner (Exercise #31).

★ Straight 1–2 strides.

★ Ride the long diagonal (Exercise #32).

★ Change posting at the center.

★ Turn left, and ride straight 1–2 strides.

★ Left corner.

★ Straight for half the short end.

★ Large circle to the left.

★ Straight for the rest of the short end.

★ Left corner.

★ Straight 1–2 strides.

★ Ride the long diagonal.

★ Change posting at the center.

★ Turn right, and ride straight 1–2 strides.

★ Right corner.

★ Straight.

★ Circle, and continue the exercise.

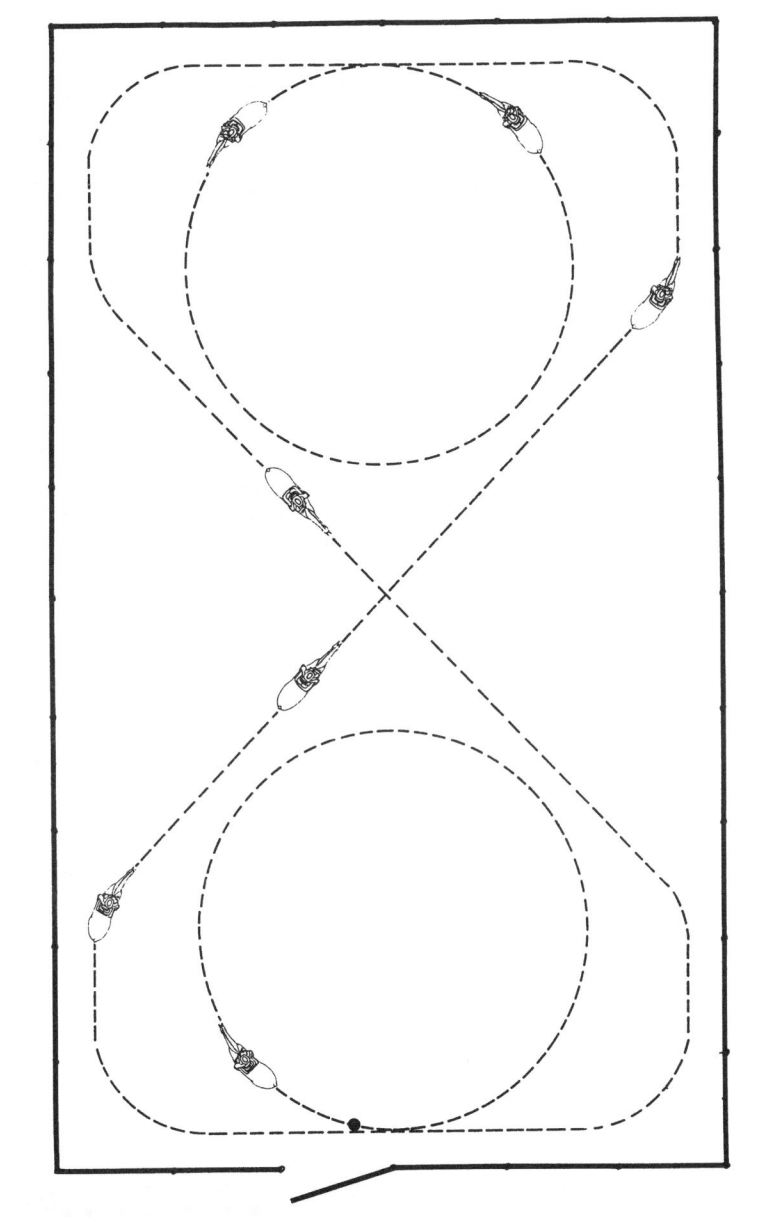

Although this Western horse is moving forward in a nice energetic trot and his frame is acceptable, his poll has dropped and his face has come behind the vertical. It would be better if his face were 5–10 degrees in front of the vertical.

VARIATION

At one of the short ends, instead of riding a large circle, perform a half turn (Exercise #43) so you will be riding the exercise in the opposite direction.

NOTE

This is one exercise that can't be overdone. It is a great warm-up for both horse and rider. You could ride this exercise 10 times or more in a row and continue to derive benefit if you stay focused and keep your horse on the aids.

BENEFITS

★ Develops forward energy.

★ Teaches the horse to maintain consistent rhythm in spite of a change of direction.

★ Provides a simple exercise that gets the horse off the rail.

Half Turn

How to Ride the Exercise

Half turn to the right:

★ Leave the rail and perform a half volte right (Exercise #37).

★ At the widest part of volte, ride a diagonal line back toward track.

★ Initiate left flexion.

Half turn in reverse:

★ Leave the rail using mild right bend.

★ Straighten and ride a diagonal line until you are about 20 feet from the rail.

★ Initiate bend to left.

★ Ride a half volte to left.

★ Straighten.

Arena map, clockwise from lower left:

★ Proper half turn

★ Improper half turn with bulge and delayed straightening

★ Proper half turn in reverse

★ Improper half turn in reverse with delayed straightening, resulting in a light-bulb shape

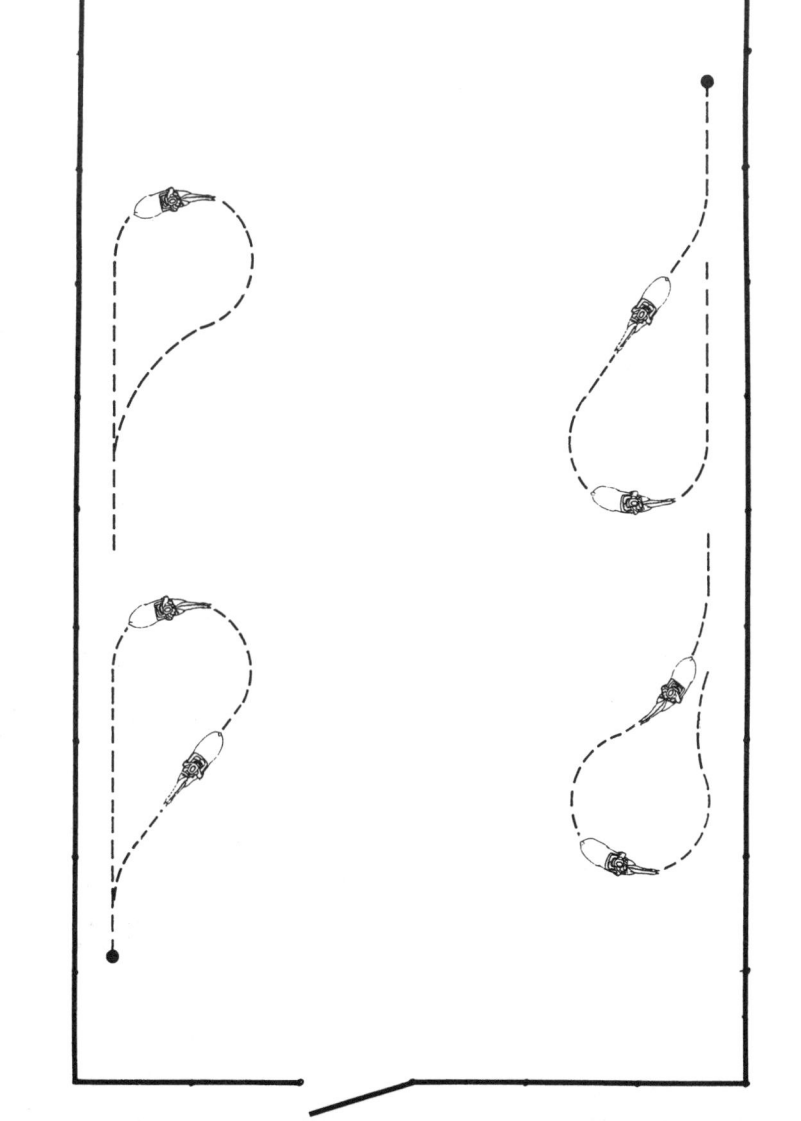

At the moment the horse leaves the rail for a half turn to the right, he is flexed right. Note that although the rider has weighted her right heel, she has not collapsed her body. Therefore, the horse stays up on his left shoulder throughout the turn.

NOTE

A half turn should look more like an ice cream cone than a tear drop or a light bulb.

BENEFIT

Provides a more concise and immediate way to change direction than on a diagonal or figure 8.

CAUTION

Many horses slow down their rhythm in a half turn. This usually occurs for one of two reasons. The young horse decreases his tempo because he interprets increased bit pressure as a signal to slow down. He hasn't learned to differentiate the various pressures on the bit. The horse that is lazy or out-of-condition will slow down because it requires more energy to perform a half turn in balance and at the correct tempo than it does to perform one sloppily. Keep your forward driving aids on your horse so he doesn't lose rhythm in the turn.

Change of Bend — Single Loop

HOW TO RIDE THE EXERCISE

★ Working trot (Exercises #6 and #7).

★ Right corner (Exercise #31).

★ Continue right bend.

★ Gradually straighten bend until at midpoint of long side, horse is straight and parallel to the rail, about 20 feet off the rail.

★ Introduce left bend and gradually work your way toward the next corner.

★ Straighten for one stride.

★ Right corner.

VARIATION

Ride the same exercise across the short end.

Ride the exercise at a walk to establish the amount of appropriate bend necessary to complete the exercise.

Perform the same exercise on the quarter line and the center line.

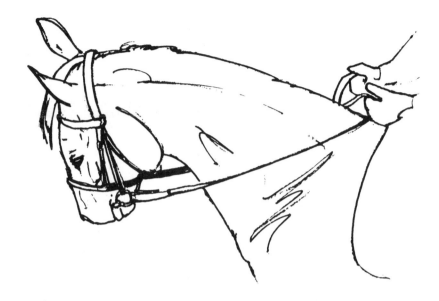

This drawing depicts the moment when the horse is bending left and working his way back to the rail. Note that there is left bend created by the action of the rider's hand on the left rein, yet the horse stays up and balanced on the right rein. This is the amount of bend that is appropriate for a shallow loop.

BENEFIT

Change of bend — single loop is used for suppling.

CAUTION

Do not rush this exercise. Be sure your horse performs it correctly before moving on to more demanding changes of bend. Performed correctly, a change of bend consists of the following throughout the exercise:

★ a poll that is at a consistent level

★ a steady rhythm

★ an even feel on both reins

★ the horse traveling "straight" (see Exercise #30).

NOTE

The change of bend is an important link to the upcoming lessons: counter-canter and lead changes.

Change of Bend — Shallow Loop

HOW TO RIDE THE EXERCISE

★ Jog (Exercise #7).

★ Right corner (Exercise #31).

★ Continue shallow right bend and trot off the rail.

★ When horse is about 10 feet off the rail, change to left bend and continue until 20 feet off the rail.

★ Maintain left bend until horse is 10 feet from the rail.

★ Change to right bend.

★ With right bend, trot toward the rail and leave it again.

★ When the horse is 10 feet off the rail, change to left bend.

★ Continue as arena size permits.

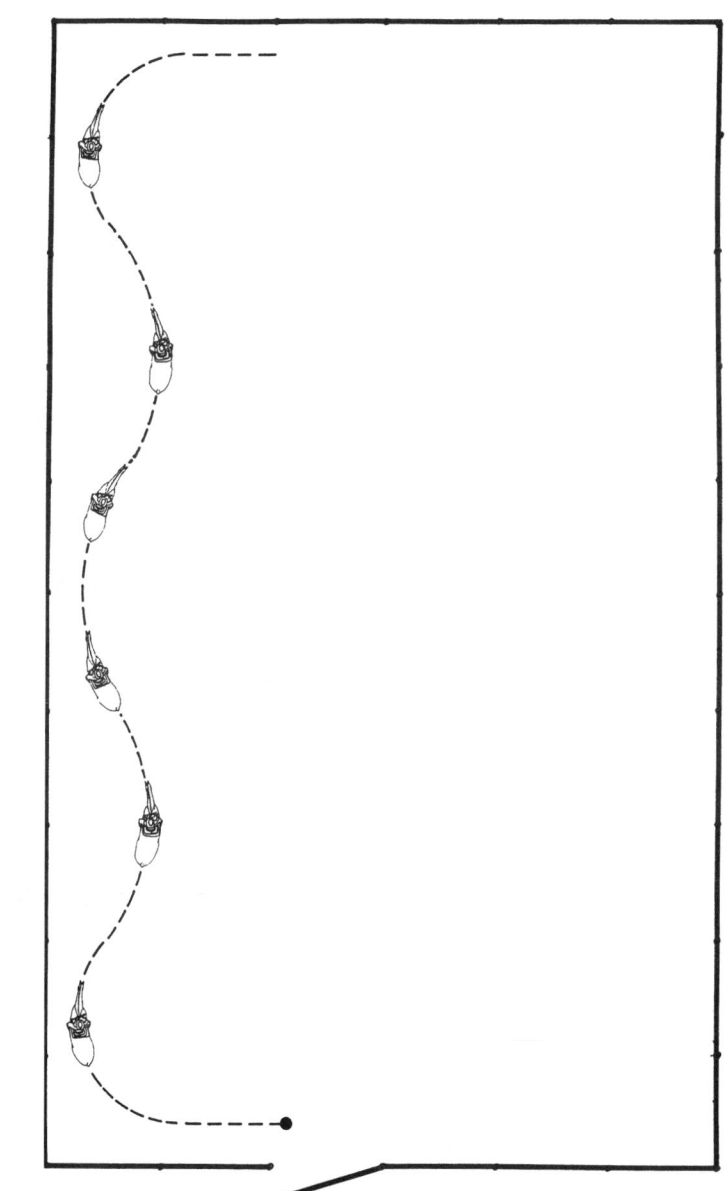

This Western rider, using one hand and a curb bridle, relies almost entirely on subtle weight and leg aids to change the bend in her horse. Here is a front view of the horse just after he has rejoined the rail in right bend and is leaving the rail in right bend.

VARIATION

At first you might only perform one shallow loop on a long side and add loops only if you can maintain rhythm (see Exercise #44).

Perform on the quarter line and center line.

NOTE

There are no truly straight strides in the loop portion of this exercise.

Be sure your predominant aids are your legs and weight, with your rein aids acting as a guiding influence only.

BENEFIT

Develops a fluidity of aids and responses between rider and horse in bending. This is the beginning of "dancing with your horse"!

Change of Rein out of a Circle

HOW TO RIDE THE EXERCISE

★ Trot (Exercise #7).

★ Ride a medium circle to the right (Exercise #36).

★ As you finish the circle, change from right to left bend (Exercise #45).

★ Ride a medium circle and a half to the left.

★ As you finish, change from left bend to right bend.

★ Ride a medium circle to the right.

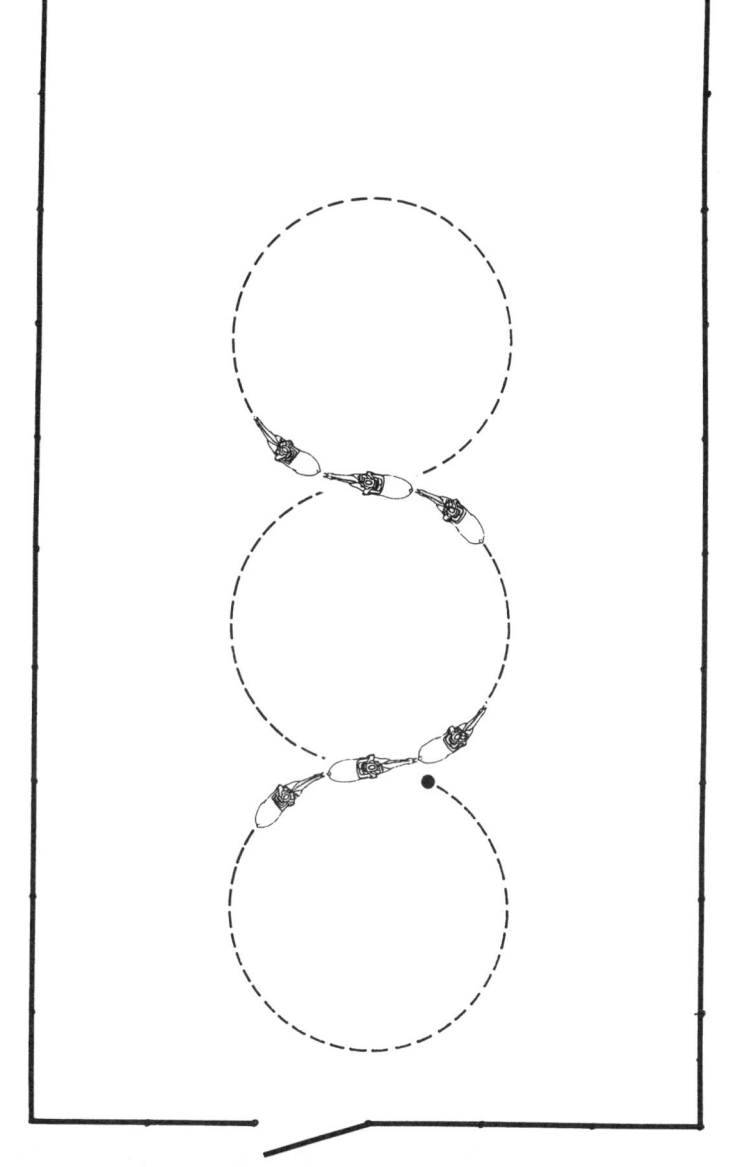

At this moment, the horse has just finished the middle circle to the left and is now being bent to the right to start the third circle, to the right.

BENEFIT

As a variation to the figure 8 pattern (Exercise #38), here the horse's bend is changed within a stride, without a straight stride in between.

This type of change requires more collection.

Change of Rein in a Circle

How to Ride the Exercise

★ Trot (Exercise #7) a large circle (66 feet) to the left (Exercise #35).

★ At the point of the circle closest to the long side, turn into the circle and trot a 33-foot half circle (Exercise #36) to the left.

★ As you finish the half circle, you should be approaching the center of the large circle.

★ Change from left bend to right bend (Exercise #45).

★ Trot a 33-foot half circle to the right.

★ Rejoin the original large circle, now tracking right.

VARIATION

You can practice the pattern at a walk, making "deeper" dips in place of the half circle, giving you a "longer diagonal" between the two half circles so you have plenty of time to change your bend properly.

CAUTION

Be careful not to leg yield as you change bend. Keep a true linear alignment.

This horse was bent left and has passed through the "diagonal" between the two half circles. Now the rider is introducing right bend with the right rein and the right leg. Note the left rein holds the horse's left shoulder up, limits flexion to the right, and prevents the horse from suddenly falling on the right shoulder when the bend is changed to the right.

Five-Loop Serpentine

HOW TO RIDE THE EXERCISE

★ Working trot sitting (Exercise #6) straight (Exercise #30) along the short end.

★ Trot first corner (Exercise #31) to the left.

★ Continue the bend of the corner until you've made a half circle to the left approximately 35 feet in diameter.

★ Trot straight across the arena until you are about 30 feet from the long side.

★ Change your leg, rein, and weight aids to right bend.

★ Bend the horse to the right and trot a half circle to the right approximately 35 feet in diameter (Exercise #36).

★ Trot straight across and continue, alternating right and left half circles that are connected by straight lines.

VARIATION

★ Can be ridden at a posting trot for younger horses and/or riders that have not developed a steady sitting trot seat. Posting must be changed on each straight line.

★ When ridden properly at the sitting trot, the benefits of bending and harmony between horse and rider are greatest.

★ This can also be ridden at the lope or canter with simple or flying lead changes on the straight lines or as a counter-canter exercise (Exercise #54).

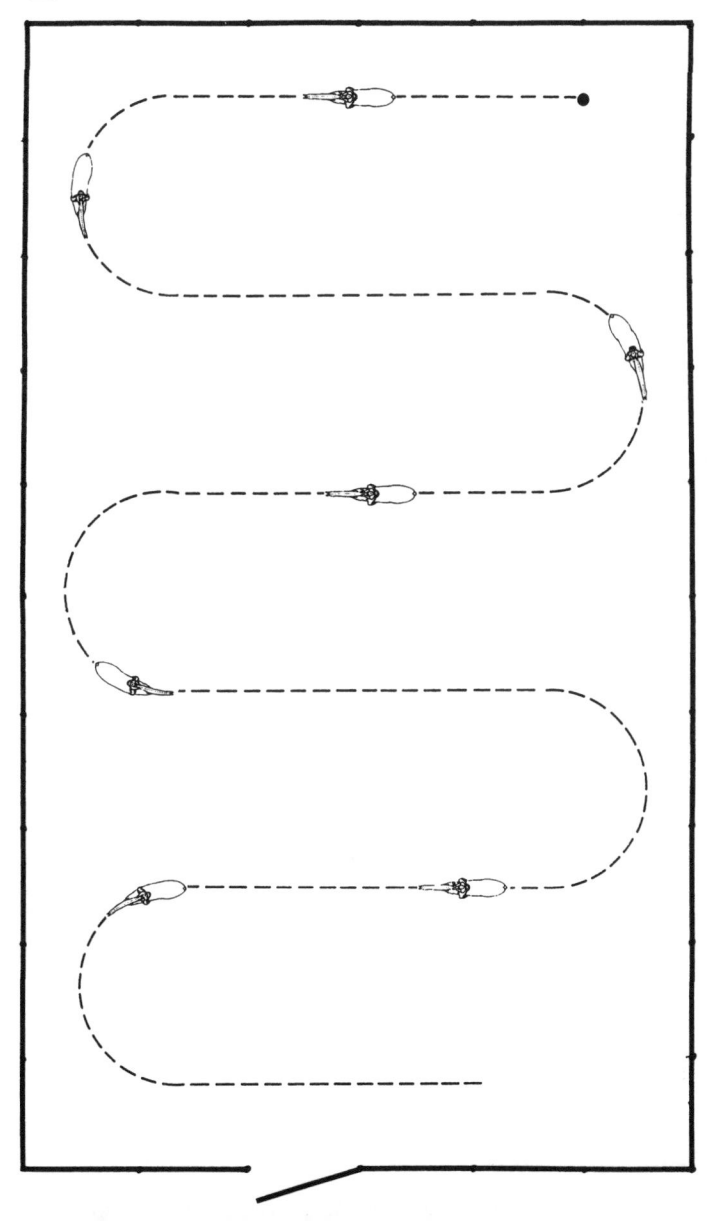

Coming around a left loop and making an active, supple half circle, this horse is bending nicely from head to tail and reaching well underneath with the left hind.

NOTE

★ The number and size of loops will be dictated by the size of your arena, the gait you choose, and the horse's level of training (bend and collection).

★ In most cases, the loops of a serpentine should be of equal size.

BENEFITS

★ The alternating change of bend is a good suppling exercise for the horse.

★ Training-level dressage.

Long Serpentine

How to Ride the Exercise

★ Jog (Exercise #7) straight (Exercise #30) up the long side of the arena.

★ About 25 feet from the far end, jog a 30-foot half circle (Exercise #36) to the right.

★ Jog straight down the arena on a track 30 feet from your original track.

★ About 25 feet from the gate end, jog a 30-foot half circle to the left.

★ Jog straight up the arena on a track 60 feet from your original track.

★ Continue.

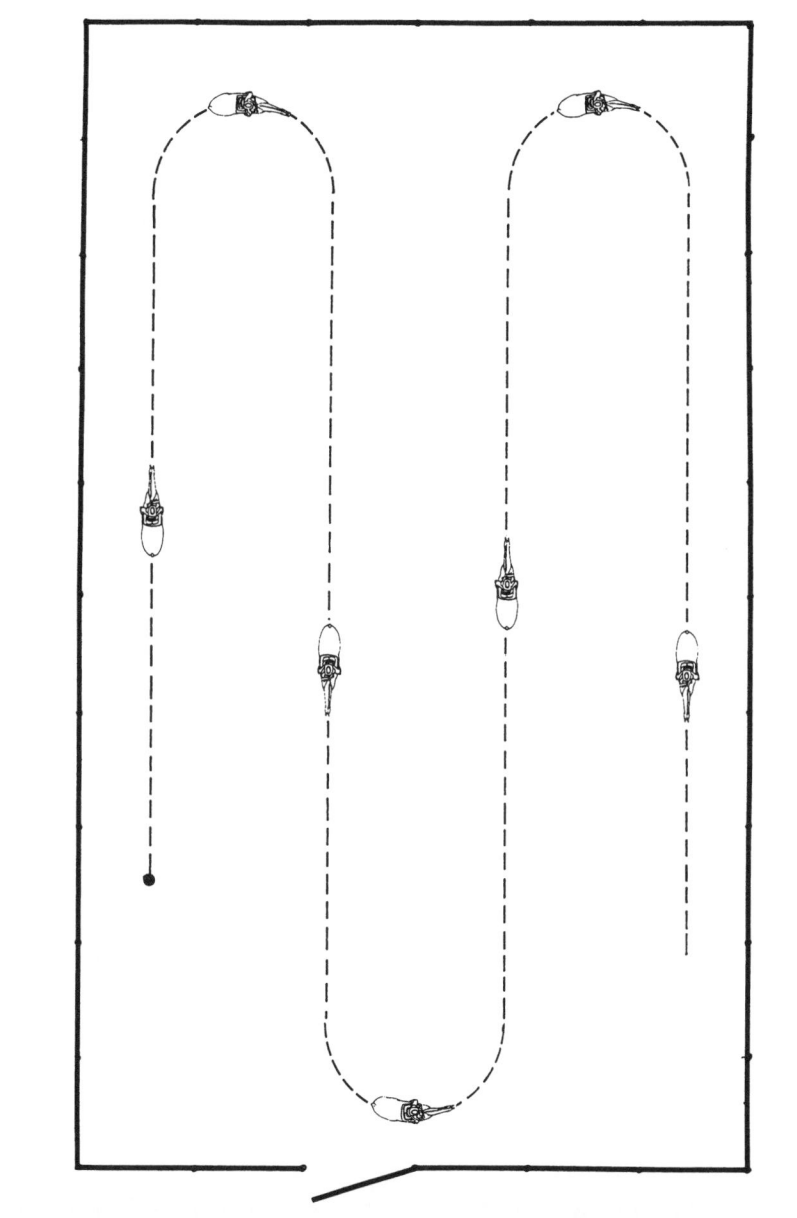

This shows the moment when the horse is coming out of the half circle to the right. The rider is beginning to think about the aids for straightening. She is ready to use a left rein to counteract the right bend created by the right rein. She is decreasing right leg pressure from the right bend and is getting ready to drive evenly forward with both legs and seat bones.

Benefit

This is the best "let's get it straight" exercise for you and your horse because you cannot rely on the arena rail to keep you straight.

As you ride from one short end to the other, keep these things in mind (see Exercise #1):

★ Can you feel equal weight on both of your seat bones?

★ Are your shoulders even and level?

★ Are your legs in the same position on the sides of the horse?

★ Is there equal weight in both of your heels?

★ Is your chin up, your sternum elevated, and are you looking forward and projecting forward?

Quarter Turn

HOW TO RIDE THE EXERCISE

★ Collected trot forward (Exercise #9).

★ Right corner (Exercise #31).

★ Straight to midpoint of long side (Exercise #30).

★ Half halt (Exercise #14).

★ Quarter turn right.

   • Rein aids are between those for a volte (Exercise #37) and a turn on the haunches (Exercise #69), but without any lateral movement of the legs. The horse should stay on the line of the exercise.

   • Momentarily lift both reins in a decisive position flexion.

   • Take care to maintain contact on left rein so the horse doesn't overbend to right.

   • Strong right seat bone, weight deep through knee and heel.

   • Strong right leg at the girth to give the horse a "post" to turn around.

   • Left leg at the girth to maintain impulsion through the turn.

★ Be ready as you are 60 degrees through the turn to begin applying straightening aids.

★ When the 90-degree turn is complete, head straight across the arena.

★ The aids for a left quarter turn will be the reverse of above.

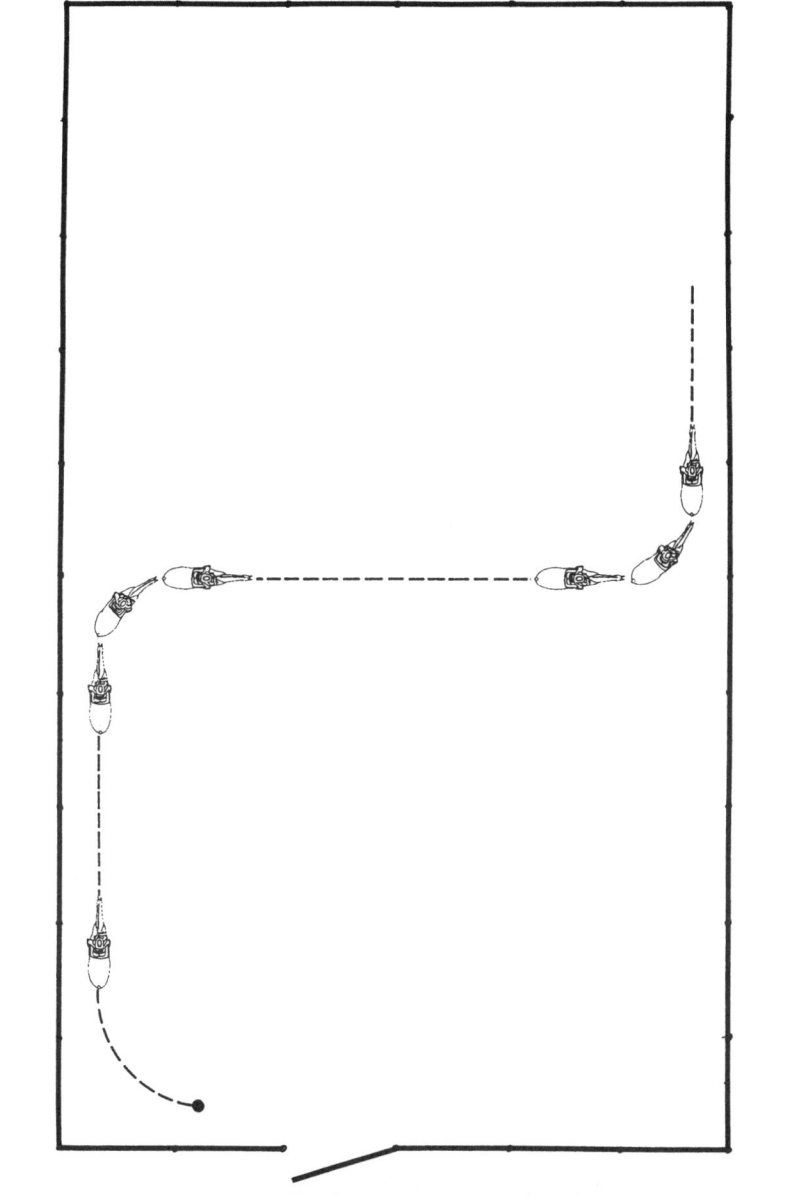

NOTE

★ This exercise must be ridden in collected gaits.

★ You can practice at the walk.

★ Only the most highly schooled horses should be asked to perform a quarter turn at the canter.

In this poor attempt at a quarter turn to the left, the rider has used far too much left rein, causing the horse to "rubber neck" — that is, bend the neck in response to the extreme rein aid yet continue straight forward with the body. To correct, the rider must prepare the horse with half halts and rely more on weight and leg aids for the actual turn to take place uniformly through the horse's body. See drawing in Exercise #85. For contrast, see drawings in Exercises #31, #34, #36, and #43.

Counter-Flex

HOW TO RIDE THE EXERCISE

★ Working trot, sitting (Exercises #6 and #7).

★ Right corner with normal bend (Exercise #31).

★ Straight 1–2 strides (Exercise #30).

★ Counter-flex 2–3 strides.

  • While hind legs continue to follow front legs and stay on the line of the exercise, the neck and head are brought to the left with a left direct rein and right supporting rein.

★ Straight 1–2 strides.

★ Counter-flex 2–3 strides.

★ Straight 1–2 strides.

★ Right corner with regular bend.

★ Straight 1 stride.

★ Counter-flex 2–3 strides.

★ Straight 1 stride.

★ Counter-flex around the corner and for 1 stride beyond.

★ Straight 4–5 strides.

★ Counter-flex 3–4 strides.

★ Straight 1 stride.

★ Right corner normal bend.

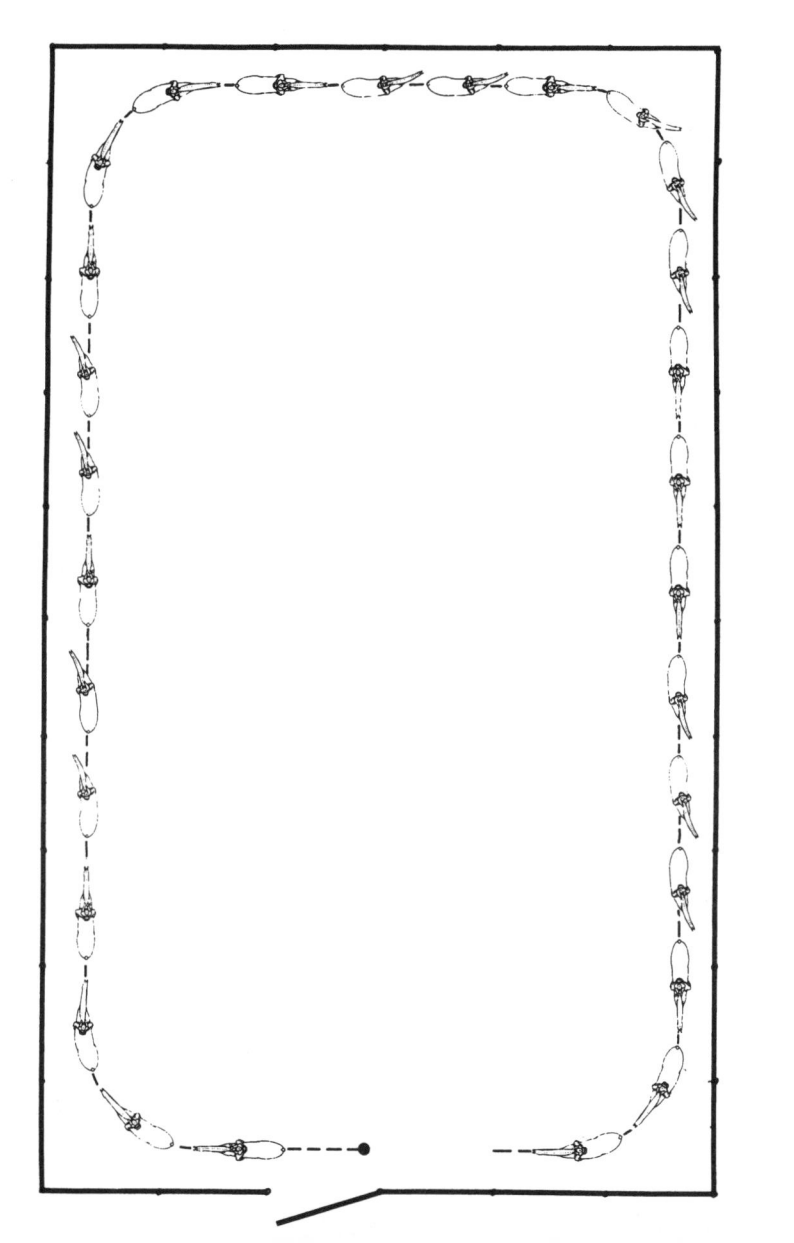

VARIATION

★ Can be performed at the walk and canter.

★ Vary where and for how long you ask for counter-flex.

Here the horse is walking right and is counter-flexed to the left. The amount of flexion in the neck, poll, and throat latch is perfect. Note that the horse's shoulders are not being displaced laterally by the rein aid, which is correct. The rider is taking care not to apply too much left leg because she wants her horse to keep his body straight, with the hinds following directly behind the fronts. Contrast to regular flexion in drawing in Exercise #37.

NOTE

★ Counter-flex is not a lateral movement — the hind legs follow the front legs on their normal track.

★ Sometimes it is necessary to ride the counter-flex exercise as a counter bend because as the horse's nose is brought to the left in this counter-flex exercise, the hindquarters automatically want to move to the right. The rider might have to apply a strong right leg behind the girth and is in essence bending the horse around his left leg, thus in a counter bend.

BENEFIT

The counter-flex teaches a horse to stay up on the outside rein. For example, when tracking left, if a horse overbends to the left and avoids taking contact with the right rein, counter-flex the horse to the right.

Counter-Canter — Shallow Loop

How to Ride the Exercise

★ Collected canter right lead (Exercises #12 and #20) with position right throughout.

★ Right corner (Exercise #31).

★ Up the long side (Exercise #30).

★ Right corner.

★ Short end.

★ Right corner.

★ Maintain bend (position) to right and counter-canter.

- Half halt (Exercise #14) and forward seat to keep horse balanced up front.

- Weight in right seat bone and deep into right heel.

- Right rein so horse remains flexed toward the leading foreleg (right).

- Keep right leg on to keep horse bent to right.

- Keep left leg on behind the girth to maintain right canter.

- Maintain positive contact with supporting (left) rein

  to balance and direct horse through the turns,

  to keep horse on the lines of the exercise,

  to prevent horse from falling out over the left shoulder,

  to prevent horse from over-flexing to right.

- Keep your hips parallel to horse's hips.

- Keep your shoulders parallel to horse's shoulders.

★ Return to the rail and maintain right position for a stride or two.

★ Straighten.

Here the horse has come off the corner and is cantering nicely on a left arcing loop on the right lead. Note that the horse remains flexed toward his leading foreleg (right).

BENEFITS

★ Strengthens horse's loins and engages hind legs.

★ Prepares the horse for flying change.

★ Helps in training for pirouette because it really balances the canter. The horse will be able to increase and decrease circle size easier.

★ Enhances first-level dressage.

CAUTION

★ This is not a canter on the wrong lead, since the horse is bent in the direction of his lead. Compare with drawing in Exercise #54.

★ Be sure you don't shift your weight because your horse might break gait or perform a flying lead change.

★ Don't get tense or stiff because you will cause the canter to become stilted.

★ Don't leg yield to and from the rail. You must ride your horse "forward" on the curved line.

Counter-Canter across Diagonal

HOW TO RIDE THE EXERCISE

★ Lope in a collected frame (Exercises #12 and #20) on the right lead down the long side and the short end to the second corner of the short end.

★ Start a half circle to the right and head across the short diagonal (Exercise #33).

★ Maintain right flexion (or even slight right position) even on the straight line.

★ As you approach the opposite long side, half halt (Exercise #14) and prepare for a left turn in counter-canter (Exercise #52).

   • Keep your shoulders parallel to the horse's shoulders.

   • Keep your pelvis parallel to the horse's hips.

   • Keep your weight deep in your left heel.

   • Bend the horse with your legs and keep your legs steady to help your horse keep his balance.

★ Counter-canter a rounded square to the left.

★ About two-thirds of the way up the long side, turn left and head across the short diagonal.

★ Maintain right bend.

★ When you reach the corner, ride the corner in a normal bend.

★ After the corner, straighten.

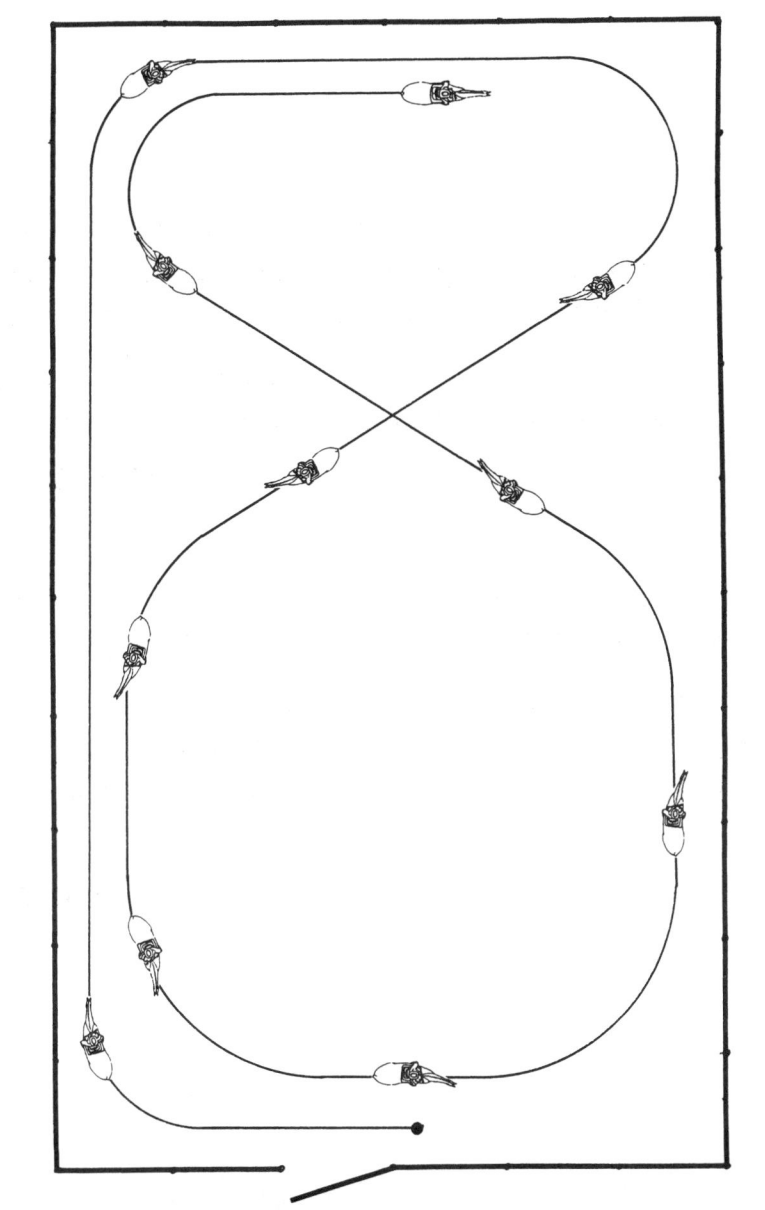

This example of a Western counter-canter to the left on the right lead takes place on the rounded square just across from the starting dot. The horse is mildly flexed to the right an appropriate amount for the degree of contact. If he were ridden with more contact and in a more collected frame, the degree of his right flexion would be greater.

NOTE

In descriptions of counter-cantering, the terms *outside* and *inside* can be confusing. *Inside* refers to the shorter side of the horse, the one he is bent toward. In this exercise it is the right. *Outside* refers to the side that is longer — in this case, the left.

The rider's outside (left) leg must be very effective so the horse continues to canter forward with good impulsion.

CAUTION

★ A common error is the horse being too straight without any bending toward the lead.

★ It is important that the rhythm be equal throughout. The speed on the straight lines should not be faster than that on the circular components.

Counter-Canter Serpentine

HOW TO RIDE THE EXERCISE

★ Collected canter (Exercise #12) right lead.

★ Canter a medium half circle to the right (Exercise #36).

★ Maintain right bend and canter straight.

★ Counter-canter (Exercise #52) a large half circle (Exercise #35) to the left.

★ Maintain right bend and canter straight.

★ Canter a medium half circle to the right.

★ Straighten.

★ Collected canter right corner.

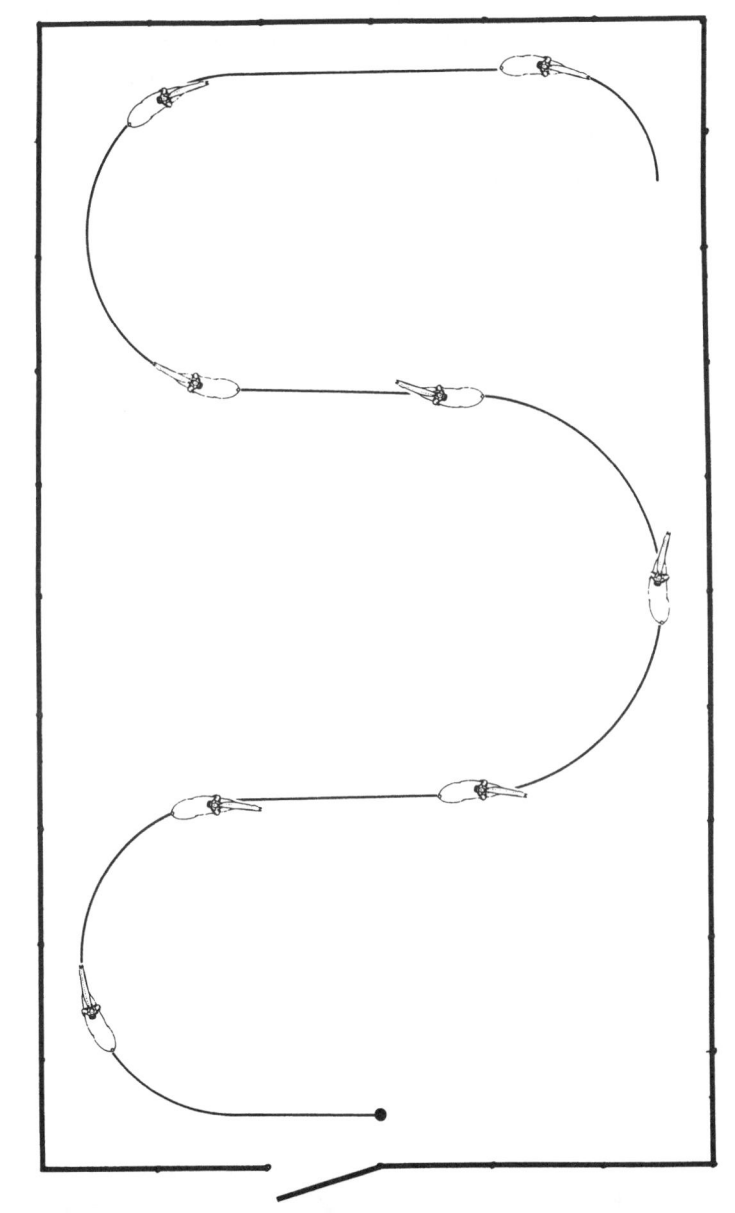

Here is a horse at the midpoint of the biggest loop of the serpentine. The horse is cantering on the right lead to the left yet is flexed to the left! This is basically cantering on the wrong lead, not counter-cantering. Compare with drawing in Exercise #52.

NOTE

★ The horse's hind legs must still follow the tracks of the front legs and stay on the line of the exercise. The poll and tail must be on the line at all times.

★ If a horse does not do well, go back to easier counter-canter exercises for a period of weeks.

★ If a horse loses his balance, he pushes out with his outside shoulder to counterbalance his imbalance.

CAUTION

★ If the hindquarters swing off the line, use a stronger outside (left) leg behind the girth.

★ If the forehand overbends toward the lead, use less inside (right) rein.

★ Don't change the degree of bend as the horse changes direction. It must be consistent throughout the pattern.

★ Never let the horse's neck bend more than his body.

★ *Never* let a horse counter-canter while counter-flexed (example: circling right on the left lead yet flexed right) as it is counterproductive to his physical development and he may cross-canter, break gait, or change lead.

Lateral Work

Lateral work is designed to teach the horse to move sideways in response to a sideways driving leg aid — one applied on the same side of his body is a predominant rein aid. An example of this is the application of the left leg and left rein to cause the horse to move to the right. Lateral work supples the horse and eventually straightens him.

Lateral movements contain varying degrees of lateral flexion and bend as well as sideways movement, from the minimal "in position" to the full sideways movement of a sidepass.

Instead of the hind legs following in the tracks of the front legs as in straight and circular work, in lateral work the front legs are offset to the hinds or vice versa. Lateral movements are often called "two-tracking," but in reality, all lateral movements are really "three-tracking" or "four-tracking." Here's why: If you were to stand behind a horse that is walking straight and you looked at the tracks that he left, there would be two tracks. One from the left legs and one from the right legs. Therefore, a horse that is traveling straight ahead could actually be said to be "two-tracking."

When a horse offsets his forehand to his hindquarters (such as in a shoulder in Exercise #62), one foreleg comes inside of the track of the other foreleg and creates a new track, so now the horse is "three-tracking."

In some maneuvers (such as travers in Exercise #65 and in renvers in Exercise #68), a combination of bend and forehand or hindquarters positioning will cause each leg to travel on a separate track, so the horse is "four-tracking."

In training a horse to perform quality maneuvers, the lessons are by degrees. To perform a correct shoulder in, a horse is first taught to carry himself "in position" and then "shoulder fore." Both are stages on the way to the shoulder in. "In position" (see drawing in Exercise #37) is a very mild version of the shoulder fore but with little or no displacement of the forelegs.

Turns such as the turns on the forehand and haunches, the pivot, pirouette, and turnaround are all lateral movements because the horse is moving sideways in some fashion.

It is important to note that the Western and English versions of performing maneuvers have slight differences. Contrast the Western two-step with the English leg yield. Also note the differences between the English turn on the haunches and the Western pivot.

Turn on the Forehand

HOW TO RIDE THE EXERCISE

★ Walk (Exercise #2).

★ Right corner (Exercise #31) at a walk.

★ Drift off the track so you are about 10–15 feet from the rail and have room for the turn.

★ Halt (Exercise #15).

★ Turn on the forehand 180 degrees with left flexion and hindquarters moving to the right.

  • Flex horse's head to the left with a shortened left rein.

  • Weight left seat bone.

  • Use left leg actively behind the cinch to push the hindquarters to the right.

  • Use right leg at the girth to keep the horse

    moving in a forward walk rhythm,

    from rushing sideways to the right,

    from backing up.

VARIATION

★ Do directly from a walk without a halt in between.

★ Perform with horse straight, not flexed to the left (more difficult).

★ Perform with horse flexed to the right (most difficult).

NOTE

In a turn on the forehand where the hindquarters move right and the horse is flexed left (as on arena map):

★ Footfall pattern is left hind, left front, right hind, right front.

★ The pivot point is the left front foot; the left front remains relatively stationary, lifting up and setting down (not swiveling) in place.

★ The right front walks a tiny forward half circle around the left front.

★ The hind legs walk a half circle around the front legs.

★ The left hind crosses over and in front of the right hind.

BENEFITS

★ Turning on the forehand is an essential suppling, obedience, and positioning (straightening) exercise.

★ It teaches the horse to respond to sideways driving and lateral aids.

This is an example of nicely balanced turn on the forehand, hindquarters moving left and horse flexed right (opposite of arena map). The right front foot is the pivot point of the turn. The right hind moves left from the rider's right leg. The footfall pattern is right hind (crossing in front of left hind), right front (lifting up and reorienting but not stepping sideways), left hind (uncrossing from behind), and left front (small step forward and to the right).

CAUTION

★ Keep this turn very forward. Don't let your horse avoid the aids and back out of the turn.

★ At the beginning, let him do a walk around, forward turn on the forehand before you require one absolutely in place.

★ If a horse backs up, he will be unable to cross over behind and his pivot point will be lost.

★ A too-forward turn can be easily counteracted by increasing pressure on the outside (right) rein.

Western Two-Step

HOW TO RIDE THE EXERCISE

★ Walk (Exercise #2).

★ Straight (Exercise #30).

★ Right corner (Exercise #31).

★ Straight for one stride.

★ Perform the two-step for 3−4 strides.

★ Aids similar to leg yield (Exercise #57) but with

  • more flexion (and even bend) away from the
    direction of movement (more left rein).

  • more sideways movement, so more active left leg.

★ Ride straight for a few strides.

★ Two-step and repeat.

★ After last two-step, change to right bend (Exercise #31).

★ Straight.

VARIATION

Can be performed at trot and lope.

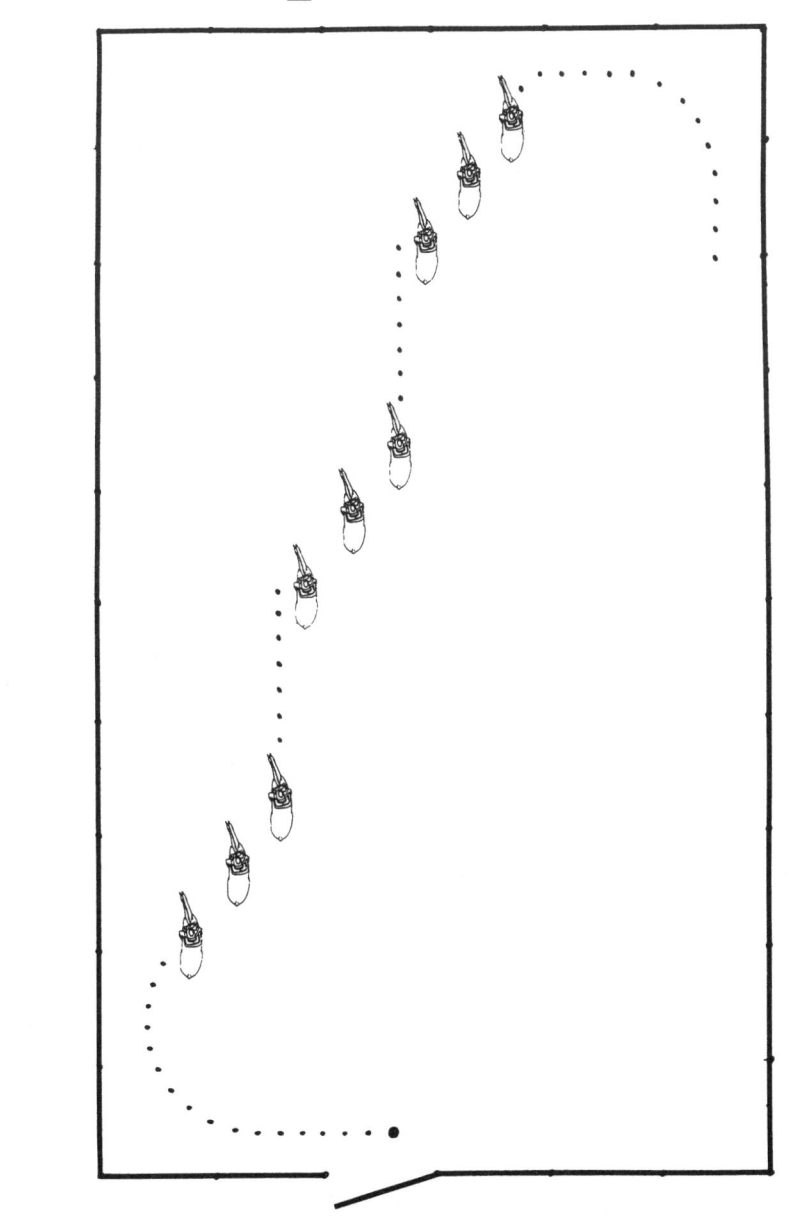

This energetic yet balanced two-step performed at the walk shows great forward and sideways response to the rider's active left leg. Note that the right front leg is just getting ready to land and the left hind has already lifted and is getting ready for its sideways swing to the right. The rider is asking for left flexion with the left rein but is limiting it with the right rein, so the horse doesn't fall on or bulge the right shoulder. Compare to drawing in Exercise #57.

NOTE

★ This basic lateral movement is sometimes referred to as the "two-track." (Two-tracking is defined in the introduction to this section.)

★ The line of forward movement is parallel to the arena rail.

BENEFITS

★ Teaches the horse to move away from leg while moving forward.

★ Can be used as a prelude to leg yield, sidepass, and turn on the hindquarters.

CAUTION

★ Because of the increased counter flexion, there is an easier chance for the outside shoulder to bulge.

★ It is difficult for a horse to move with this much sideways reach and stay in balance, so be on the lookout for overload: irregular rhythm, rushing, head way down, balking.

Leg Yield

HOW TO RIDE THE EXERCISE

★ Working trot, sitting (Exercise #7).

★ Straight (Exercise #30).

★ Corner (Exercise #31).

★ Straight.

★ Half halt (Exercise #14).

★ Leg yield to the right with forward driving aids:

  • Left seat bone.

  • Left leg behind the girth and actively pushing sideways each time the left hind lifts and starts a forward/sideways step.

  • Right rein guides direction of travel and prevents bulging right shoulder.

  • Right leg prevents rushing away from the left leg and keeps the horse moving forward.

  • Left rein slight flexion left added as last aid and lightly because the horse is basically ridden straight between the reins.

★ Straighten and ride forward.

This is an attempt at a leg yield to the left from the rider's right leg. However, there are many things wrong with this picture. The rider has collapsed her right side: Her shoulder has fallen and she has likely raised her heel in giving the right leg aid. She is taking too much with the right rein and not supporting enough with the left rein. The horse is making a valiant attempt at complying with the rider's leg aid in spite of incorrect rein aids. Note that his nose is tilted to the right and his left ear is lower than his right ear because of this. See drawings in Exercises #56, #58, #59, #60, #83, and #87. See the related half pass and sidepass exercises.

VARIATIONS

Practice first at the walk to become familiar with the application and timing of your aids.

Rather than riding the leg yield on a diagonal line, ride the leg yield directly along the wall or rail. Either have the horse flexed slightly toward the rail and have him yield from your leg by the rail, or have the horse flexed slightly toward the inside of the arena and have the horse yield from your leg on the inside of the arena.

NOTE

In a leg yield to the right, the horse is flexed very slightly to the left, the body is straight, and the horse is moving to the right from the rider's left leg. The horse's left legs cross over the right legs. The forehand is very slightly in advance of the hindquarters. The horse remains parallel to the arena rail in this version of the leg yield exercise.

BENEFITS

★ Teaches obedience to sideways driving aids.

★ Serves as a suppling exercise to show horse how to perform with loose, free movement.

★ Is useful later for initial straightening.

Leg Yield Refresher

HOW TO RIDE THE EXERCISE

★ Walk (Exercise #2).

★ Turn right on the quarter line or center line (Exercise #31) with normal right bend.

★ Ride straight for one stride.

★ Change to left flexion (if leg yield) or left bend (if two step).

★ Leg yield (Exercise #57) up the arena on a straight line from your left leg for 40 to 80 feet. (Note: the arena map depicts counter bend.)

★ Halt or half halt (Exercise #14).

★ Turn on the forehand 180 degrees with horse flexed left and hindquarters moving to the right, paying special attention to the use of an effective supporting right rein.

★ Leg yield down the arena on a straight line, which should be right on top of the original leg yield line.

★ Straighten horse and walk forward.

VARIATION

An easier version would be to go from the right turn up the quarter line into a leg yield from the right leg with right flexion. The turn on the forehand would be in the opposite direction.

The version diagrammed on the arena map makes for a more distinct change of aids, and although it may be more difficult for the rider, if done correctly it provides a greater benefit for the horse.

NOTE

The turn on the forehand should occur when there is resistance, reluctance, or sluggishness to the rider's sideways driving leg. Maybe you will only ride a few feet of leg yield before performing a turn on the forehand.

BENEFIT

Use this to "tune up" the horse to your sideways driving leg aids so he will perform a more energetic and correct leg yield, sidepass, and other maneuvers with lateral movements.

This is a very mild leg yield from the rider's right leg with very slight right flexion. The horse should respond by placing his left front leg to the left of its normal track. If the rider wanted more of a response, she could use the leg yield refresher.

Leg Yield on a Circle

HOW TO RIDE THE EXERCISE

★ Walk a 60–80 foot circle to the right (Exercise #35).

★ Weight your right seat bone.

★ Move your right leg behind the girth and push the hindquarters out of the circle (Exercise #57).

★ Flex the horse to the right with the right rein.

★ With the left rein, keep the forehand from moving into the circle.

★ Regulate the flexion and mild bend with the left rein.

★ Half halt (Exercise #14) with the left rein each time you use your right leg.

★ Use your left leg to keep the walk forward and to prevent the leg yield from becoming a turn on the forehand.

VARIATION

See the variations under "Note," below.

Here the horse is yielding to the rider's (outside) right leg on a circle to the left. This brings the hindquarters into the circle and keeps the forehand on the circle line. The question of direction of bend and the use of the rider's weight will depend on the gait, size of circle, and the degree of collection. In this drawing, the rider has slightly weighted the left seat bone by looking left to correspond to the left bend of the rein aids and circle. Her right leg is only asking for a mild crossover with the right hind leg. If the rider wanted to shift the hindquarters into the circle more, she could use a stronger right leg and flex the horse straight or to the right.

NOTE

There are two distinctly different ways to use the leg yield on a circle.

One is depicted by the arena map and instructions: The horse is yielding to the rider's (inside) right leg on a circle to the *right*. This places the hindquarters outside the circle and keeps the forehand on the circle line. The right legs are crossing over in front of the left legs as the horse moves forward on the circle to the right.

The other way to use a leg yield on a circle is depicted by the drawing. The horse is circling to the left, and the rider moves the hindquarters in with right leg.

BENEFIT

The circular figure combined with the leg yield movement results in greater crossover and suppling effect.

Zigzag Two-Step

HOW TO RIDE THE EXERCISE

★ Trot (Exercise #7).

★ Trot corner to the right (Exercise #31).

★ Trot straight (Exercise #30) 20 feet or so.

★ Counter bend left.

★ Two-step to about 20 feet off the rail (Exercise #56).

★ Ride straight one stride.

★ Counter bend right.

★ Two-step back to the rail.

★ Ride straight, both corners of the far end.

★ As soon as straight after second corner, flex left.

★ Two-step to about 20 feet off the rail.

★ Ride straight one stride.

★ Flex right.

★ Two-step back to the rail.

★ Repeat sequence.

★ Trot actively forward through the corner and across the gate end.

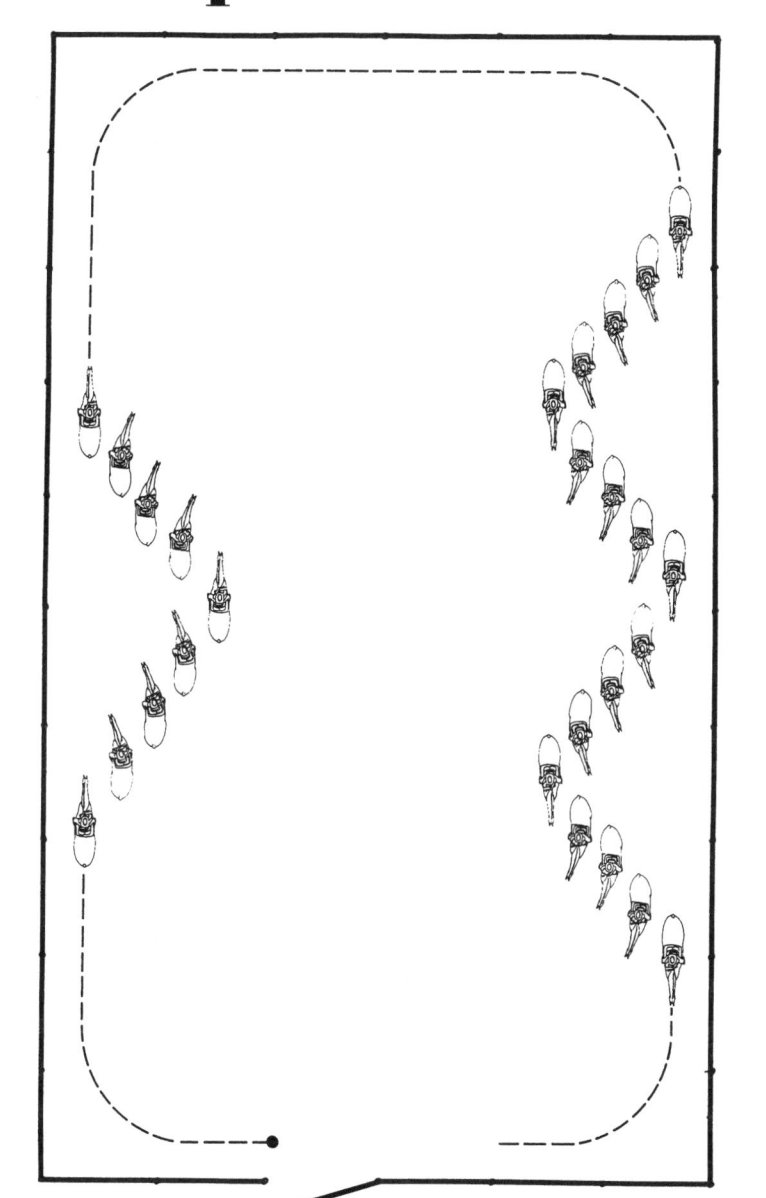

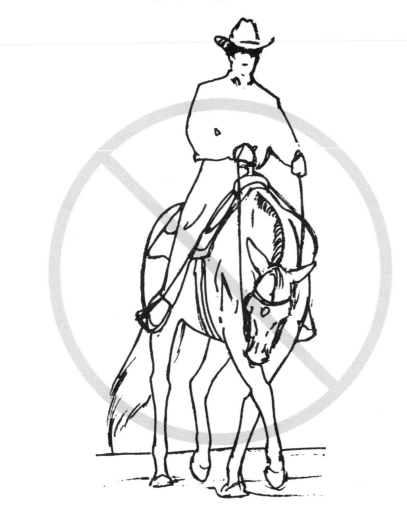

This drawing shows a moment coming down the second long side where the horse is two-stepping back to the rail. The benefit of the exercise is nullified because the horse is not responding with an energetic sideways and forward reach of his hind leg. Worse yet, he has dropped severely behind the bit and lost all forward contact and motion. It is more beneficial to ride this exercise with minimal bend in the neck. He needs to be ridden actively forward in a straight line so his poll is at least as high as his withers. See drawing in Exercise #56.

VARIATION

★ Practice this exercise at the walk first, asking for just a few steps at a time.

★ Practice this exercise at both a walk and trot in leg yield (Exercise #57) configuration rather than two-step — that is, riding the horse straight and with minimal flexion.

NOTE

Remember that the two-step has a great deal more flexion and bend and more sideways movement than a true leg yield. In either instance, the forehand should slightly lead the hindquarters.

BENEFIT

Tests and improves the horse's response to forward/sideways driving aids. A good lead-in to sidepass or half pass.

CAUTION

Use a strong outside leg to keep the movement really forward.

In Position and Shoulder Fore

How to Ride the Exercise

★ Track left at the lope (Exercise #10).

★ Left corner (Exercise #31).

★ Ride straight (Exercise #30).

★ Shoulder fore.

  • Forward driving seat with slightly more weight on left seat bone.

  • Left leg activating left hind leg.

  • Left leg pushing horse onto right rein.

  • Right rein restrains and brings horse's shoulders (to the left) in from the track.

  • Right leg prevents the hindquarters from falling out to the right.

  • Left rein keeps horse straight, but indicates a slight left direction and bend by holding the rein slightly away from withers.

★ Straighten by bringing the forehand back in front of the hindquarters.

VARIATION

Start the shoulder fore immediately after the left corner to take advantage of the left bend and automatic position for the shoulder fore.

This front view of a shoulder fore left under Western tack shows very light contact and minimal bend with the right front stepping on a track between the hind legs. This is in contrast to the shoulder in drawing in Exercise #62, which has three tracks.

NOTE

★ In position produces no crossover, and shoulder fore produces little crossover.

★ Shoulder fore and shoulder in are not forms of leg yielding! The horse's forehand is put in position by the reins, and the rider maintains the inward position with the seat and the legs. The rider's aids do not actively ask for sideways steps as in the leg yield, but crossover does occur because of the horse's position. In shoulder fore the horse's inside legs step toward the center of the horse's body. In shoulder in they actually cross over because of the greater inside position.

BENEFIT

In position and shoulder fore straighten the horse for later work; a prelude to shoulder in.

Shoulder In

HOW TO RIDE THE EXERCISE

★ Trot (Exercise #6) to the right, immediately after the corner.

★ Perform a shoulder in right.

　• Bring horse's forehand in 30–35 degrees maximum so the left shoulder is in front of the right hind leg.

　• Weight right seat bone slightly.

　• Right leg at the girth

　　pushes the horse forward,

　　activates the right hind leg,

　　maintains the position and the subsequent forward and sideways movement of the right hind,

　　creates right bend.

★ Left leg behind the girth prevents the left hind from stepping to the left. (Don't depend on the rail or wall to do this for you!)

★ Left rein controls tempo and degree of bend in the neck.

★ Right rein guides the horse in to the right and maintains the degree of right bend.

★ Straighten horse by bringing forehand back to the original track.

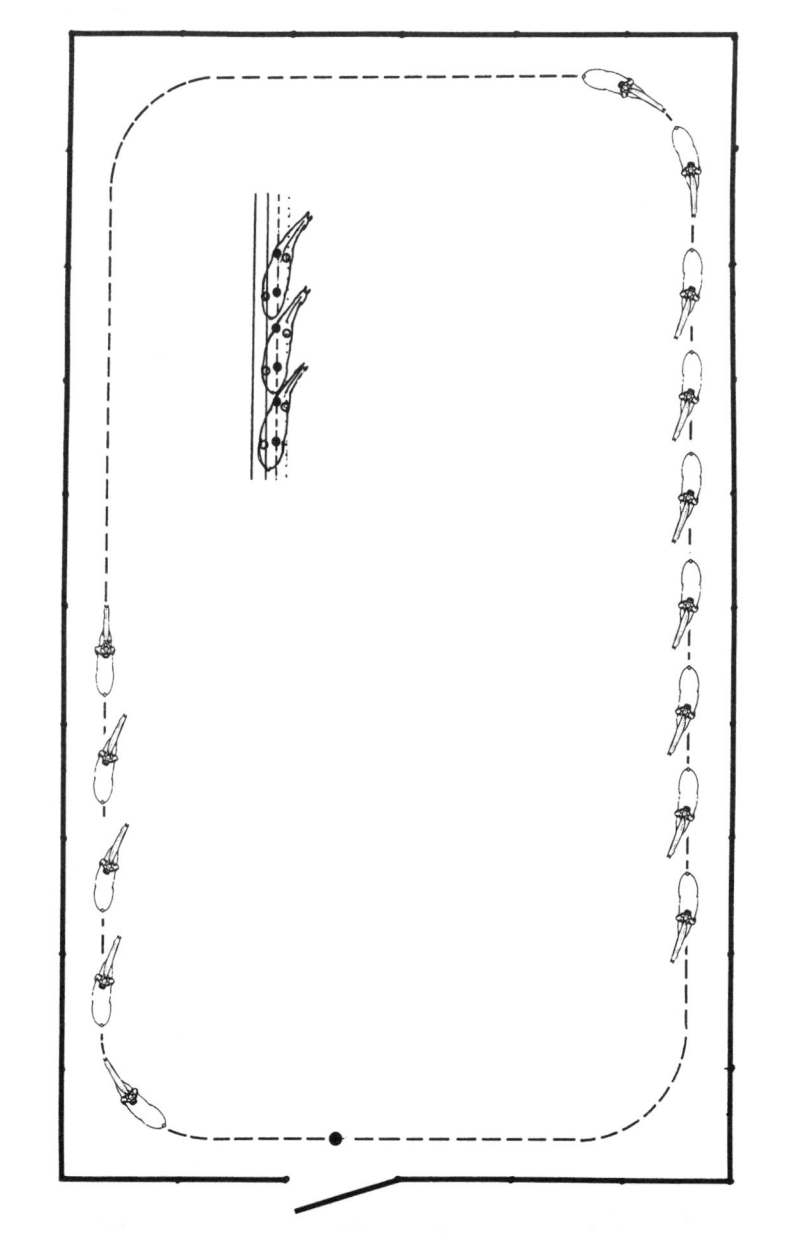

VARIATION

Be sure to ride shoulder in down the center line, the quarter line, and so forth, to prevent the horse (and you) from becoming dependent on the rail.

The shoulder in right with the three distinct tracks as listed above. The horse is balanced well between his left and right shoulders.

NOTE

★ There are three tracks in a shoulder in right:

1. Left hind

2. Right hind and left front

3. Right front

★ The right legs cross in front of the left legs with the right hind reaching well forward toward the left front.

BENEFIT

The cornerstone of training for straightening, collection, and hind leg activity.

CAUTION

★ If the inside rein is too strong, the horse will be overbent and will bulge on the outside shoulder making it look like a "neck in" rather than a "shoulder in."

★ If the horse tilts his head (when tracking right, the right ear will be lower), it is usually because the left rein is too strong. Lighten both reins, lift the right rein momentarily, and resume.

★ If the horse gets behind the bit or shortens his stride, return to the straight track and ride actively forward.

Shoulder In and Circle

HOW TO RIDE THE EXERCISE

★ Collected trot (Exercise #9).

★ Small circle (Exercise #37) in the first corner.

★ Come out of the circle in a shoulder-in (Exercise #62) position.

★ Ride shoulder in up the long side for about 40 feet.

★ Straighten (Exercise #30) for one stride, then create right bend.

★ Ride a small circle with regular right bend.

★ Come out of the circle in shoulder in.

★ Ride shoulder in for about 40 feet.

★ Ride straight for at least one stride before the corner.

★ Ride the corner with a regular right bend.

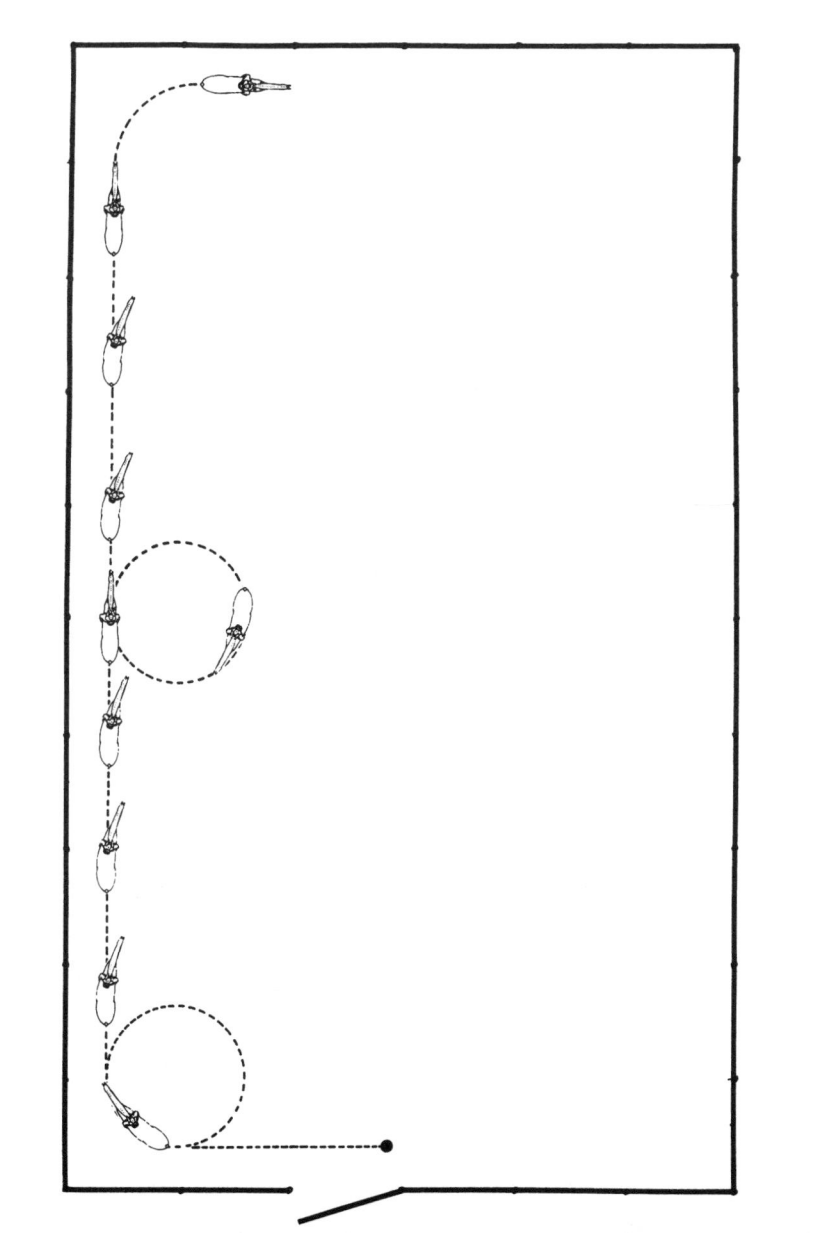

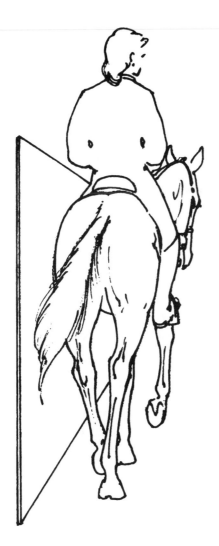

VARIATION

Practice at a walk and working trot (increasing size of circles) first to develop coordination of aids. Then perform exercise at the canter.

BENEFIT

Develops good habits for both horse and rider as to the specific differences in traveling on a straight line and on a curved line in both straight and laterally displaced positions.

Shoulder in right at the working trot. From the rear shows the three tracks and right position. To get the most from this exercise, the horse should be more active and collected.

Shoulder In on a Circle

HOW TO RIDE THE EXERCISE

★ Start a large circle to the right (Exercise #35) at an active trot (Exercise #7).

★ Ride the large circle once around with normal right bend.

★ When you pass your starting point, ride the circle in a shoulder-in (Exercise #62) position.

★ Shoulders come inside the circle.

★ Hindquarters stay on the circle line.

★ Resume regular right bend.

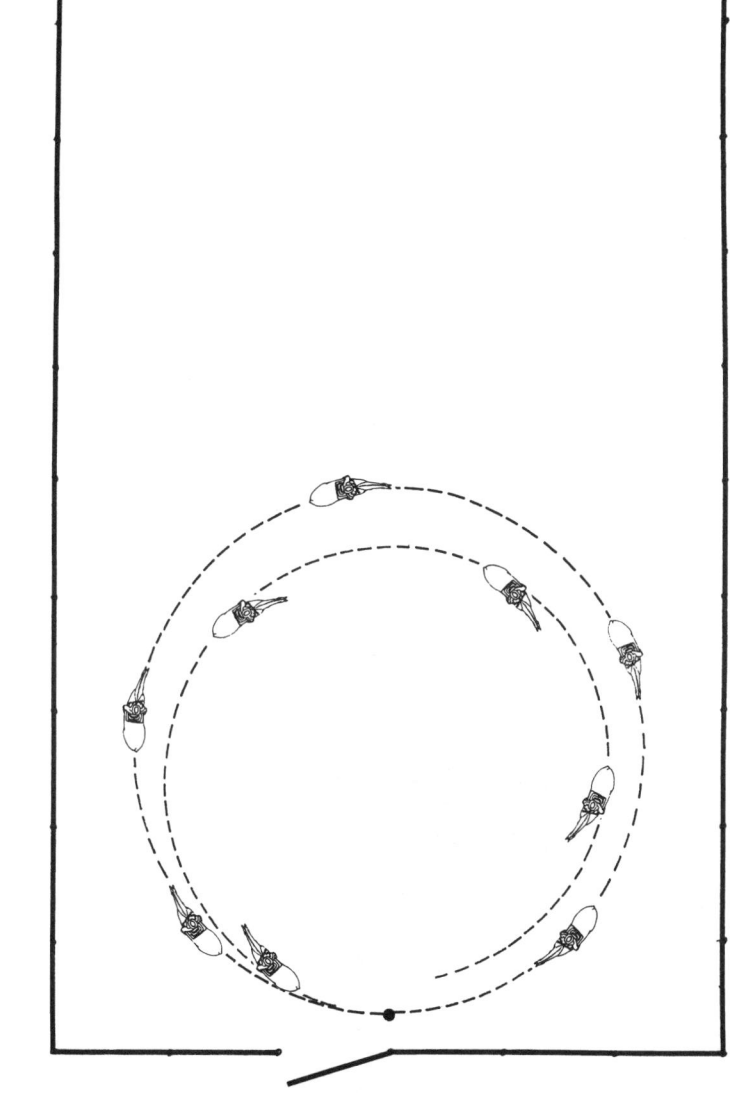

*Drawing **A** shows an example of a "neck in" rather than a shoulder in. The horse is overbent to the right. The rider's hand comes dangerously close to crossing the horse's midline. The rider's left leg should be behind the cinch to drive the horse actively into the left rein. To correct, the rider should bring the right hand in the vicinity of the withers, thus lightening the right rein. The horse should be driven actively forward with half halts on the outside rein.*

A

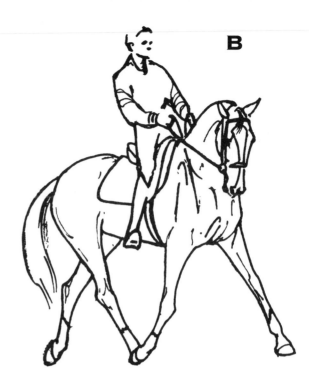

B

*In drawing **B**, shoulder in on a circle to the right, the diagonal pair landing (right hind and left front) constitutes one track. The right front is inside that track and the left hind outside.*

For contrast, see drawings in Exercises #62 and #63.

NOTE

Be sure to use more left leg than normal to prevent the hindquarters from falling out of the circle.

BENEFITS

★ Especially good exercise for a horse that doesn't take an even contact with both reins.

★ You should really be able to feel (in your seat and hand) the horse step from his right hind to his left front.

CAUTION

Don't use too much right rein or it could cause the left shoulder to bulge and the hindquarters to fall out of the circle line.

Travers (Haunches In)

How to Ride the Exercise

★ Collected trot (Exercise #9) straight.

★ Corner to right (Exercise #31).

★ Half halt (Exercise #14).

★ Travers:

- Right leg at the girth to keep the right hind active and maintain bend.

- Right rein for right flexion.

- Left leg behind the girth pushing in rhythm with the gait as the left hind is leaving the ground to move the hindquarters in off the track.

- Left rein controls the degree of bend to the right.

- Left rein keeps the neck secure at its base so no "rubber-necking" occurs.

- Weight is slightly to the right and forward.

★ Straighten by bringing the forehand in front of the hindquarters so now the track is a few feet inside the original track.

★ If desired, move the straightened horse sideways back to the original track with the right leg.

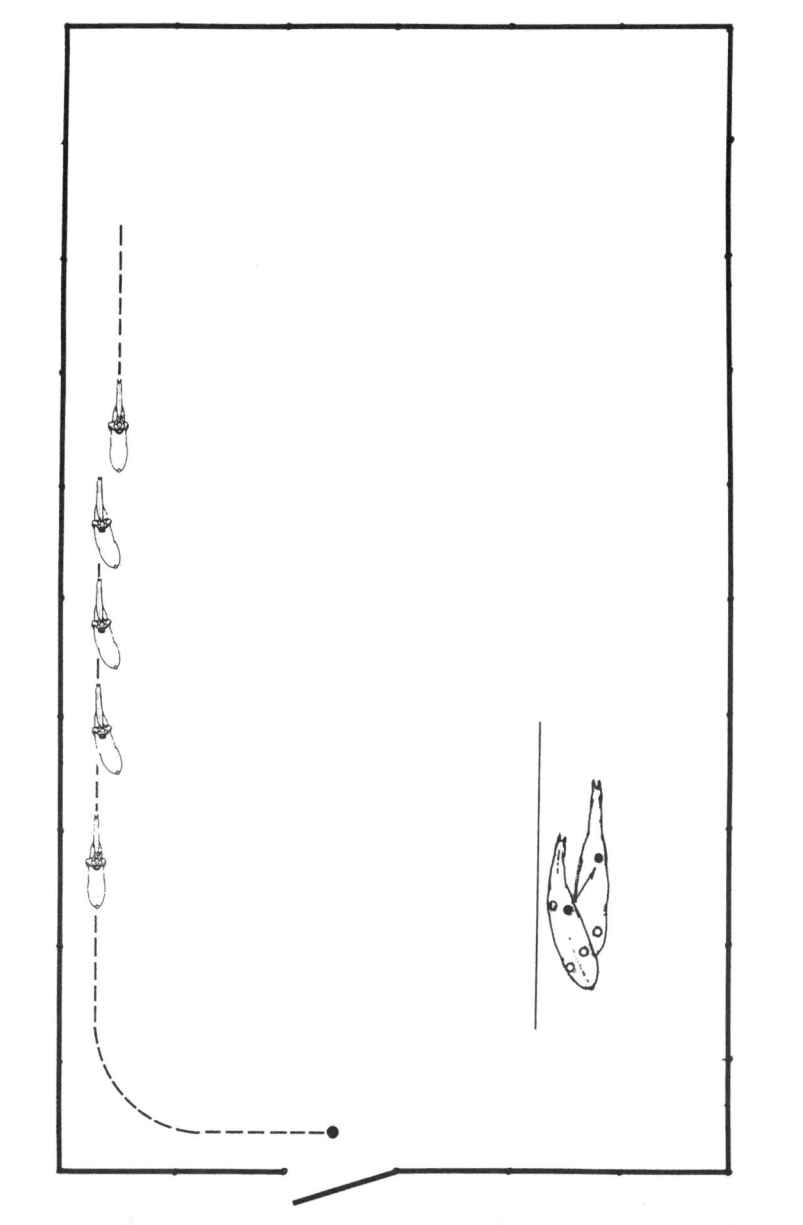

VARIATIONS

★ Practice first at the walk to become familiar with the aids. This exercise is best at collected trot. If used exclusively at the canter, it may encourage the horse to carry his haunches in during normal canter, so beware.

★ This exercise can be easier to start immediately after the corner, "holding" the bend of the corner to get started.

This front view of a very nice travers right at the trot clearly shows the four tracks outlined. The rider should be made aware of her head tilt, and she really should be looking forward in the direction of travel.

NOTE

The four tracks in a travers to the right are (from the rail inward): left front, right front, left hind, right hind. The left hind travels on a path very close to that of the right front. The horse is bent to the right. The left legs cross over the right legs.

BENEFITS

★ Helps perfect the shoulder in.

★ Works on straightness, engagement of the hindquarters, and collection.

★ Increases the engagement of the inside hind leg: The joints bend more and the leg carries more weight.

CAUTION

★ It is an error to bend the neck extremely at the shoulder. To remedy, add more right leg and left rein.

★ It is an error to bring the hindquarters in too much to the right because the gait will lose rhythm and often the horse steps sideways to the right with the right (inside) hind leg, defeating the purpose of strengthening the inside hind leg to carry more weight.

★ Common rider errors are collapsing the right side and bringing the right hand over the mane to the left.

Shoulder In and Travers on Long Serpentine

HOW TO RIDE THE EXERCISE

★ Ride collected trot (Exercise #9) down the long side of the arena in a long serpentine (Exercise #49) pattern.

★ Ride the corner (Exercise #31) to the right with regular bend.

★ Turn up the center line.

★ Retain the shoulder-in (Exercise #62) position from the turn.

★ Ride shoulder in up the center line for about 60 feet.

★ Straighten (Exercise #30) by bringing the forehand in front of the hindquarters on the original line of travel.

★ Ride straight ahead for about 60 feet.

★ Turn left with regular bend, and continue the turn down the quarter line.

★ Retain the travers (Exercise #65) position from the turn.

★ Ride travers for about 60 feet.

★ Straighten by bringing the forehand in front of the hindquarters, resulting in a new line of travel.

★ Ride straight ahead.

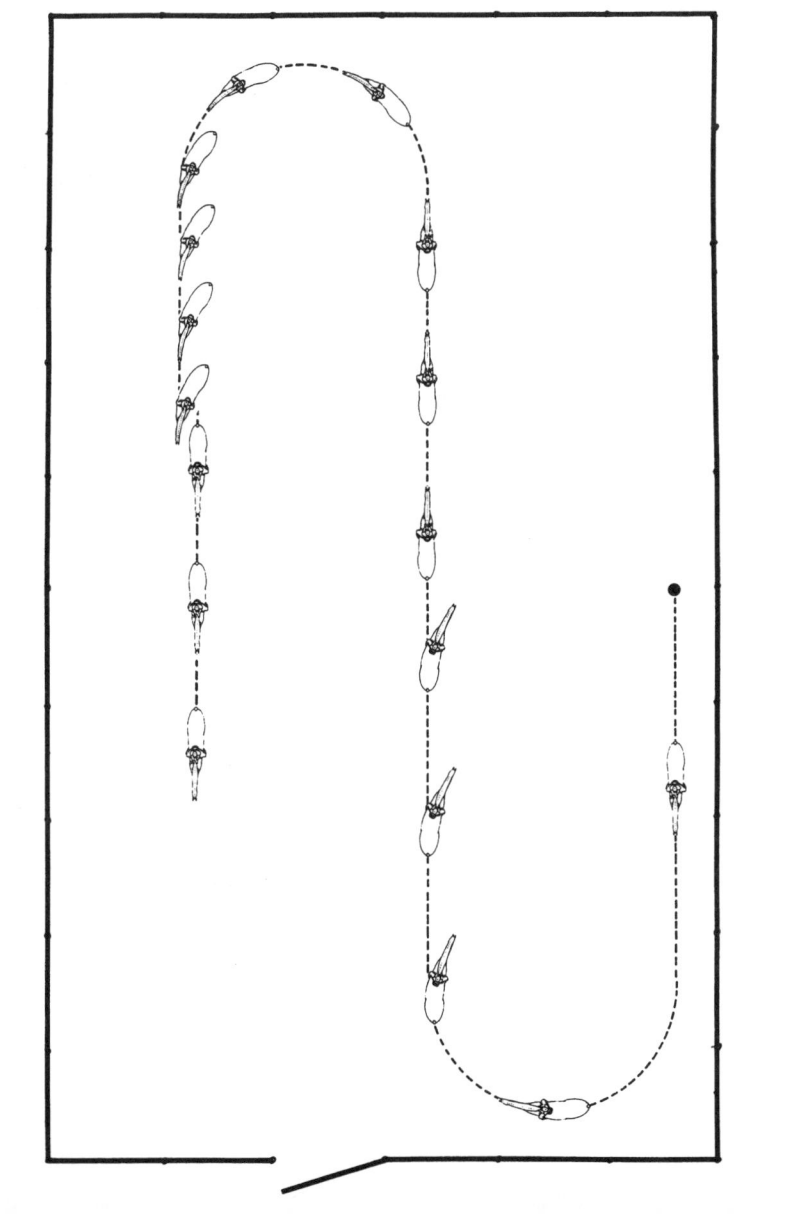

This shows an attempt at a collected trot, but the gait has deteriorated into an unattractive pulling match. The rider is using far too much rein. The horse has broken at the poll and is severely behind the vertical. He is pushing against the rider's strong rein aids with the muscles on the underside of his neck. Although the flexion of his legs might make one think the gait is "collected," the fact that his croup is high, his back is hollow, and he is pushing strongly downhill shows he is not at all collected. This horse needs a lot of forward work and properly applied half halts before a rider should attempt Exercise #66 with him.

BENEFIT

Shows the rider the importance of the difference in straightening after a shoulder in and travers.

Walk-Volte-Travers

HOW TO RIDE THE EXERCISE

★ Walk (Exercise #15).

★ Ride the corner (Exercise #31).

★ Collected walk (Exercise #4).

★ Volte (small circle) (Exercise #37).

★ Come out of circle in travers (Exercise #65).

★ Travers 40 feet or so.

★ Straighten by aligning forehand with hindquarters.

★ Straight forward working walk.

VARIATION

Perform at a collected trot or collected canter.

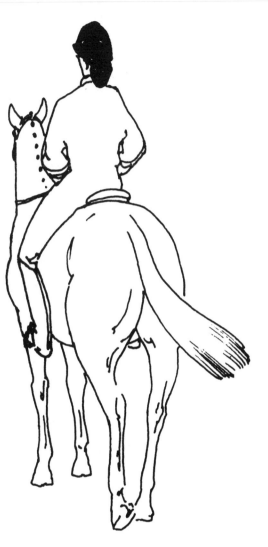

Travers tracking right at a collected walk. Note the distinct four tracks from the rail: left front, right front, left hind, and right hind. The left legs cross over and in front of the right legs and land in this order: left hind, left front, right hind, right front. The horse is flexed right and is bent around the rider's right leg. The rider's left leg could be a bit farther back to bend the haunches to the right a little more. The rider is looking straight ahead, which helps keep her upper body erect.

BENEFIT

This exercise shows the horse in clear terms what you want in travers.

Renvers (Haunches Out)

HOW TO RIDE THE EXERCISE

★ Collected trot (Exercise #9) straight (Exercise #30), then corner (Exercise #31).

★ Straight, collected walk (Exercise #4).

★ Shoulder in (Exercise #62).

★ Half pirouette (Exercise #69), ending on original track (note arena map drawing is offset for clarity).

★ Renvers, returning on original track along rail without changing the bend of the pirouette.

Half halt (Exercise #14).

Weight right seat bone.

Right leg at the girth

• to give the horse a point to bend around,

• keeps steps with the right hind lively.

Left leg

• behind girth to keep the hindquarters on the track,

• bends the horse around the right leg,

• prevents sideways steps.

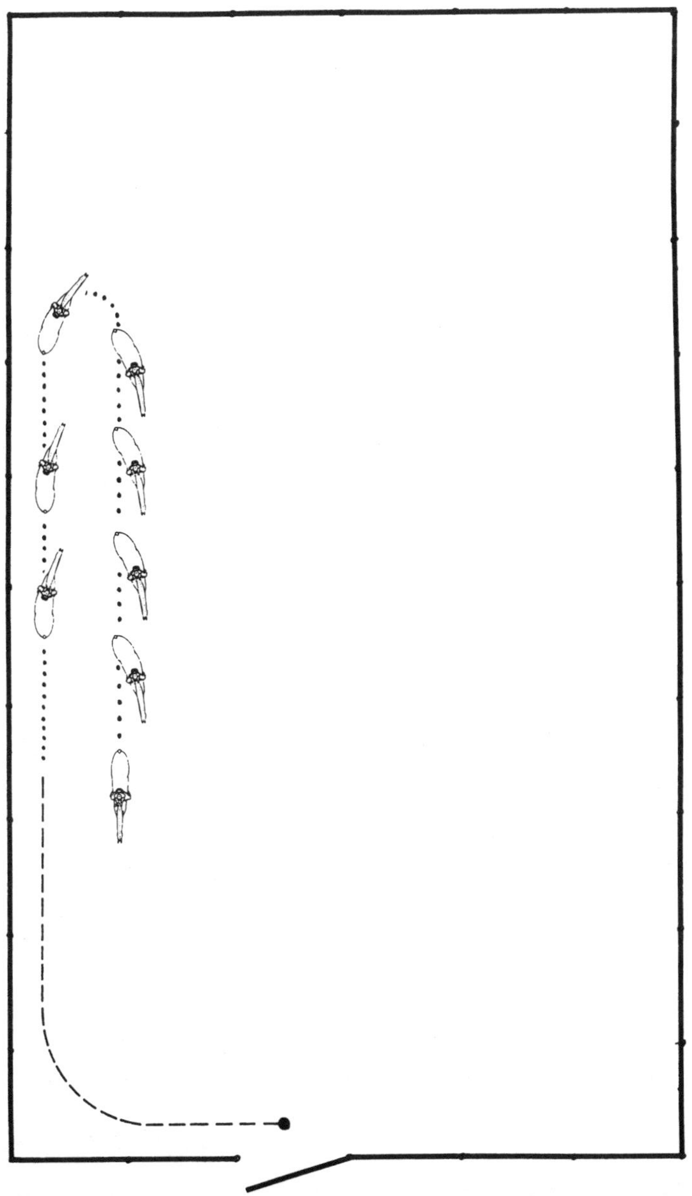

Right rein to create right flexion.

Left rein

- to keep the shoulder in off the track,

- to maintain left/right balance,

- to regulate the degree of bend.

Rider's left shoulder forward.

★ To finish, align forehand by bringing it back in front of the hindquarters.

Drive with both legs.

Right opening rein.

Left leg at the girth.

Renvers at the collected walk tracking left, with right bend. The rail would be on the rider's right. The four tracks are (from the rail) right hind, left hind, right front, left front. All legs step close to the horse's center of gravity, which is a line between the tracks of the left hind and right front.

VARIATION

After correct practice at the walk, perform at a collected trot. This exercise can also be ridden in collected canter.

NOTE

Renvers is a four-track movement. The haunches are on the track, the forehand is a half-step in to the left from the haunches, but the bend is to the right (opposite to the line of travel, which is to the left). Here the horse is bent to the right and is tracking on a line to the left.

BENEFITS

★ Renvers is a good means of developing lateral bend because the hindquarters are "held" by the arena rail or wall and the rider can effectively work on controlling the left shoulder.

★ Renvers is also a good exercise to show the rider the difference between shoulder in and haunches out.

CAUTION

★ Too much bend in the neck will cause loss of rhythm because the horse is stepping sideways too much and not forward enough.

★ A head tilt to the right requires rein adjustment with forward driving aids. Lighten both reins, lift the right one momentarily, and drive forward.

Walk Pirouette

HOW TO RIDE THE EXERCISE

★ Collected walk (Exercise #4) up the long side.

★ At the midpoint, half halt (Exercise #14).

★ Walk pirouette right.

• Flex the horse to the right, and guide him into the turn with the right rein.

• Left rein controls degree of right flexion but allows movement for turn to right.

• Weight right seat bone.

• Keep upper body straight.

• Left shoulder forward.

• Right leg at the girth to keep the turn forward.

• Left leg slightly behind the girth

supporting the hindquarters,

preventing the left hind leg from stepping sideways to the left,

activating the hindquarters to step forward and sideways to the right in a small half circle.

★ Finish the turn one horse-width off the original track.

★ Straighten and walk forward.

VARIATION

If the exercise is performed at a collected trot, the actual pirouette is performed at a collected walk. The horse should not come to a full halt before or after the turn.

In this walk pirouette to the right, although the horse is exhibiting great crossover in front, he is stiff behind and appears to be "standing on his inside hind" (or possibly his outside) instead of walking in time. Because of the extreme crossover, the horse's front end appears to be tilted to the right but his nose is counter-flexed to the left. The rider should use a lower left rein away from the horse's neck to keep the horse up on the left shoulder, and she should use leg aids to maintain the four-beat rhythm of the walk. See also drawings in Exercises #70, #71, #90, #91, and #92.

NOTES

Footfall pattern of a walk pirouette to the right is the same as the walk: left hind, left front, right hind, right front. The horse is flexed to the right. The pivot point is the right hind. The right hind moves up and down nearly in the same spot or slightly in front of it with each stride. The left hind walks a tiny half circle around the right hind. The forehand moves in a half circle to the right with the left front crossing over in front of the right front.

The difference between a *pivot point* and a pivot foot is as follows: The leg of a pivot point marks time by lifting up and setting down in rhythm with the four-beat walk. A pivot foot, on the other hand, swivels in place. It is locked or planted in place. In a walk pirouette, a pivot foot is not desirable. If the horse is pivoting on the foot, he is said to be "standing on the inside hind leg." In a Western pivot (Exercise #71), a pivot foot is desirable.

BENEFIT

The walk pirouette creates collection.

CAUTION

A really active outside leg might cause you to weight your outside seat bone instead of your inside seat bone. This may cause your horse to use his outside hind leg as a pivot point and could cause him to step backward with his inside hind leg to keep his balance. A forward step in a walk pirouette is a much less serious error than a backward step.

Counter-Flexed Spiral In

HOW TO RIDE THE EXERCISE

★ Begin a large circle (Exercise #35) to the right at a walk (Exercise #2) with right bend.

★ Follow a spiral pattern (Exercise #41).

★ At the halfway point of the first circle, change from right bend to straight (Exercise #30).

★ As you approach the starting point, change from straight to counter-flex with left flexion (Exercise #51).

★ Spiral in with the horse in the counter-flexed position.

★ When you get to the center you can ask for a few steps of counter-flexed turn on the hindquarters (Exercise #69).

★ Immediately straighten and ride forward out of the circle.

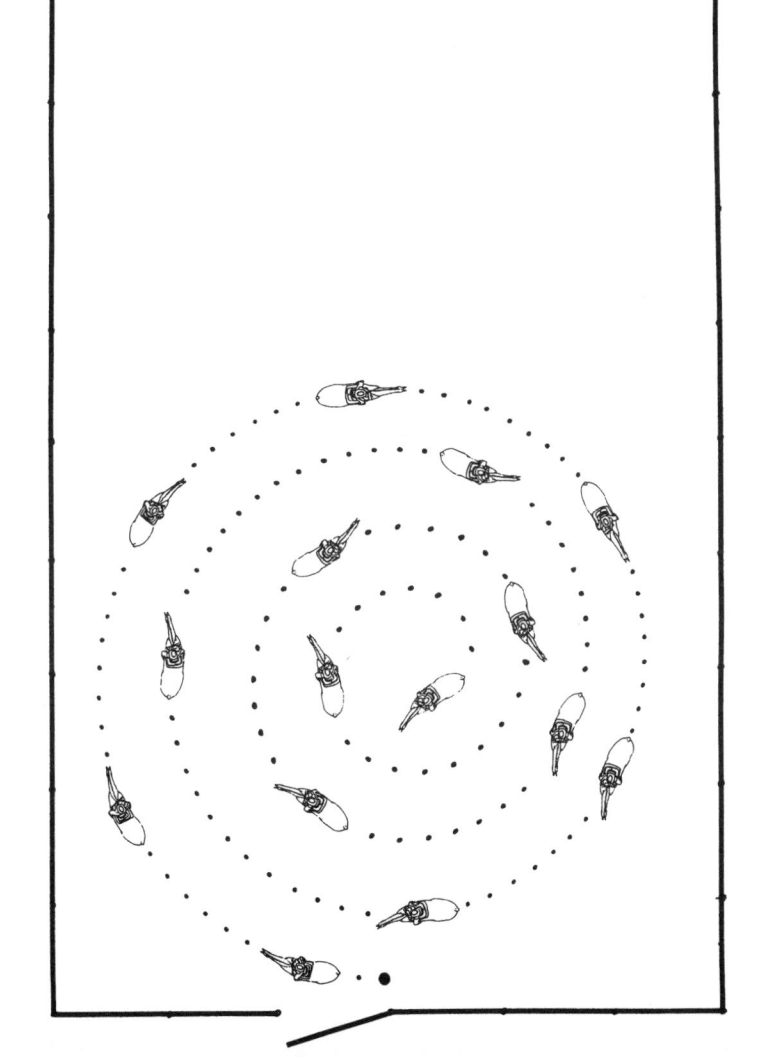

This is a good example of Western counter-flex or "reverse arc" used to start horses in their hindquarter work. Horse is spiraling to the right while counter-flexed to the left.

NOTE

Since the hindquarters stay on the track, there is less crossover behind than in front.

Hold well with the right leg to prevent a sideways step of the right hind.

BENEFIT

The counter-flexed spiral in is an easy way to teach a horse to move his front legs laterally and to cross over in preparation for pivots or turnarounds.

Hindquarter Pivot

How to Ride the Exercise

★ Walk (Exercise #2) around the corner (Exercise #31) and straight up the long side.

★ Check (Exercise #14).

★ Slight position right.

★ Hindquarter pivot.

★ Weight on right seat bone to hold pivot foot down.

★ Lift reins up and back to weight hindquarters and lock pivot foot.

★ Left leg at or slightly in front of the cinch to initiate right turn.

★ Right leg passive but ready to correct or prevent sideways step of the right hind.

NOTE

When a horse pivots, he ends up on the same track he started. In contrast, when performing a walk pirouette (Exercise #69), the horse ends up on a new track a horse's width away from the original track.

CAUTION

Don't let the horse back up during the pivot or he will be forced to pick up his pivot foot. There is a fine line between settling the weight *on* the hindquarters and forcing the horse's weight backward *past* the hindquarters.

In this very fine pivot to the right, the right hind leg is well under the horse's body and the horse's body is straight. The rider's upper body could be a little more upright if it wouldn't cause the horse to take a step backwards to re-balance. See drawings in Exercises #69, #90, #91, and #92.

Rollback

HOW TO RIDE THE EXERCISE

★ Lope (Exercises #10 and #20) right lead up the long side of the arena.

★ Near the center of the long side, drift about 10 feet off the rail.

★ Check (Exercise #14) several times to shift the horse's weight to his hindquarters.

★ Without asking for a halt and with the forehand directly in front of the hindquarters, turn 180 degrees to the left.

• Left rein to provide direction.

• Right rein to guide the front end around.

• Right leg to push the forehand sideways.

★ After 90 degrees of the turn, release rein aids to prevent overturning.

★ Lope left lead.

VARIATION

Practice at the walk and trot first to become familiar with the aids.

NOTE

A rollback is described as a set and turn at a lope as opposed to a halt and turn or a sliding stop and turn.

Starting on the rail and then drifting off the rail is better than riding the whole exercise on a straight line that is off the rail. Drifting off the rail keeps the horse's body straight but aimed slightly to the right, which sets the horse up for a better rollback to the left.

Don't let the hindquarters swing to the right on the "set" or it will ruin your chances of planting the (left hind) pivot foot.

Prevent overbend to the left by providing some positive resistance with the right rein, which actually keeps the horse straight and guides him through the turn.

During the turn, it is important that the inside pivot foot (left hind) bear the weight all through the turn so when the turn is finished, the right hind is free to initiate the left lead by driving off strongly as beat number one of the lope stride.

BENEFIT

Really shows a horse what balancing on his hindquarters feels like. When done properly, it can strengthen the loin and back, provided you don't strain the horse's hind legs.

A good deep set to the hindquarters shown by the angle of the hocks and the space under the saddle as the horse breaks at the loin. However, the horse should be more on the right rein to keep him straighter. The left hind should be more under the center of gravity, not splayed out to the left. The rider's weight is too far to the right, causing the horse to be imbalanced. See drawing in Exercise #97.

Sidepass

HOW TO RIDE THE EXERCISE

★ Walk (Exercise #2) around the corner (Exercise #31) and up the long side of the arena.

★ Once your horse is straight (Exercise #30), turn on the forehand 90 degrees, with the horse flexed left and hindquarters moving to the right (Exercise #55).

★ When facing the arena rail

• weight your left seat bone,

• sidepass right 3–4 strides, modifying the aids for leg yield (Exercise #57) to achieve a full sideways movement.

★ With the horse still flexed left, turn on the hindquarters to the right (Exercises #69 and #71).

★ Ride straight, then the corner.

★ Ride one stride straight.

★ Ride one stride flexed left.

★ Turn on the forehand (see above).

★ When horse is facing the rail, straighten his body.

• Sit evenly on both seat bones.

• Sidepass to the right 3–4 steps, possibly using an occasional right opening rein.

★ Flex slightly right and turn on the hindquarters (Exercise #69).

★ Ride straight, then corner, and straight.

★ With right flexion, perform a turn on the forehand with hindquarters moving right.

★ Retain right flexion and sidepass right 3–4 strides.

   • Weight right seat bone.

★ Retain right flexion and turn on the hindquarters 90 degrees to the right.

★ Straighten and walk forward.

VARIATIONS

★ Vary the flexion in the turn on the forehand, hindquarters, and sidepass.

★ Jog between the segments to liven up the horse.

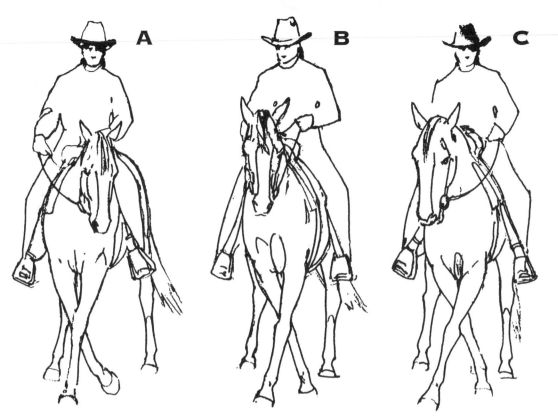

NOTE

Foot sequence in sidepass to the right is the same as the walk. Horse might start off taking a small step to the right with the right front.

1. Left hind crosses over in front of the right hind.

2. Left front crosses over in front of the right front.

3. Right hind uncrosses from behind the left hind and steps to the right.

4. Right front uncrosses from behind the left front and steps to the right.

Note: Numbers 2 and 3 happen almost in unison, allowing the horse to retain his balance.

In this sidepass to the right, the three flexions are demonstrated. All occur during foot sequence number 2 of the sidepass as outlined in Note.

A. *Counter-flexed — easiest.*

B. *Straight — moderately difficult.*

C. *Flexion into direction of movement — most difficult.*

See drawings in Exercises #86 and #89.

Half Pass

HOW TO RIDE THE EXERCISE

★ Collected trot (Exercise #9).

★ Coming out of the corner, half halt (Exercise #14).

★ Half pass to the right.

Look slightly in the direction of travel.

Ride shoulder fore (Exercise #61) or shoulder in (Exercise #62) for a few strides if necessary to be sure the shoulder is leading. (This is exaggerated on the arena map to make the point.)

Weight right seat bone and heel.

Right leg at the girth

  • to keep right hind moving actively forward,

  • to maintain the right bend.

Left leg behind the girth pushing in rhythm with trot stride.

Left rein

  • controls bend,

  • secures neck at the base,

  • maintains balance and rhythm.

The right front leg should take the first sideways step.

★ Straighten by releasing the shoulder fore aids and continue travers (Exercise #65) aids for half a stride, then finish straightening.

★ Ride straight ahead.

In this half pass to the right at the trot, note the great forward and sideways reach. The horse's body is quite straight, balanced, and collected. The rider is looking in the direction of movement, has the right seat bone weighted, and the left leg is behind the girth pushing sideways in time with the trot stride. The horse could have more right flexion up front.

NOTE

Practice at walk to learn aids, then at collected trot and collected canter.

In a half pass to the right, the horse moves forward and sideways to the right around the rider's right leg, the horse flexed and bent to the right. The horse's body is basically parallel to the rail with the shoulders slightly in advance of the hindquarters.

BENEFITS

★ Supples the horse evenly on both sides.

★ Develops straightness and balance.

★ Develops collection and strength of the inside hind leg.

CAUTION

★ Don't be tempted to weight your *left* seat bone and heel and try to push the horse over to the right for a half pass right.

★ Take care not to overbend to the right or to let the right hand cross over the mane to the left.

★ If the horse is not bent around your right leg, you are basically performing an incorrect version of leg yield!

Half Pass Refresher

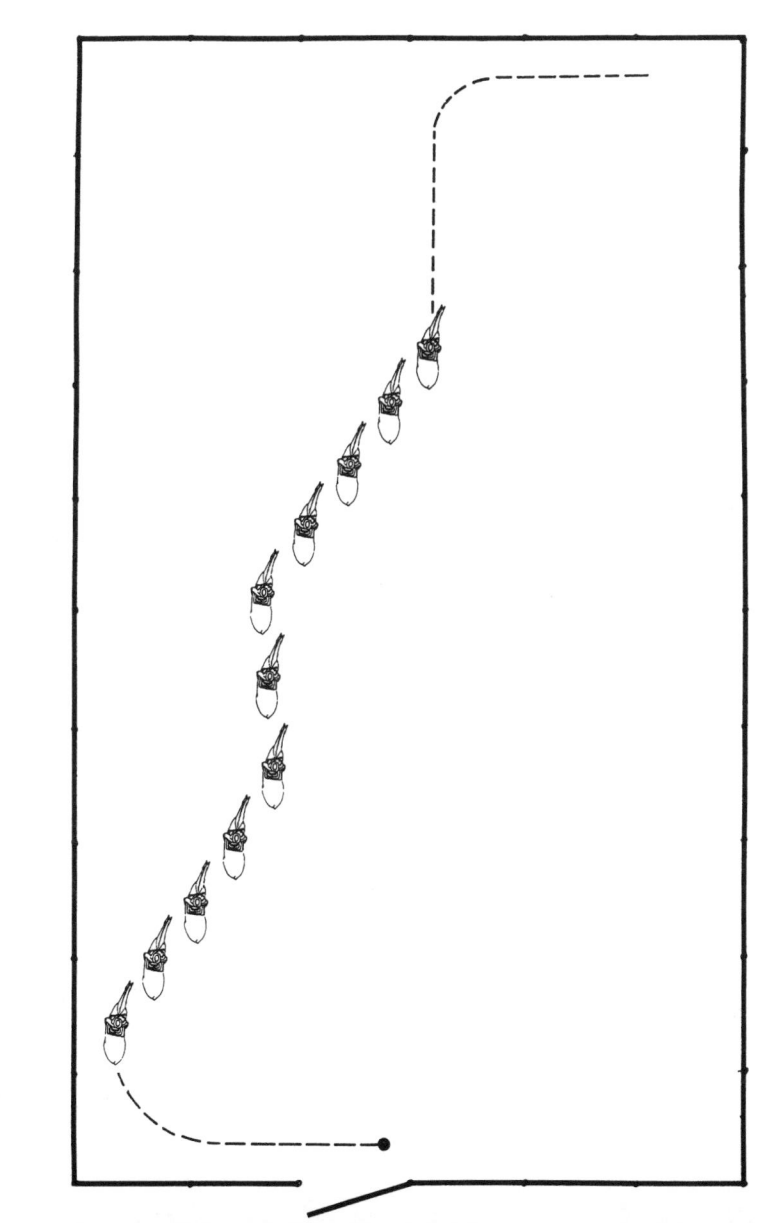

How to Ride the Exercise

★ Collected trot (Exercise #9).

★ Corner (Exercise #31).

★ From corner, go into half pass right (Exercise #74).

★ After a few strides of half pass, go into a shoulder in (Exercise #62) on a straight line.

★ When the horse regains right bend and forward movement, return to the half pass right.

★ Repeat as necessary.

Variations

★ Instead of a shoulder in, ride a full volte to the right and then continue the half pass.

★ This exercise can be practiced at a walk, collected trot, and collected canter.

This attempt at a half pass to the right has deteriorated into an unbalanced movement that needs the straightening and collecting benefits of a shoulder-in refresher. The horse has fallen on the right shoulder, is overbent to the right, his poll and forehand have fallen, and there appears to be too much sideways movement and not enough forward movement. For contrast see drawing in Exercise #74.

NOTE

Some of the common problems with a half pass and their solutions are:

★ The horse does not stay bent around the rider's inside leg. For example, when going to the right, instead of the horse's body bending evenly to the right, the horse's forehand faces straight ahead or to the left. Solution: Ride the shoulder in to re-establish bend to the right.

★ The horse loses rhythm and begins slowing down. Solution: Drive the horse actively forward with both legs into a very forward gait.

★ The horse overbends to the right (when half passing to the right) and falls on the inside (right) shoulder. Solution: Use a strong right leg at the girth and re-establish contact with the outside (left) rein via a shoulder in.

BENEFIT

This ensures the horse is correctly bent around the inside leg, is up on the outside rein, and is moving forward.

Zigzag Half Pass

HOW TO RIDE THE EXERCISE

★ Collected trot (Exercise #9) around corner (Exercise #31).

★ Half halt (Exercise #14).

★ Shoulder fore (Exercise #61) out of corner.

★ Half pass right (Exercise #74).

★ Straighten and ride straight 1–3 strides.

★ Flex the horse to the new direction (left).

★ Shoulder fore to left.

★ Half pass left.

★ Straighten.

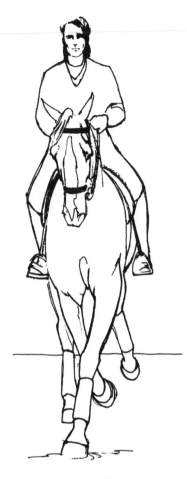

Here the rider has just completed a half pass right and is straightening her horse in preparation for a half pass left. There is still a tiny bit of right flexion remaining, but the rider is straightening the horse with her left rein. She has released the sideways driving aids of her left leg and is "catching" the horse's body with her right leg. By the time the horse moves the right front and left hind forward, his head and body will be completely straight. See drawing in Exercise #74.

NOTE

On the straight line, the horse's hindquarters must be absolutely straight with the forehand *before* initiating new bend. Then be sure the forehand is in position (shoulder fore) to advance properly before initiating the new half pass. Otherwise the hindquarters may lead.

This exercise is also called "counter change of hand."

BENEFIT

Zigzag half pass is a requirement for fourth-level dressage.

CAUTION

Don't continue the half pass if it deteriorates. Instead, ride actively forward in shoulder in, travers, or in a circle, then try again.

Working Pirouette (Pre-Pirouette)

HOW TO RIDE THE EXERCISE

In preparation for this exercise:

★ Walk (Exercise #4) a small circle in travers (Exercise #65).

★ Walk a normal circle.

★ Ride a small circle in collected canter (Exercise #12).

★ Then canter a straight line in travers.

★ Canter a straight line in shoulder in (Exercise #62).

★ Then canter a small to medium circle (Exercise #36) in travers.

★ Canter a small to medium circle in shoulder in.

For the actual exercise:

★ Canter a straight line, then spiral in (Exercise #41) at a collected canter (in position right or shoulder fore), ending up in a working pirouette.

★ Ride out of the circle portion by riding travers on a line.

★ Straighten.

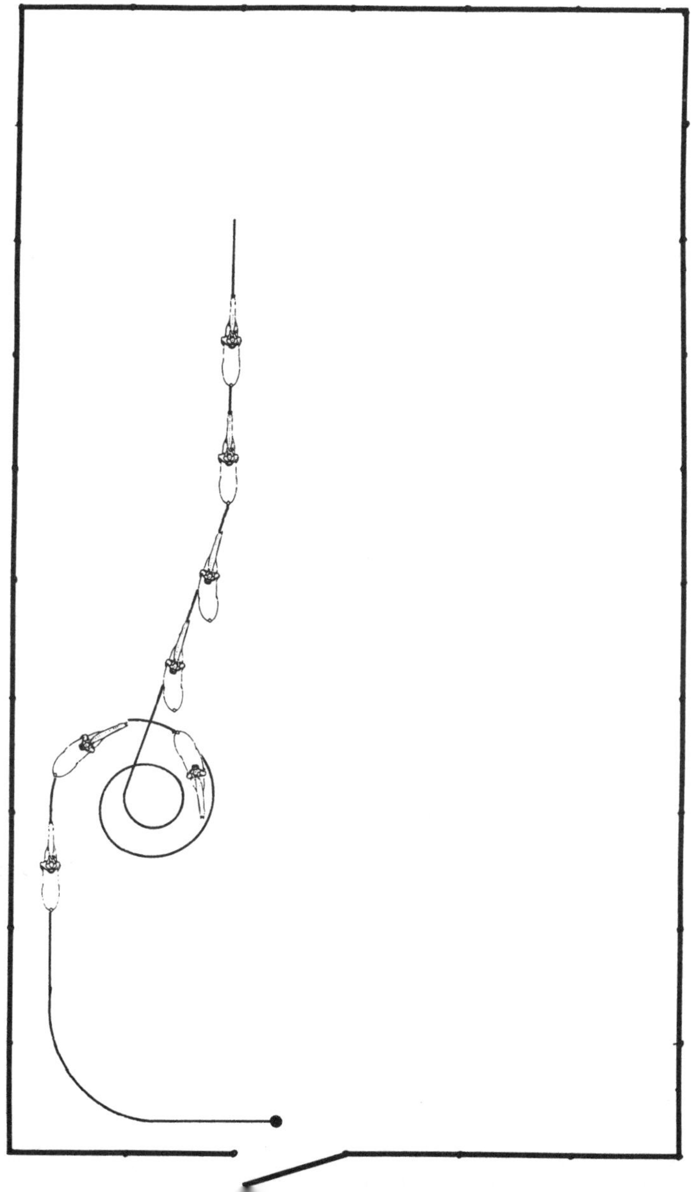

In this beginning of a working pirouette to the right, the horse is in position right. The rider's left leg is being used far behind the girth to keep the hindquarters from moving left and to initiate the small canter circle to the right.

NOTE

In a working pirouette, the hindquarters canter an 8- to 10-foot circle rather than cantering "on the spot," as in a finished pirouette.

BENEFIT

Working pirouette is a good preparation for the canter pirouette work.

CAUTION

Never force a horse around with the reins. He should remain light and "come around" in response to your slight re-balancing aids (seat and leg).

Half-Canter Pirouette

HOW TO RIDE THE EXERCISE

★ Ride a very collected, cadenced canter (Exercise #12) right lead up the long side about 20–30 feet off the rail.

★ Prevent travers (Exercise #65) by riding shoulder in (Exercise #62), if necessary.

★ About 30 feet from the short end, half halt (Exercise #14).

★ Half pirouette.

Right leg at the girth with steady pressure.

Left leg behind the girth (even farther behind than for canter right lead)

  • to prevent the left hind from moving sideways to the left,

  • to bend the horse around the rider's right leg,

  • to initiate and maintain sideways movement (to the right) for the pirouette.

Right rein

  • to develop the necessary flexion,

  • to indicate the direction of the turn.

Left rein

  • controls the degree of right flexion and bend,

  • keeps the hindquarters cantering a particular size circle,

  • maintains the rhythm.

Keep weight centered and upper body erect.

- ★ When the half pirouette is complete, straighten with right leg to left rein.
- ★ Re-establish the activity of the canter if it was lost during the pirouette.

For the most part, things are going well in this pirouette to the right. However, because the horse is bent so much to the right and because the rider is weighting her right side, I get the impression that the horse's left hind leg could pop sideways (to the left) on the next beat. It doesn't look as if the rider's left leg is in good enough contact to prevent it, either. See drawings in Exercises #77, #79, and #80.

NOTE

- ★ A half pirouette should require 3–4 strides of canter to complete.

- ★ At first, only ask for a working pirouette (Exercise #77).

- ★ The clear three-beat canter must be maintained. The horse must be able to be ridden out of the pirouette at any moment. This requires that he work with "bent haunches," with his weight well back and ready to spring out.

BENEFIT

Trains and conditions the horse to carry more weight with the inside hind leg.

CAUTION

- ★ If the pirouette becomes labored, it will be a four-beat movement.

- ★ If the rider's weight is taken to the left (outside) to "push" the horse around to the right, the rider imbalances the horse to the left hind leg and the rider often collapses her right side.

- ★ If the rider's weight is taken too much to the right seat bone, it will imbalance the horse and he will rush, lose rhythm, and make the hindquarters swing to the left.

Three-Quarter Pirouette

How to Ride the Exercise

★ Canter right lead (Exercise #12).

★ Regular bend around the corner (Exercise #31).

★ Canter straight 100 feet or more (Exercise #30).

★ Half halts as necessary (Exercise #14).

★ Position right.

★ Half pirouette (180 degrees) to the right (Exercise #78).

★ Straighten.

★ Canter 80 feet or more.

★ Half halts as necessary.

★ Position right.

★ Three-quarter pirouette to the right (270 degrees).

★ Canter with right flexion.

★ Straighten.

★ About 20 feet before the long side, lead change (Exercise #95).

★ Canter left lead around the corner.

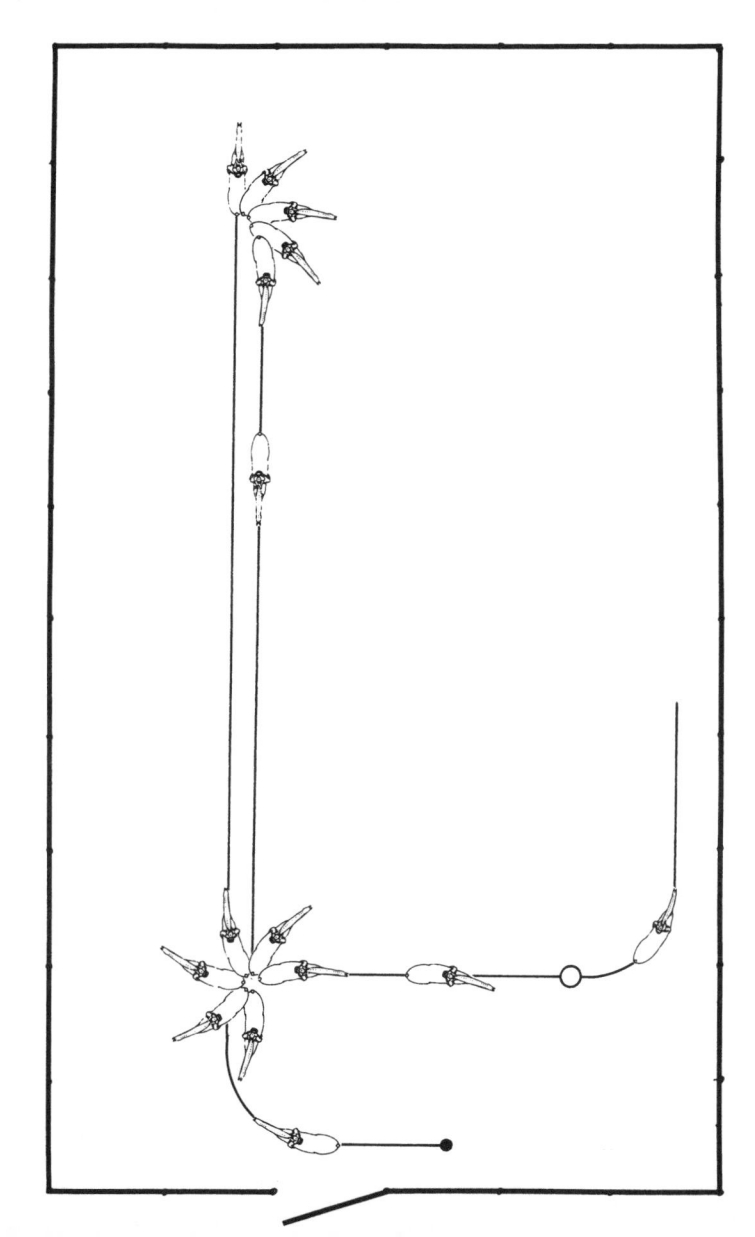

This is a nice example of a collected and straight pirouette to the right. Note, however, that the diagonal pair has broken with the right hind, landing in advance of the left front and indicating that the true three-beat rhythm might be just a bit labored.

NOTE

It should take 3–4 strides to complete the half pirouette and 5–6 to complete the three-quarter pirouette.

VARIATION

★ Canter.

★ Halt.

★ Walk half pirouette.

★ Canter.

★ Halt.

★ Walk three-quarter pirouette.

★ Canter.

★ Simple change.

CAUTION

If you find the canter slows down too much in the pirouettes, go back to canter volte (#37) to strengthen your horse's balance and hindquarter carrying capacity. Avoid the temptation to pull on the reins when you begin the pirouette. Instead, as you approach the pirouette, think of more forward driving aids to round and energize your horse.

Remember, do not try to pull your horse around in the turn. This will only throw him off balance and bind up the movement of his shoulders. Bring the horse around with your leg and seat aids primarily.

Full Canter Pirouette

HOW TO RIDE THE EXERCISE

★ Collected canter (Exercise #12) through the corner
(Exercise #31).

★ Half pass to the right (Exercise #74), making sure your
horse's inside hind (right) is well under his mass.

★ Full pirouette (Exercise #78).

• Right leg to maintain forward impulsion.

• Left leg as for half pirouette (Exercise #78).

• Right rein can be carried a bit higher than the left to cause
the horse to flex vertically at the poll (in accordance with the
degree of collection of the pirouette) without overbending to
the right.

★ From pirouette, go into half pass right.

★ Straighten (Exercise #74).

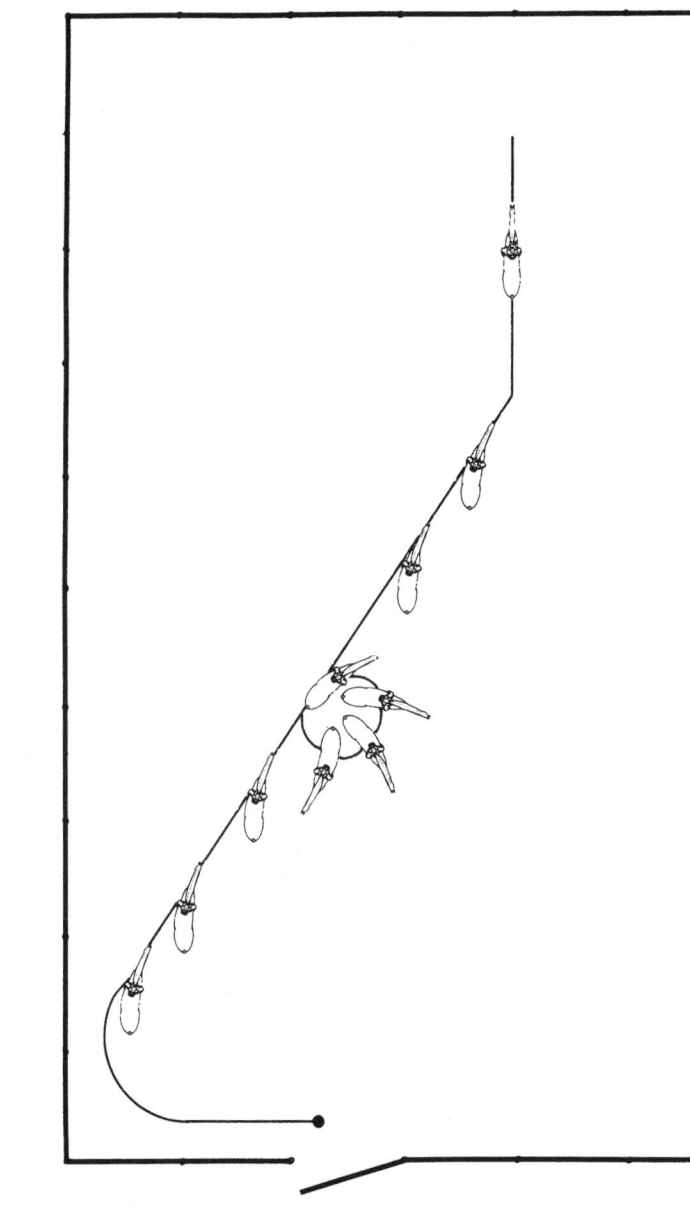

In this, the beginning steps of a canter pirouette to the right, the horse's inside hind is well placed and the rider's aids are effectively positioning the horse for the beginning of the turn. The first step sideways should be with the leading foreleg (right).

NOTE

A full pirouette will take from 6–8 strides of canter.

BENEFIT

The full canter pirouette can improve Prix St. George dressage.

CAUTION

The main problems are the hindquarters swinging to the left, a loss of bend to the right, and a loss of the three-beat rhythm. If at any time there is a loss of forward motion in the pirouette, ride forward out of it in an active canter.

Mini-Patterns

The mini-patterns in this section combine exercises covered in gaits, transitions, circles, and lateral work. When you start putting all the components together, you will find an unlimited variety of routines for you and your horse.

Flying change work is included as a group of exercises at the end of this section.

Guess What

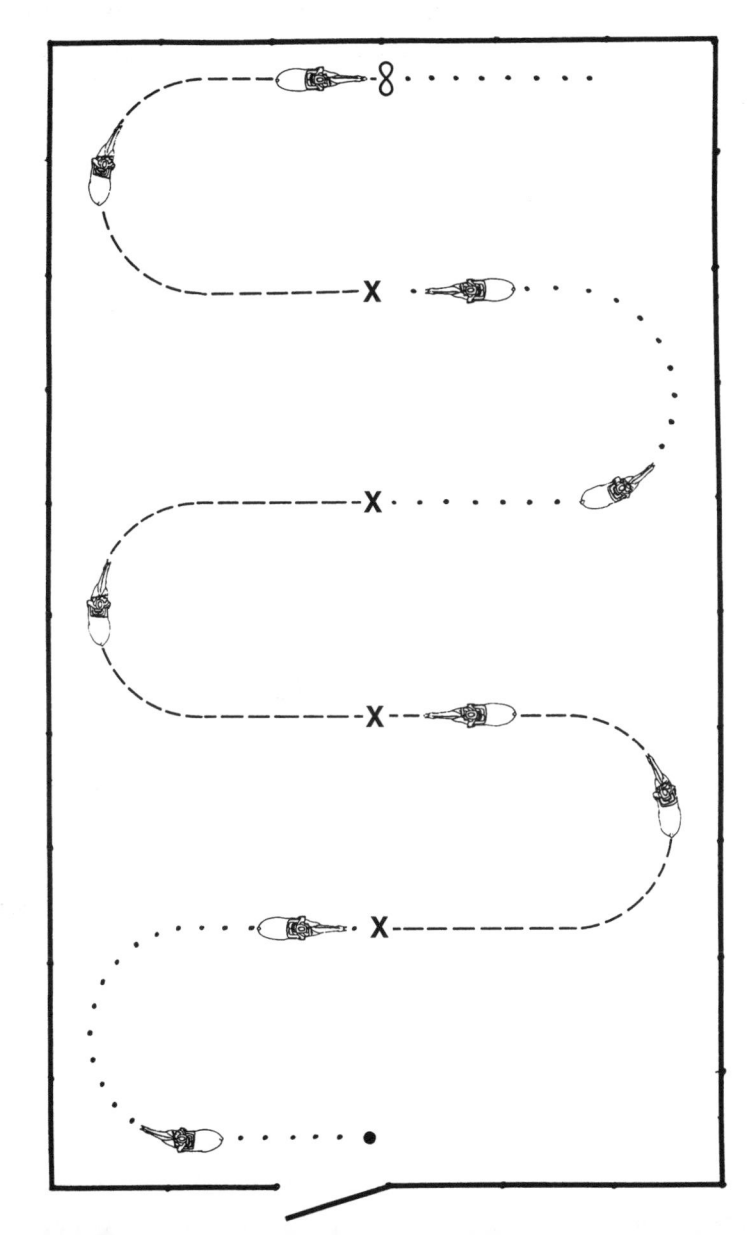

HOW TO RIDE THE EXERCISE

★ Walk (Exercise #2) and follow pattern for five-loop serpentine (Exercise #48).

★ After first loop, in the center of the straight line, halt.

★ Trot (Exercise #6) and ride second loop.

★ At center, halt (Exercise #19).

★ Trot and ride third loop.

★ At center, halt.

★ Walk and ride fourth loop (Exercise #15).

★ At center, halt.

★ Trot and ride fifth loop.

★ At center of short end, half halt (Exercise #14).

★ Walk forward.

VARIATION

Use any combinations of transitions. Vary the placement of halts.

As you are tracking down the straight lines of the serpentine, be sure your horse walks forward energetically. This is a working/extended Western walk on light contact.

BENEFIT

This is a great set-up for teaching a half halt.

CAUTION

To prevent anticipation, vary the sequence and locations of halt, walk, and trot.

Don't lose the exact serpentine shape as you add maneuvers and customize this exercise. It is tempting to make an exercise more challenging by adding many transitions or more complex ones but it is best to first perform the simple version very well and then gradually increase the difficulty.

Serpentine at Trot with Leg Yield

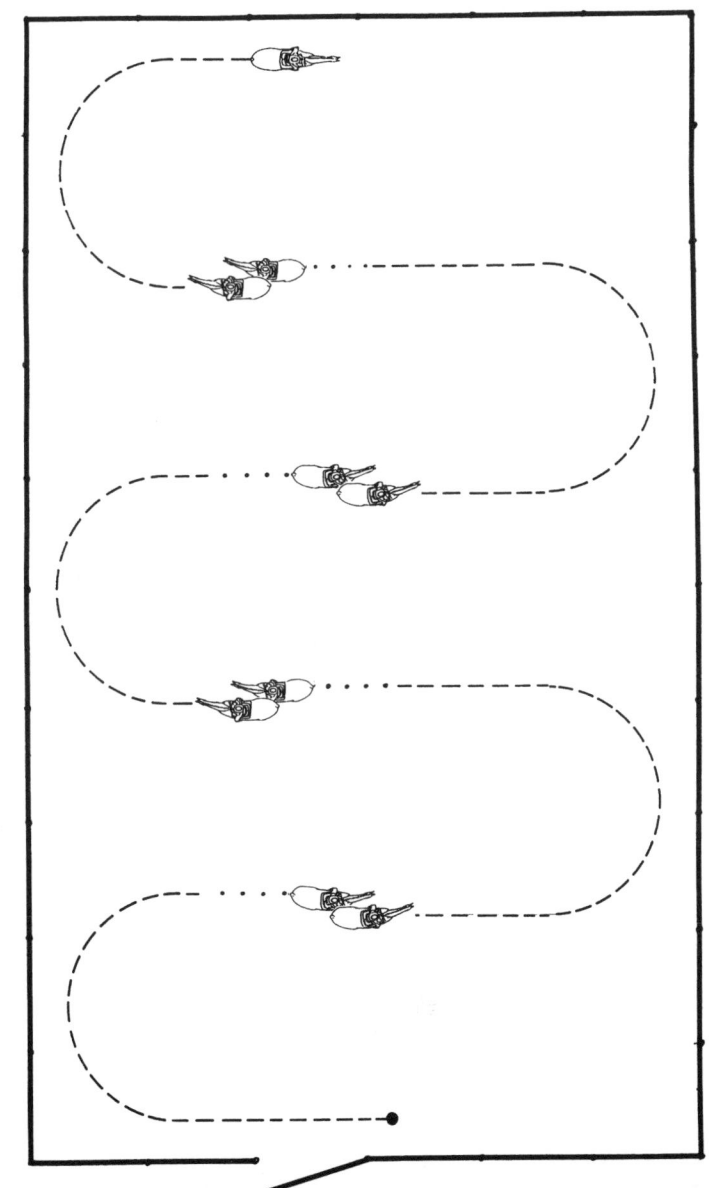

HOW TO RIDE THE EXERCISE

★ Proceed at working trot (Exercises #6 and #7).

★ Follow pattern of five-loop serpentine (Exercise #48).

★ Just after you finish the first loop and your horse is straight, walk 2–3 strides.

★ Leg yield to the right at the walk (Exercise #57) 2–3 steps.

★ Straighten and trot straight ahead, resuming the serpentine pattern.

★ After the second loop, when horse is straight, walk 2–3 strides.

★ Leg yield to the left at the walk 2–3 steps.

★ Straighten and trot straight ahead, resuming serpentine.

★ Repeat until the pattern is complete.

BENEFITS

★ Serpentine at trot with leg yield teaches horse to pay attention on the straight line of the serpentine.

★ Properly done, the horse comes under with hind legs on the downward transition and steps well under his belly in the leg yield, so the exercise is a great hind-end engager.

★ The leg yield puts the horse up on a new outside rein and therefore prepares him for a new bend without falling into the inside.

CAUTION

★ Make the walk-trot transition smooth and forward so your horse doesn't come above the bit.

★ If the horse begins to anticipate, vary where you begin the walk.

VARIATION

★ Replace all trot work with canter.

When you ask your Western horse to leg yield in a curb bit and instead he resists by coming above the bit, you probably need to practice a simple leg yield exercise using a snaffle bit.

Circle and Leg Yield

HOW TO RIDE THE EXERCISE

★ Ride a large circle (Exercise #35) to the right at a working trot (Exercise #6).

★ When you return to the point you started, turn right into the circle.

★ Straighten (Exercise #30) and ride your horse straight one stride.

★ Flex left and leg yield (Exercise #57) to the right approximately to the quarter line.

★ Straighten and ride forward 60 feet.

★ Turn left and begin a large circle to the left.

★ When you return to the point you started the circle, turn left into the circle.

★ Ride your horse straight one stride.

★ Flex left and leg yield to the right to the quarter line.

★ Straighten and ride forward.

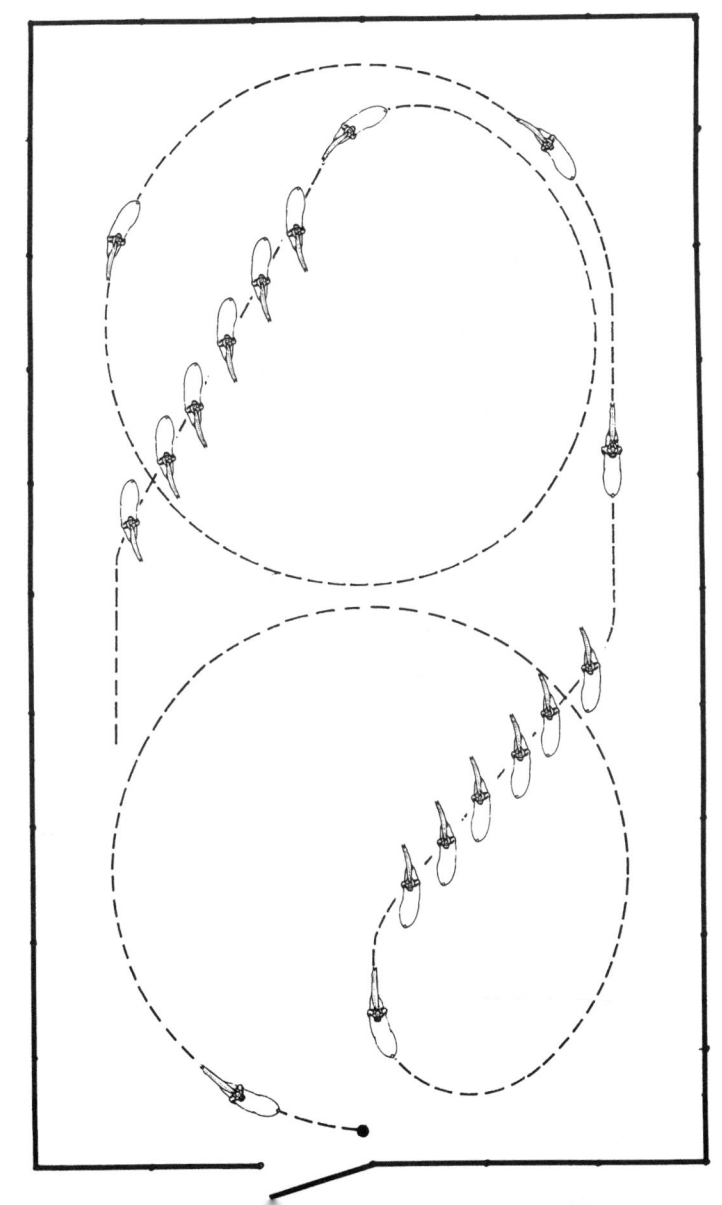

This is a close-up of left flexion. Note that the flexion occurs in the poll-throatlatch area, not the neck–shoulder area.

NOTE

Which way does the leg yield to the right begin more easily and correctly, from the right turn or the left turn? The answer will help you design future work for you and your horse.

The leg yield to the right from the left turn is a more natural progression because both involve left flexion.

You can post on the circle work, but you should ride sitting trot for the leg yield portion.

When going from the right circle to the leg yield to the right (with left flexion), take care to make the transition smooth and systematic. From the right bend, be sure to ride straight one stride, sitting evenly on both seat bones. Then initiate left flexion with your rein aids. Finally, add your left leg to ask for forward movement to the right.

Simple Change Serpentine

HOW TO RIDE THE EXERCISE

★ Canter right lead (Exercise #20) and follow pattern for five-loop serpentine (Exercise #48).

★ After the first loop, ride straight (Exercise #30) ahead 20 feet.

★ Walk one stride (Exercise #20).

★ Canter left lead.

★ After second loop, ride straight ahead 20 feet.

★ Walk one stride.

★ Canter right lead.

★ Continue until the serpentine pattern is complete.

VARIATIONS

★ Make the simple change through a trot rather than a walk.

★ Counter-canter some of the loops.

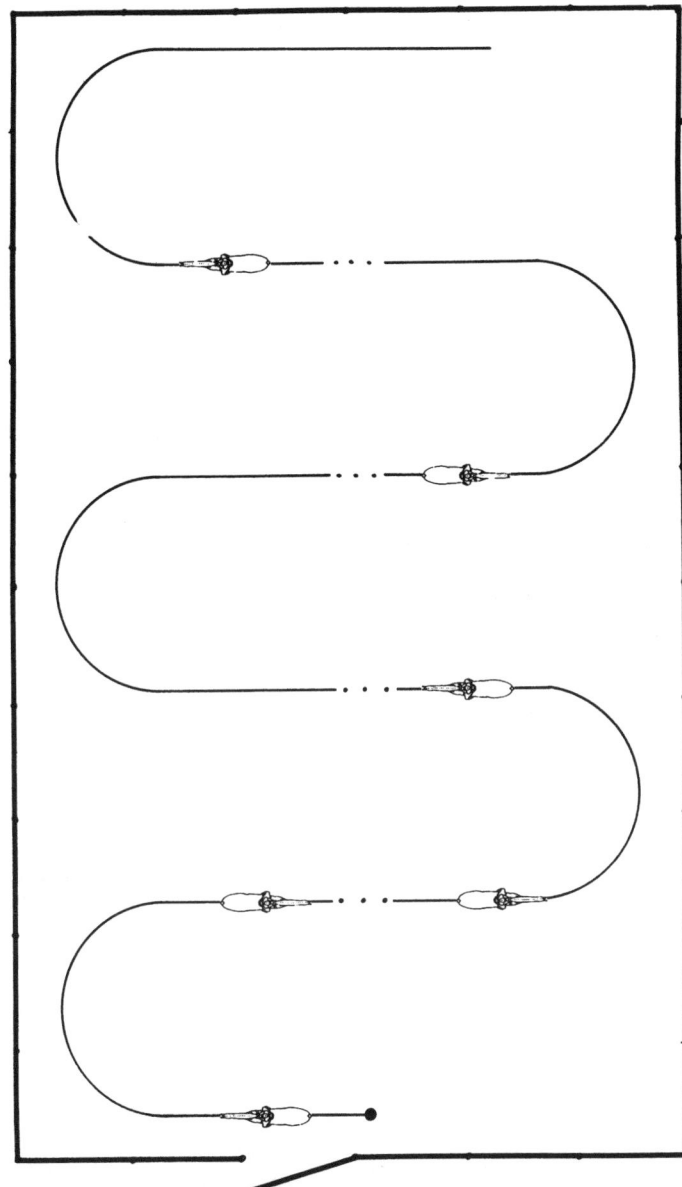

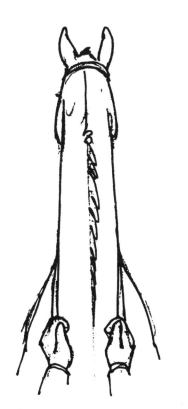

A close-up of bilateral (both sides) direct rein used on the straight line portion of the serpentine.

CAUTION

Horses can begin to anticipate the downward transition, so vary with other serpentine pattern exercises.

Leave yourself plenty of time and space to straighten in between the old bend (old lead) and new bend (new lead). Maintain the exact serpentine shape. The tendency is to cut across on a diagonal from one loop to another rather than adhere to a very straight line. Be ever vigilant and focus on a post or point across the arena.

Square Serpentine

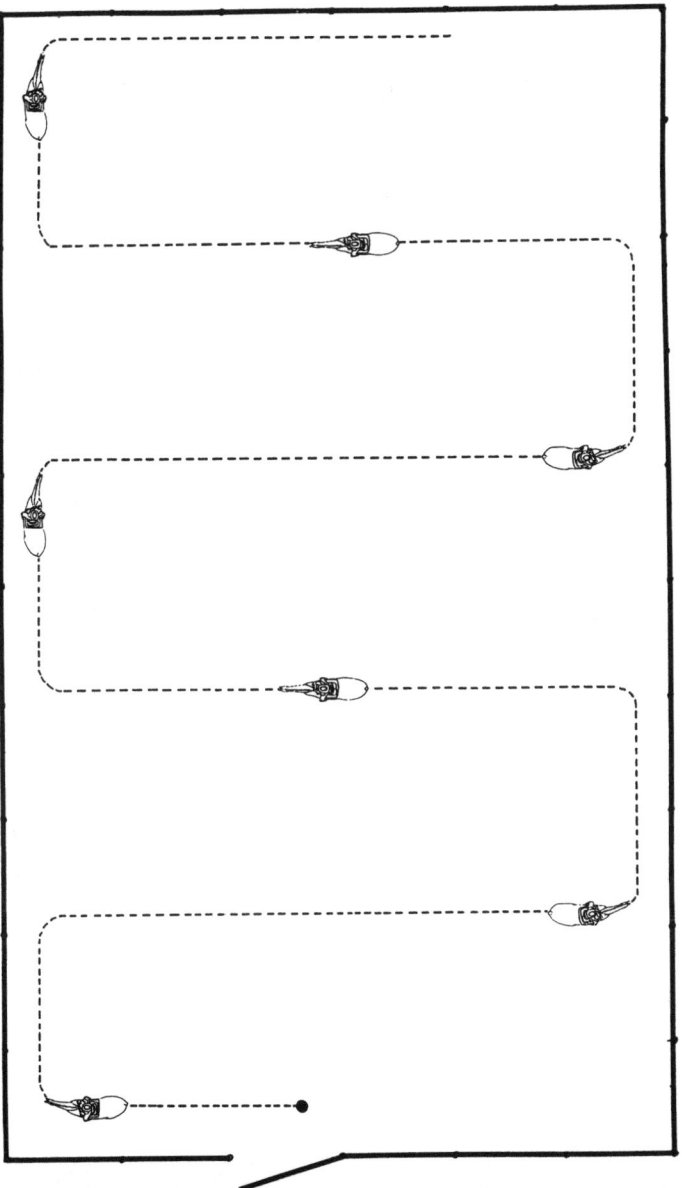

HOW TO RIDE THE EXERCISE

★ Proceed at a collected trot (Exercise #9).

★ Quarter turn (50) to the right at the corner.

★ Ride straight 20–25 feet (Exercise #30).

★ Quarter turn right.

★ Ride straight across the arena (100 feet).

★ Quarter turn left when you reach the opposite rail.

★ Ride straight 20–25 feet.

★ Quarter turn left.

★ Ride straight across the arena (100 feet).

★ Quarter turn right.

★ Continue until the serpentine pattern is complete.

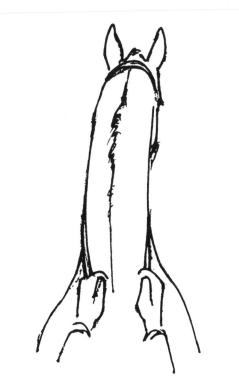

A close-up of rein aids for a quarter turn to the right. Right direct rein to create right flexion. Left supporting rein to limit right flexion and assist the right rein in maintaining necessary vertical flexion (in the poll and throatlatch).

NOTE

This exercise (the quarter turns, at least) must be performed at a *collected* gait.

BENEFITS

★ If ridden in a true collected trot, the horse's inside hind leg will be strengthened during the turns.

★ Square serpentine is a good exercise to teach the rider to focus straight ahead.

CAUTION

★ Be careful you do not use too much rein in the turns or your horse will start prancing or mincing at the trot.

★ Do not overbend the front end in an attempt to make the sharp turn.

★ Take your time and perform each turn in balance and rhythm.

Two Squares

HOW TO RIDE THE EXERCISE

Square 1:

★ Ride forward at the collected walk (Exercise #4) about 40 feet.

★ Halt.

★ Sidepass right 40 feet (Exercise #73) with the horse straight.

★ Halt.

★ Back 40 feet (Exercise #13).

★ Halt.

★ Sidepass left 40 feet.

Square 2:

★ Ride forward at a collected walk (Exercise #4) about 20 feet.

★ Quarter turn (Exercise #50) right.

★ Ride forward 40 feet.

★ Quarter turn right.

★ Ride forward 40 feet.

★ Quarter turn right.

★ Ride forward 40 feet.

★ Quarter turn right.

★ Ride forward 20 feet.

★ Halt.

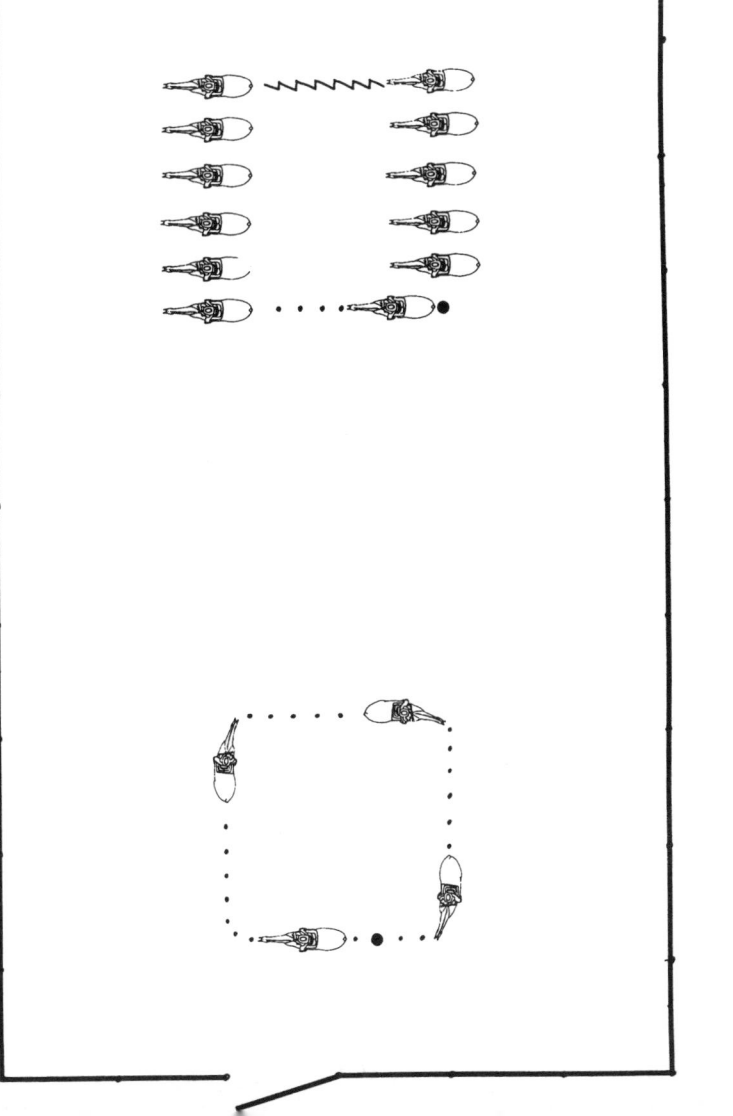

VARIATION

You may need to flex your horse away from the direction of movement in the sidepass at first because it is easier. Then you can progress to a straight sidepass and finally to a sidepass with the horse flexed into the direction of movement. (See drawing.)

A close-up of the rein aids for a sidepass to the left with the horse flexed into the direction of movement. The left direct rein creates left flexion. The right indirect rein (moving toward the horse's midline but not crossing over his mane) initiates (along with right leg aid) and maintains sideways movement to the left. See drawings in Exercises #73 and #89.

NOTE

★ Set cones for corners of the 40-foot square.

★ Look at the arena rails as you sidepass to help keep you and your horse straight.

BENEFIT — SQUARE 1

This exercise can slow down and iron out any rhythm and bend problems your horse may have in sidepass.

BENEFITS — SQUARE 2

★ This exercise can really punctuate the use of

   • your inside leg for sharp yet balanced turns, and

   • your outside leg to keep the hindquarters from swinging out of the turn.

★ Performing four quarter turns in a row can really make a point with your horse.

Lope Large Circle with Sidepass

HOW TO RIDE THE EXERCISE

★ Lope (Exercise #10) a large circle (Exercise #35) to the right on the right lead.

★ At the arena center, halt (Exercises #15, #19, and #20).

★ Sidepass to the right 2–3 strides (Exercise #73).

★ Lope left lead in a large circle to the left.

★ At the arena center, halt.

★ Sidepass to the left 2–3 strides.

★ Lope right lead.

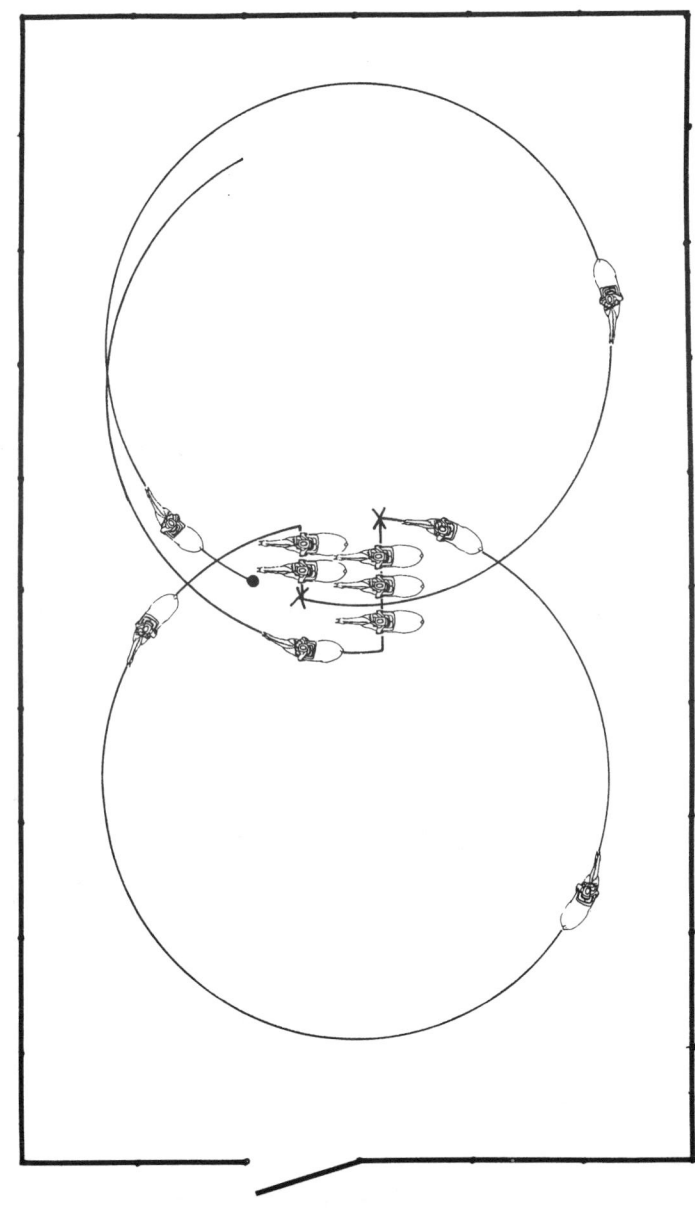

In this sidepass to the left, the horse's body is straight with slight right flexion. The right hind has just crossed the left hind and the right front will now lift and cross in front of the left front. Then, the rider will cue for lope right lead so the left hind, which would be the next leg to move, can initiate the lope.

NOTE

Keep the horse's body straight for the sidepass work, but flex him away from the direction of sideways movement.

BENEFIT

This exercise sets the horse up for proper lope position from a standstill.

CAUTION

★ To prevent anticipation, vary the exercise by loping through the center of the figure 8 sometimes. Also, simple changes can be substituted for the sidepass.

★ Eventually, only sidepass one stride in the center.

★ Finally, substitute a flying change.

Shoulder In and Lengthen

HOW TO RIDE THE EXERCISE

★ Ride collected trot (Exercise #9).

★ Medium circle (Exercise #36) in first corner.

★ Come out of the circle in shoulder-in position
(Exercise #62).

★ Ride down the long side 20–30 feet in shoulder in.

★ At the center of the long side, change to regular right bend.

★ Ride a medium circle in regular right bend.

★ Come out of the circle in shoulder-in position.

★ Ride shoulder in around both corners of the short end
of the arena.

★ After the second corner of the short end, straighten the
horse for one stride.

★ Lengthen the trot (Exercise #8) for 40–100 feet.

★ Collect the trot.

★ Ride the final corner to the right with right bend.

★ Ride forward.

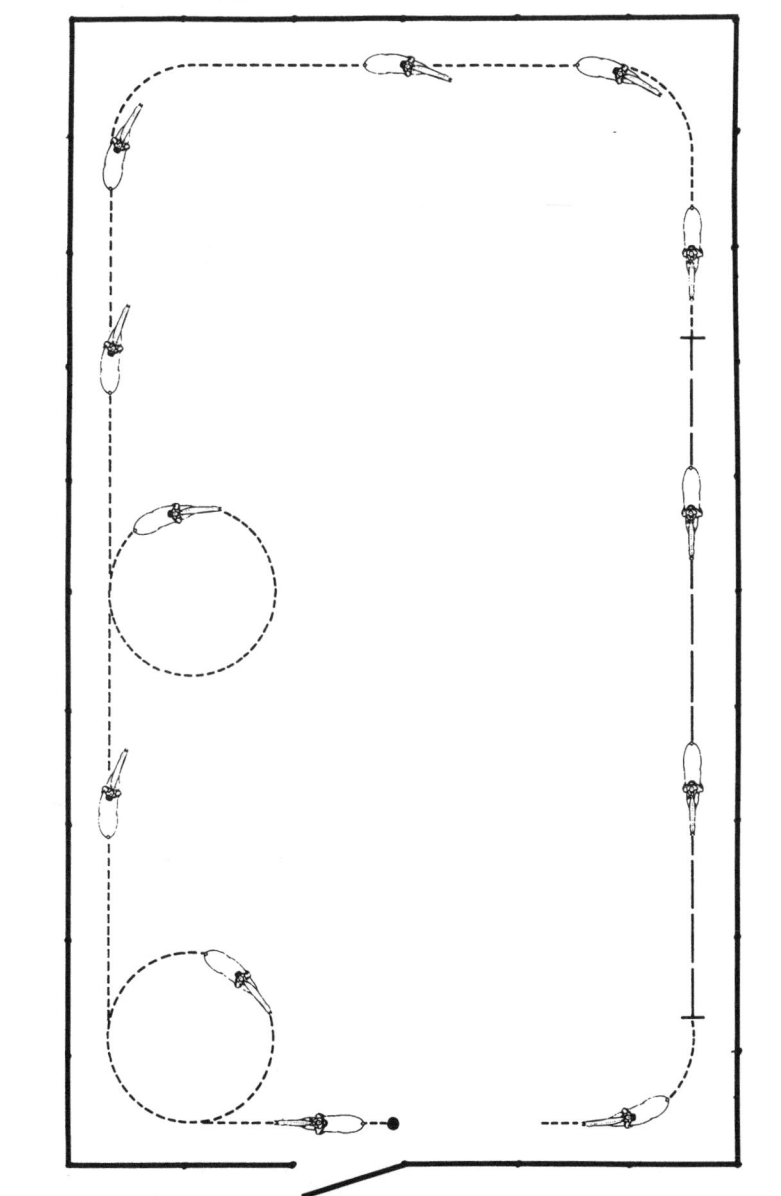

Here is a balanced, energetic, lengthened trot. The horse is reaching and not rushing. The rider's seat is steady and the horse's back is relaxed and not hollow.

NOTE

This exercise is an energizer! You store the horse's energy like a spring with the shoulder in and circle work and then release it on the lengthening down the long side.

It is a fact that initially a horse must slow down for a lengthening. This is so he can rock back on his hindquarters and prepare for the increased thrust of the extension. So right after the corner, you will apply a series of half halts to collect your horse and get him ready to really push and reach.

CAUTION

Don't *chase* the horse into a lengthened trot. Keep him balanced and organized. Don't rush the rhythm.

Sidepass and Lope the Diagonal

HOW TO RIDE THE EXERCISE

★ With the horse facing the arena rail on the long side, sidepass (Exercise #73) to the right 2–4 strides with the horse's body straight and no right or left flexion.

★ Perform a 90-degree walk-around turn on the hindquarters to the right (Exercise #69).

★ When parallel to the rail, trot 60–80 feet down the rail (Exercise #7).

★ Before the corner, lope right lead (Exercise #10).

★ Lope the corner (Exercise #31) to the right.

★ Lope the short end straight (Exercise #30).

★ Lope the corner to the right.

★ Continue to the right, turn, and lope across the long diagonal (Exercise #32).

★ About 20–30 feet from the opposite rail, trot.

★ Turn left at the rail.

★ Trot the corner to the left.

★ Trot the short end straight.

★ Trot the next corner to the left.

★ After the corner, trot 20 feet, then walk.

★ Walk straight for 20 feet.

★ Halt.

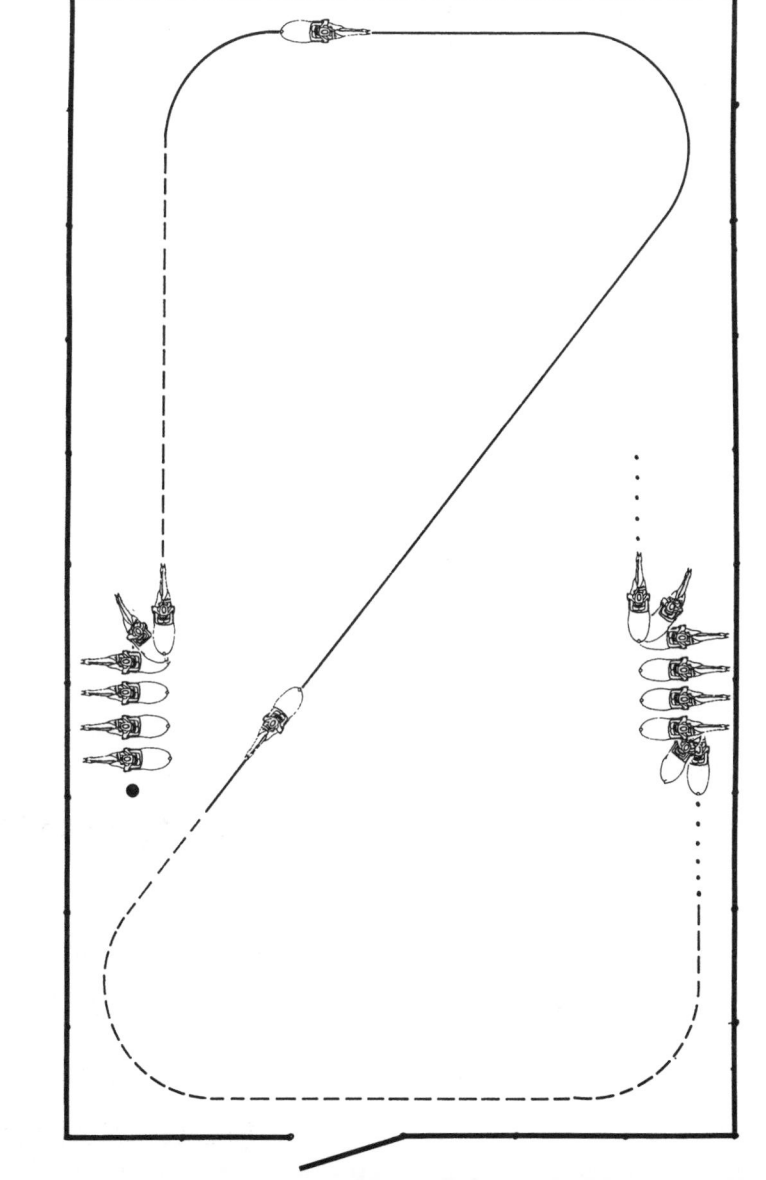

★ Turn 90 degrees on the forehand with right flexion, hindquarters moving to the left (Exercise #55).

★ Sidepass to the left 2–4 strides with the horse's body straight.

★ Make a 90-degree walk-around turn on the hindquarter to the left.

★ When parallel to the rail, walk ahead.

NOTE

Although this may seem difficult at first, it will flow naturally after you have performed it several times.

BENEFITS

★ A great combination of maneuvers and transitions.

★ A good test of your precision and accuracy.

★ An excellent preparation for trail obstacles.

CAUTION

Don't just "plow through" the entire pattern poorly. Instead, practice portions, then put it all together.

The sidepass is an alternating crossing and uncrossing of the legs with no forward movement. See drawings in Exercises #73 and #86.

Walk-360-Walk

HOW TO RIDE THE EXERCISE

★ Walk straight ahead (Exercise #30).

★ After your horse is even on all aids and moving forward energetically for 20 feet, half halt (check) (Exercise #14).

★ Introduce very slight position right.

★ Halt and simultaneously begin 360-degree walk-around turn on the hindquarters, keeping the horse fairly straight (Exercises #69 and 71).

★ When you are facing the way you began, walk straight forward.

VARIATION

Walk pirouette is a variation of Walk–360–Walk.

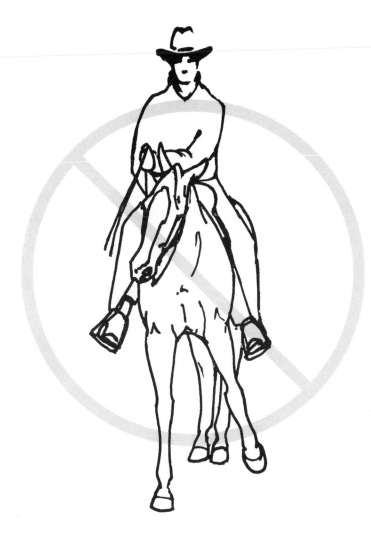

When riding with a curb bridle, take care not to apply the indirect (neck) rein improperly. Here the rider wants a 360 to the right, but by over-reining, has tilted the horse's head and thrown him off balance instead of achieving right flexion and sidepass movement to the right. Although the horse's hind feet are planted in approximately the correct position for a 360, the horse has swung his left front sideways (to the left) to counterbalance the head twist. In contrast, see drawing in Exercise #31 and other references listed there.

NOTE

A 360-degree walk-around turn allows you to develop a 1–2–3–4 walk rhythm in a hindquarter turn without the glitches and lock-ups that sometimes occur if you try to teach a pivot or turnaround without preliminary maneuvers such as this.

BENEFITS

★ Walk–360–Walk is a quiet way to teach and assess the quality of lateral movement.

★ It is also prelude to the turnaround that is a 360 (or series of 360s) with speed.

Lope–Halt–180–Lope

HOW TO RIDE THE EXERCISE

★ Lope right lead (Exercises #10 and 20).

★ Lope right corner with normal bend (Exercise #31).

★ Lope straight (Exercise #30) about 60 feet, checking lightly with every stride.

★ Double intensity check or half halt (Exercise #14).

★ Halt (Exercises #19 and 20).

★ Settle for 1–2 seconds simultaneously introducing.

★ Right flexion.

★ Perform 180-degree pivot to the right with an active left leg (Exercise #71).

★ When facing the opposite direction, continue using the left leg actively until you feel the horse's left hind leg step sideways toward the rail.

★ At the same time, change the horse's bend from right through straight to slightly left.

★ When you feel the horse securely on the right rein, lope (Exercise #20) left lead with left bend.

This is the last step of the 180 to the right. The horse is still flexed slightly right. He will step forward and to the right with his right front leg as the rider straightens him. Then the rider will flex him slightly left and ask for a step to the right with the left hind leg. The horse is then in position to push off with the right hind for the lope left lead.

VARIATION

Walk pirouette is a variation of this exercise.

Perform the exercise slightly off the rail and lope right, turn left, lope left. Although this might seem easier because the horse will already be bent left from the turn when you ask for the left lead, this variation is often more difficult because a change of flexion must occur in conjunction with the halt. Also when turning left your right leg will be at or in front of the cinch but must shift to behind the cinch for the lope depart left lead. At about the same time this shift in right leg position occurs, your left leg must move the hindquarters over to the right to position your horse for the left lead depart. All of this seems to take a greater sense of timing and accuracy than does the original version of the exercise.

NOTE

At the moment you are finishing the 180 and getting ready to lope, you are in essence going from a right turn with slight right position to a mini–leg yield to the right with left flexion to a slight left bend traveling straight ahead.

BENEFITS

★ This exercise helps get horse in position for nice, straight lope depart.

★ It is also a good way to teach lope depart from halt.

Lope-Halt-360-Lope

How to Ride the Exercise

★ Begin loping on the right lead (Exercises #10 and #20).

★ Lope straight (Exercise #30) about 20–30 feet.

★ Check your horse (Exercise #14), and re-balance his weight to the rear.

★ Make a moderately sharp turn to the right at least 20 feet off the long side.

★ Lope straight ahead 60 feet or more, checking the horse with every stride.

★ Double intensity check (Exercise #14).

★ Halt (Exercises #18 and #20).

★ Flex right.

★ Perform a 360-degree pivot (Exercise #71) to the right at a walk with precision and slow-to-moderate speed.

★ At about 340 degrees, lessen your left leg pressure and apply a right leg at the cinch to "catch" the turn to the right and to straighten the horse's body for the lope depart right lead.

★ When facing the same way you began, lope right lead.

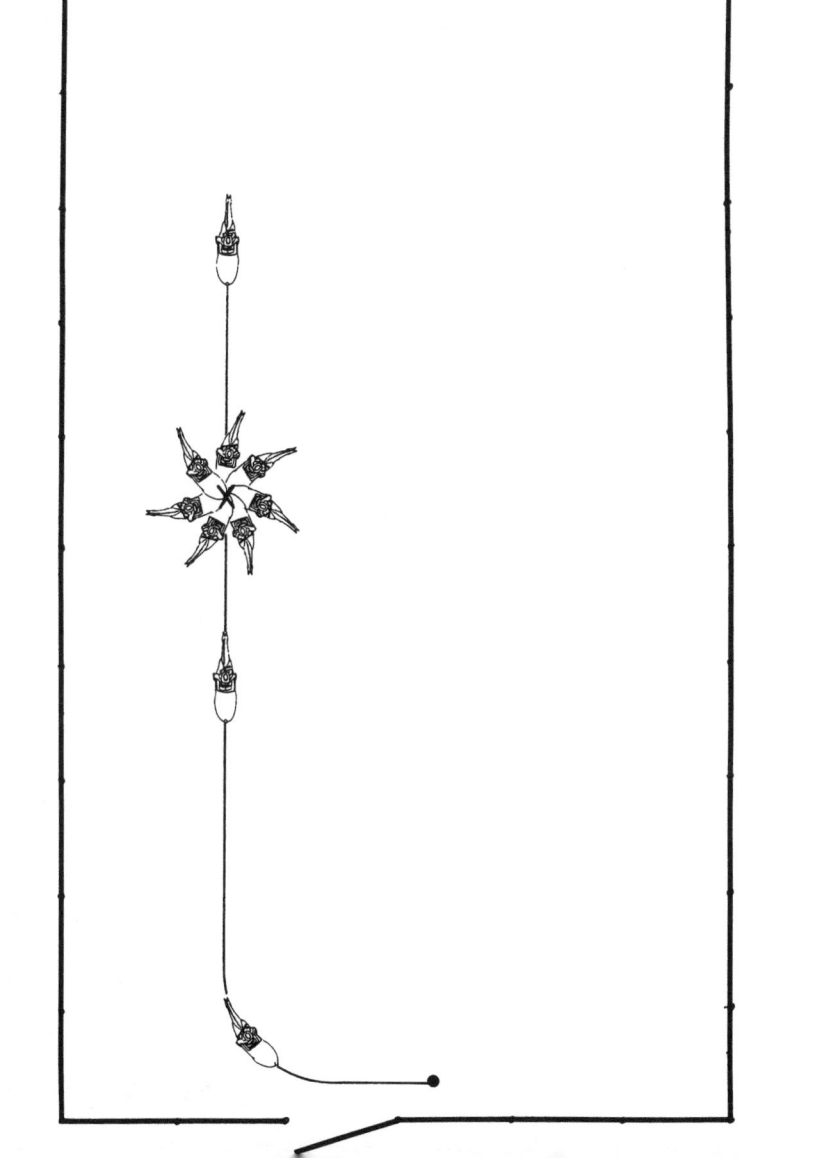

In this energetic walk-around 360 to the right, the right hind has just reoriented to the right, and the right front will next uncross and step to the right. Then the left hind will pick up and step forward and to the right. Although the horse shows a lot of bend in his turn, his body mass is balanced from left to right.

VARIATION

Walk pirouette is a variation of this exercise.

Lope out of the pivot on the left lead.

Perform the pivot to the left.

NOTE

Remember, right flexion does not mean hindquarters left!

BENEFITS

★ This exercise allows you to teach and monitor straightness during corners and the pivot.

★ Practicing this exercise will show you if your horse stays balanced from left to right in a right turn. Does he keep an even weight on his outside (left) shoulder or does he fall lazily on the inside shoulder to the right?

CAUTION

If you let the horse overbend to the right or fall in on his right shoulder, it can cause his hindquarters to come "unstuck" and swing left.

Your horse must stay up on the left rein throughout the 360 even though he is bent slightly to the right, or he won't be in position to lope on the right lead after the turn. If you find he has lost his position, you may have to dramatically straighten him, pick him up, or even leg yield one step to the left to set him up before asking for the lope right lead.

Canter Counter-Canter

HOW TO RIDE THE EXERCISE

★ Walk 2 strides (Exercise #2).

★ Canter right lead (Exercises #10 and #20).

★ Right corner (Exercise #31).

★ Canter straight 1 stride (Exercise #30).

★ Walk 1–2 strides.

★ Canter left lead.

★ Counter-canter 60 feet (Exercise #52).

★ Walk 1–2 strides.

★ Canter right lead.

★ Right corner.

★ Canter straight 1 stride.

★ Walk 1–2 strides.

★ Canter left lead.

★ Counter-canter 20 feet.

★ Walk 1–2 strides.

★ Canter right lead.

★ Right corner.

- ★ Canter straight 1 stride.

- ★ Walk 1–2 strides.

- ★ Canter right lead 30 feet.

- ★ Walk 1–2 strides.

- ★ Canter left lead.

- ★ Counter-canter 50 feet.

- ★ Counter-canter right corner.

- ★ Counter-canter straight 20 feet.

- ★ Walk.

BENEFIT

Canter counter-canter improves precision, discipline, and teaches your horse to pay attention and not anticipate.

CAUTION

A horse should have developed a really nice collected canter before this exercise is performed.

When counter-cantering to the right, the horse is on the left lead and bent left.

Canter — Half Pass — Counter Canter

HOW TO RIDE THE EXERCISE

★ Canter right lead straight (Exercises #10 and #20).

★ Canter corner to right (Exercise #31).

★ Canter straight (Exercise #30) down long side.

★ Canter corner to right.

★ Canter straight 25 feet.

★ Turn down center line.

★ Canter straight 40 feet.

★ Canter half pass to the right toward the wall (Exercise #74).

★ Finish half pass but maintain right bend and right lead canter.

★ Turn left and counter-canter toward left wall.

★ Walk *before* it becomes necessary.

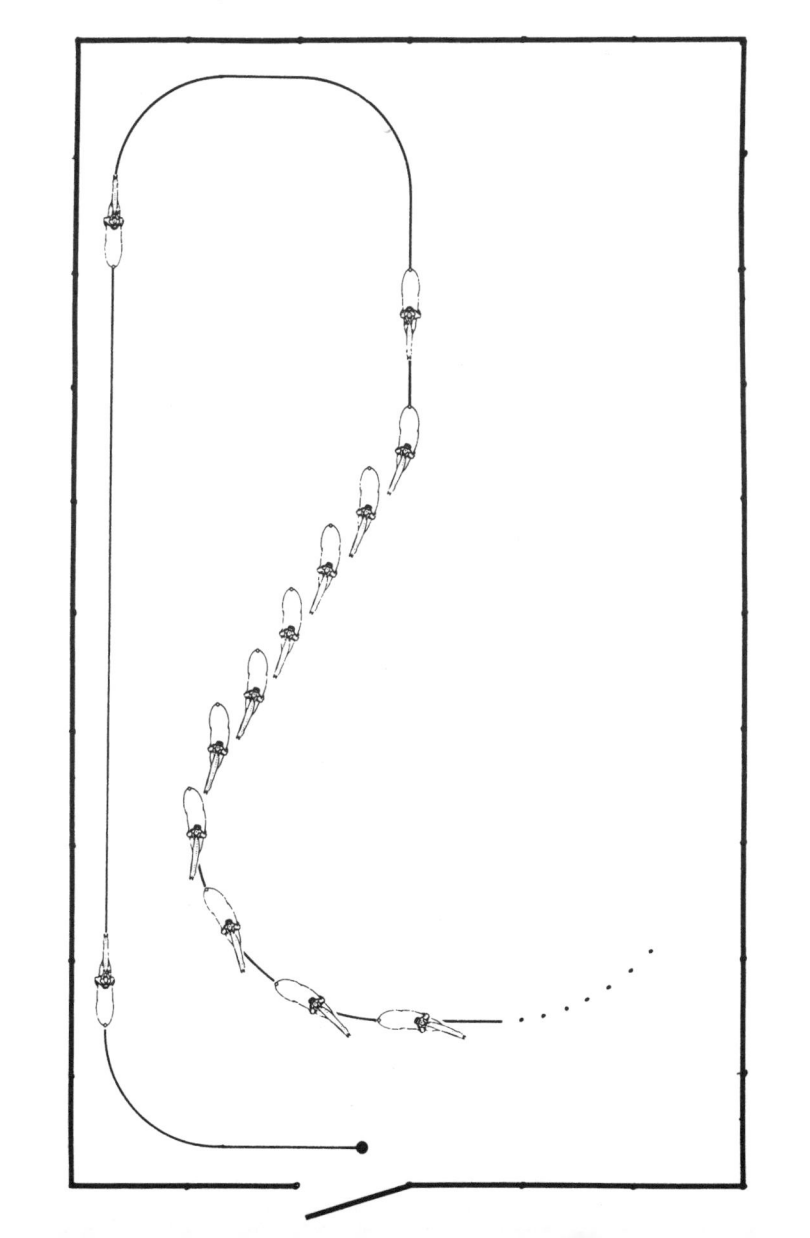

NOTE

When you have finished the half pass and are beginning the counter-canter, take care not to shift your weight to your left seat bone or your horse may break to a trot or change leads.

In this canter half pass to the right, the diagonal pair has just landed, the leading foreleg (right) is getting ready to reach forward and sideways. The horse is flexed right around the rider's right leg and is moving right from the rider's left leg behind the girth. The rider must take care not to collapse her body.

Flying Change

HOW TO RIDE THE EXERCISE

★ Canter right lead (Exercises #10 and #20).

★ Canter 65-foot circle (Exercise #35) at the short end.

★ Start across the diagonal (Exercise #32) with right bend.

★ Straighten (Exercise #30).

★ Half halt (series) (Exercise #14).

★ Before using the aids for the flying change, prepare the horse by

  • performing a half halt,

  • changing very slight flexion to left,

  • moving your new outside leg (right) behind the girth but let it remain passive temporarily,

  • being sure your new outside rein (right) supports the left flexion,

  • hesitating new inside leg (left) in its old position, holding, to help keep the horse's body straight.

★ Flying change at moment before suspension, when old leading foreleg (right) is swinging forward to land.

  • Use your new inside leg forward and active to engage new inside hind.

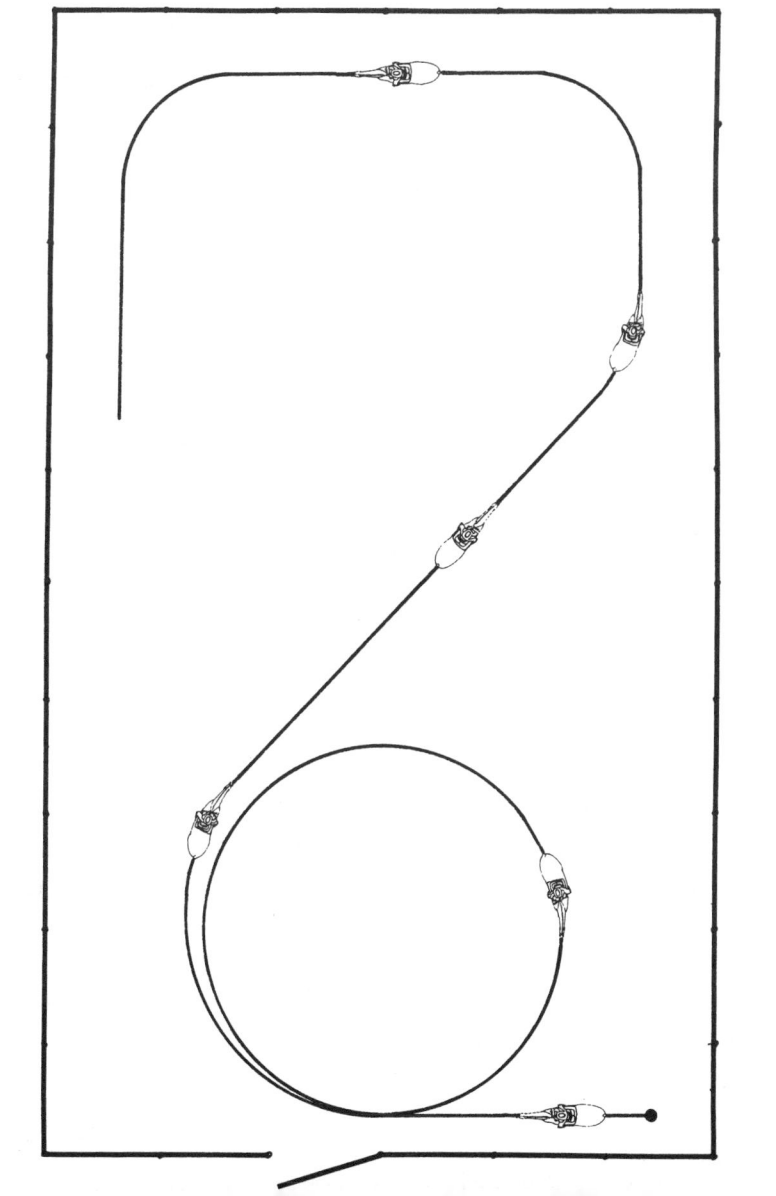

- Ease new inside rein slightly to allow new leading foreleg to stride out.

- Weight to inside seat bone without twisting.

- Outside leg active behind the girth to cause the new outside hind to jump well under and carry the horse's weight.

★ Keep canter active. Don't be a passenger.

The illustration shows the moment of a flying change from right lead to left. A nice, forward, up change. Refer to the description in Exercise #99 to learn the leg sequence in a flying change. However, note that the change in Exercise #99 is from left to right lead. See drawings in Exercises #96 through 101.

NOTE

★ A flying change occurs during the moment of suspension between two canter strides. The former inside hind (right) becomes the new outside, initiating hind, the first one to land and start the new canter, left lead.

★ Most horses tend to change more easily from right lead to left lead. However, observe whether the right lead is more balanced than the left. If so, you should probably ask for a left-to-right lead change first.

★ Flying changes are easier the more active and forward the canter.

★ Flying changes are easier and more correct the straighter the horse is before, during, and after the change.

BENEFITS

Flying change is beneficial for:

- Third-level dressage,

- Reining, Western riding, working cowhorse,

- Hunters, barrel racers, and so forth.

CAUTION

Only attempt a flying change after your horse is soft, supple, and solid in his training and will perform balanced canter departs from a walk anytime, anywhere. He should also be able to counter-canter and perform precise simple changes with a certain number of walk steps.

Flying Change after Short Diagonal

HOW TO RIDE THE EXERCISE

★ Canter right lead (Exercise #10).

★ Canter the corner to the right (Exercise #31).

★ Ride straight one stride (Exercise #30).

★ Turn across on the short diagonal (Exercise #33).

★ When you reach the opposite long side, turn left.

★ Maintain right lead and right bend (Exercise #52).

★ Ride forward one stride.

★ Flying change to left lead, left flexion (Exercise #95).

★ Ride the corners of the short end (Exercise #31).

★ After the second corner, ride straight one stride (Exercise #30).

★ Turn across on the short diagonal (Exercise #33).

★ When you reach the opposite long side, turn right, maintain left lead and left bend.

★ Ride forward one stride.

★ Flying change to right lead, right flexion.

★ Ride forward and the corner.

In the first stride after the first flying change, the horse is on the left lead showing a forward stride with slight left flexion. See drawings in Exercises #95 and #97 through #101.

CAUTION

★ Don't let the hindquarters sway sideways.

★ At first, don't practice too many flying changes at a time — one or two at the end of the session so the horse is properly prepared and then gets a rest reward.

★ If a horse runs after a change, immediately turn him into a circle and collect the canter.

Flying Change Straight at Wall

How to Ride the Exercise

★ From the center of the arena, begin to lope (Exercises #10 and #20) a large circle (Exercise #35) to the left on the left lead.

★ Instead of completing the circle, head to the opposite long side.

★ Maintain left lead, left bend.

★ About 15 feet before the arena rail or wall, flying change (Exercise #95) to right lead.

★ Change to right flexion and turn right.

★ Ride straight.

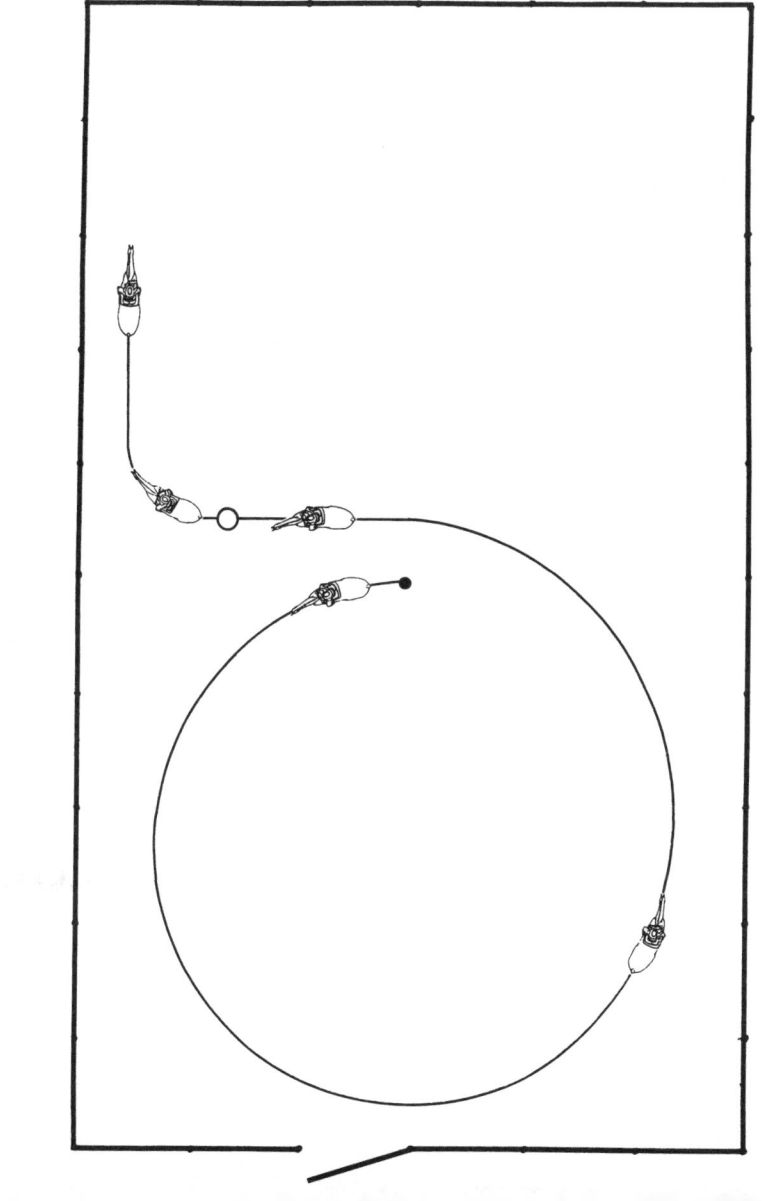

This horse was loping left lead and is being changed to the right lead. But because the "change" occurred so close to the fence, the horse is pivoting on the new inside hind as in a rollback rather than changing on the straight line and then turning, as is described in this exercise. See drawings in Exercises #72, #95, #96, and #98 through #101.

NOTE

This is a distant cousin to the rollback. Beware that it doesn't become a rollback (see drawing).

BENEFIT

The visual barrier of the upcoming wall or rail along with the use of effective and timely aids that let the horse know that he won't be turning left can help you get a horse organized for a flying change.

CAUTION

★ Don't let a horse speed up or get nervous. A horse runs off because he loses his balance and is trying to regain it.

★ The lope must be engaged (the hindquarters well under the horse) and energetic for the change to go through.

Flying Change with Sharp Corner

HOW TO RIDE THE EXERCISE

★ Lope (Exercises #10 and #20) left lead and begin a large circle (Exercise #35).

★ Instead of finishing the circle, head across the long diagonal (Exercise #32).

★ Maintain left lead and the left bend you had in the large circle (Exercise #52).

★ Check (Exercise #14) and re-balance, but don't shorten the horse's stride.

★ Aim directly at the corner.

★ About 20 feet from the corner, straighten the horse and perform a flying change (Exercise #95).

★ Lope right lead around the sharp corner (Exercise #31).

★ Lope straight ahead.

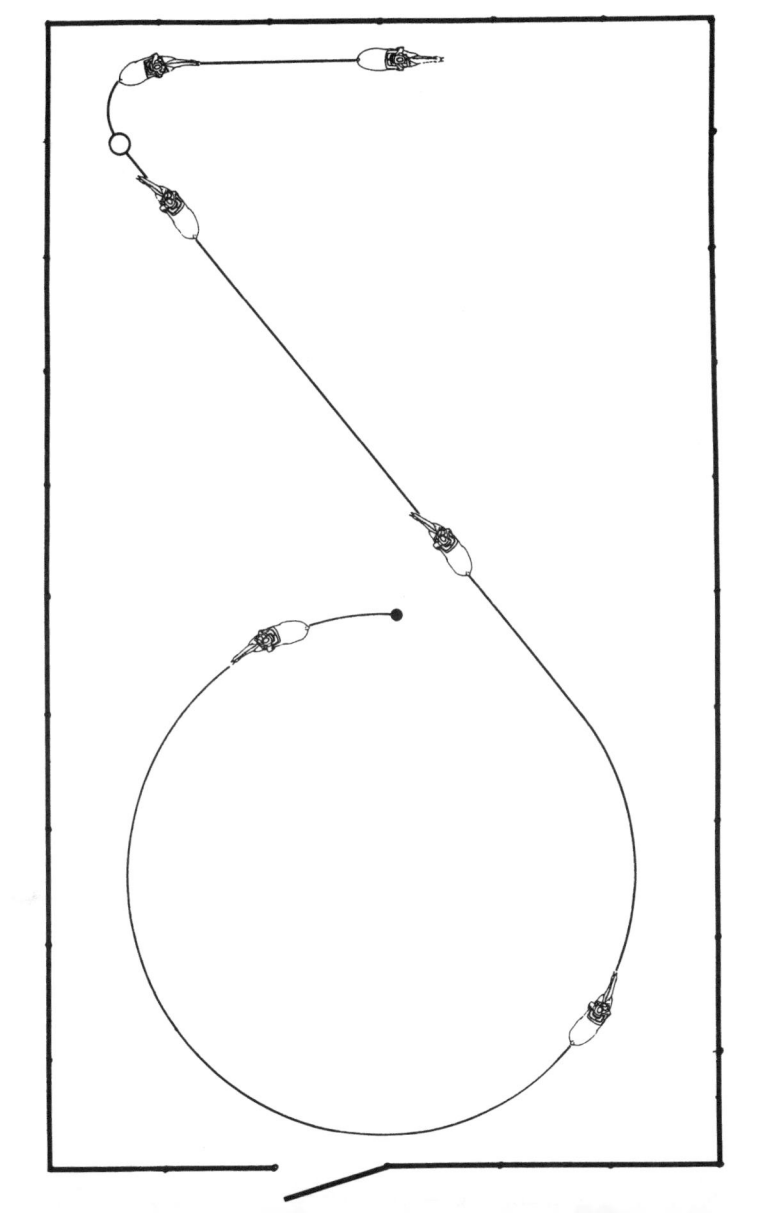

As you are heading into the corner on the left lead, your horse should still be slightly flexed to the left. Be sure his body is straight when you ask for the change. See drawings in Exercises #95 through #97 and #99 through #101.

NOTE

This is another shirt-tail cousin of the rollback, so if you get too close to the corner, the horse may have to slam on the brakes somewhat and jump out of the corner. Be ready so you don't become unbalanced and accidentally pull on his mouth.

BENEFIT

For a horse that is having difficulty changing from one particular lead to another, this may "show" him the way.

CAUTION

If a horse just trots fast instead of loping off on the right lead, *don't* push him into the lope from the fast, choppy trot. Instead, bring him down to a trot or walk, change direction so you are headed left again, lope left lead, and begin again.

Circle, Simple Change, Flying Change

HOW TO RIDE THE EXERCISE

★ Lope (Exercises #10 and #20) a very large circle (Exercise #34) to the right on the right lead.

★ After you pass your starting point, walk for a stride (Exercise #20).

★ Lope left lead with left bend on the circle to the right (counter-canter) (Exercise #52).

★ After you pass your starting point again, straighten (Exercise #30) and flying change (Exercise #95) to right lead.

★ Change to right bend.

★ Lope a circle to the right on the right lead.

NOTE

In a flying change from the left lead to the right lead, the following occurs:

★ The footfall pattern of the left lead

  • starts with the initiating hind, the right hind,

  • then left hind with right front,

  • finished by the leading foreleg, the left front.

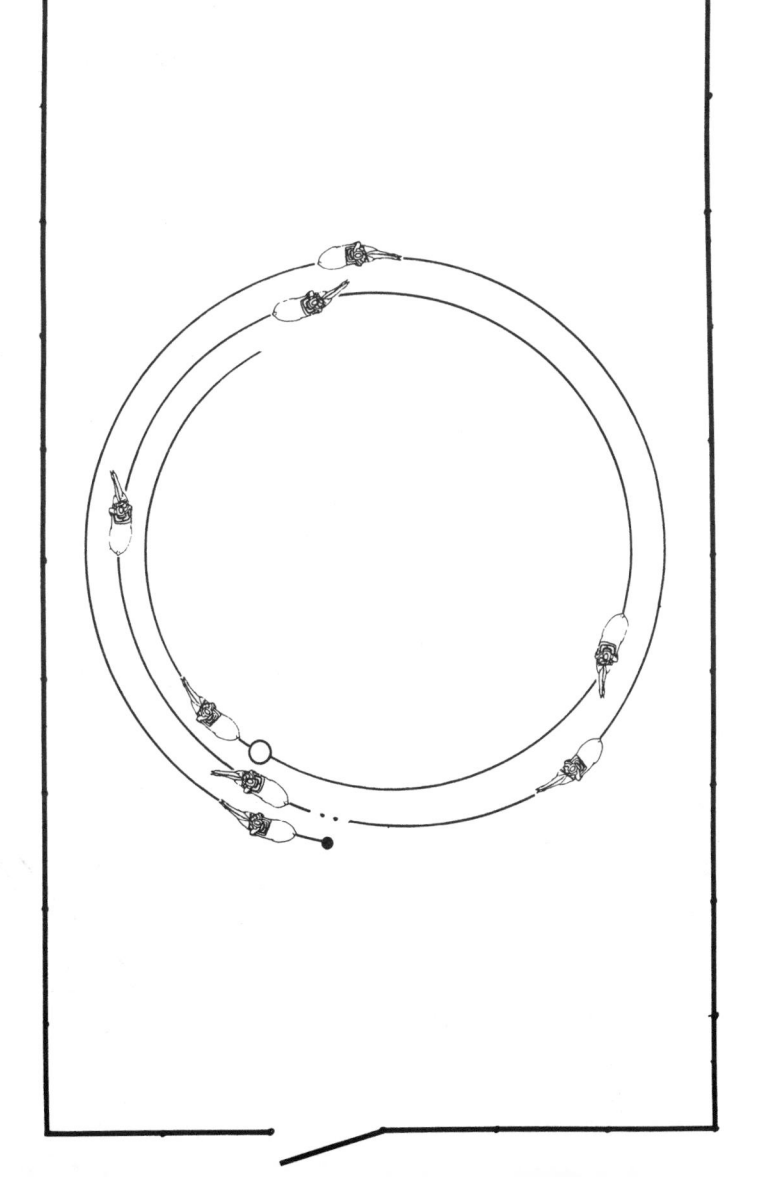

★ During the flying change, when the old leading foreleg is on the ground, all other legs are in the air. The hinds are relatively even with each other in terms of height, flexion, and how far ahead they are.

★ Then, the left hind, which was a member of the old diagonal pair, lands and becomes the new initiating hind.

★ The right hind moves in front of the left hind as this occurs.

★ The right front is already in front of the left front and is flexed.

★ The new diagonal pair (right hind and left front) is getting organized to land together, but until they actually land, it appears that the hind will land before the front. When the diagonal pair actually hits the ground, though, the legs are in unison. However, the left front lands closer under the horse's body than it does in a usual canter stride, so the diagonal pair lands closer to each other during a lead change than they would normally.

★ The new leading foreleg, the right front, really reaches ahead in the lead-change stride, and this is accentuated by the fact that the left front leg landed farther back than normal. So the span between the two front legs is greater than usual.

★ In the canter stride following the lead change, the stride becomes normalized in reaching and timing: left hind, then right hind and left front, finished by the right front.

See drawing in Exercise #95 for an example of this moment.

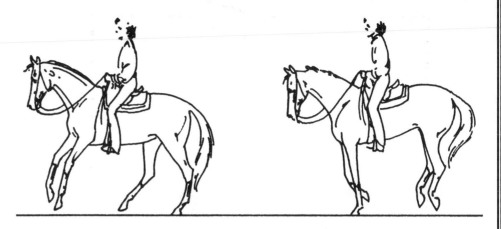

The horse on the right is in the last moment of a lope left lead (leading foreleg, left, is on the ground). The other legs are as they would be for a left lead.

The drawing on the left shows the moment just after the flying change to the right lead. Initiating hind (left) has landed. Diagonal pair (right hind and left front) are getting organized and the right front will land last.

BENEFITS

★ This exercise develops suppleness, strength, and balance.

★ Circle, simple change, flying change develops discipline and discourages anticipation.

CAUTION

★ Keep the circle very large at first. The smaller the circle, the more collected the lope must be.

★ Maintain an even tempo. Don't slow down during the counter-canter, and don't rush after the flying change.

Circle, Diagonal, Flying Change

HOW TO RIDE THE EXERCISE

★ Track right on the long side.

★ Collected canter right lead (Exercises #12 and #20).

★ Canter a medium circle in the first corner (Exercise #36).

★ Canter the short end (Exercise #31).

★ Canter a medium circle in the second corner.

★ Come off the circle and head across the long diagonal (Exercise #32).

★ Maintain right lead and right position (Exercise #52).

★ After you pass the center, straighten and flying change to left lead (Exercise #95).

★ Change to left position.

★ Finish the diagonal.

★ Canter a medium circle in the third corner (Exercise #36).

★ Canter the short end.

★ Canter a small circle in the fourth corner.

★ Come off the circle and head across the long diagonal.

★ Maintain left lead and left position.

★ After you pass the center, straighten and flying change to right lead.

★ Change to right position.

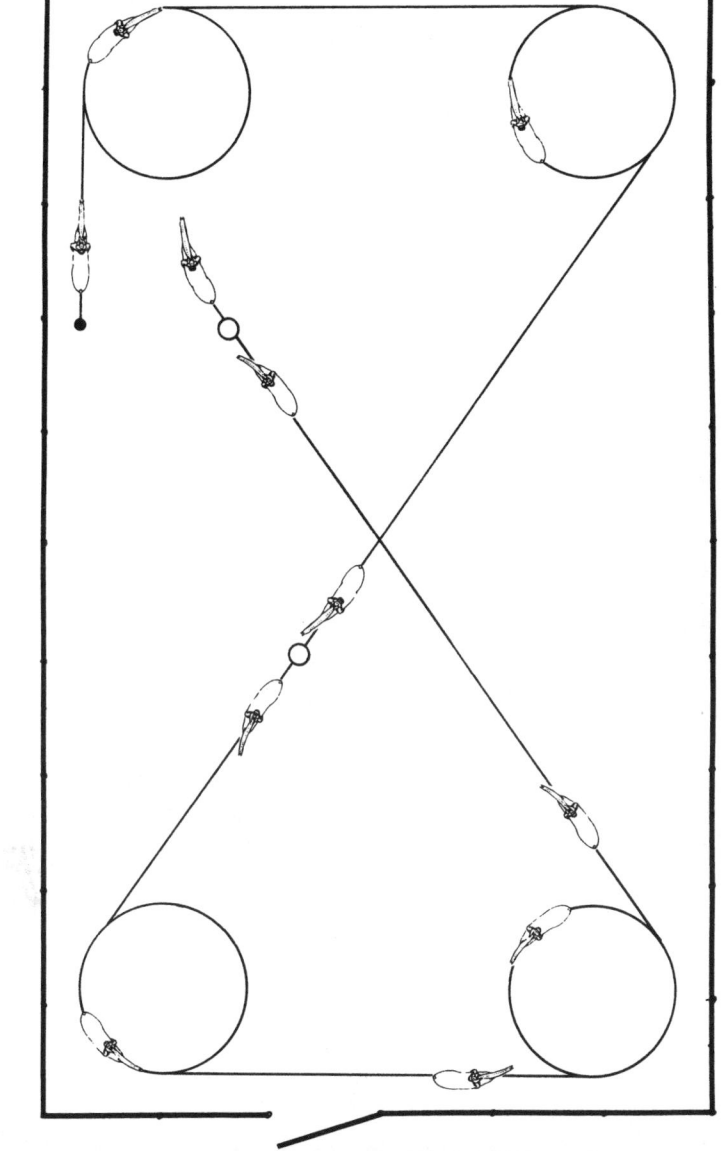

VARIATION

This is an excellent exercise in working trot to practice the change of flexion, bend, or position, or for collected to extended trot on the diagonals.

NOTE

If a horse has a problem changing, use a more active, forward tempo or try the changes out of the arena (across a pasture or down a road) on long lines.

CAUTION

Beware that you do not pull back on the reins and compress the horse's forehand as this will make it impossible for him to perform a forward, free, flying change because his forehand will be restricted.

If the hindquarters are thrown up too much during the last phase of the canter stride, the horse's weight will come too much on the forehand and it will be difficult for the hindquarters to get in position and in rhythm for a smooth change. Such a "kicking up" is often an evasion of (lack of acceptance of) the seat aids. See drawing in Exercise #99.

Canter Half Pass — Lead Change

HOW TO RIDE THE EXERCISE

★ Lope right lead (Exercises #12 and #20) in a large circle (Exercise #35) to the right.

★ After passing the starting point, leave the circle.

★ Ride your horse straight 1–2 strides (Exercise #30) parallel with the long side.

★ Half pass to the right (Exercise #74).

★ Straighten for one stride.

★ Walk 1–2 strides.

★ Lope left lead and begin a large circle to the left (Exercises #84 and #95).

VARIATION

Substitute a flying change for the simple change.

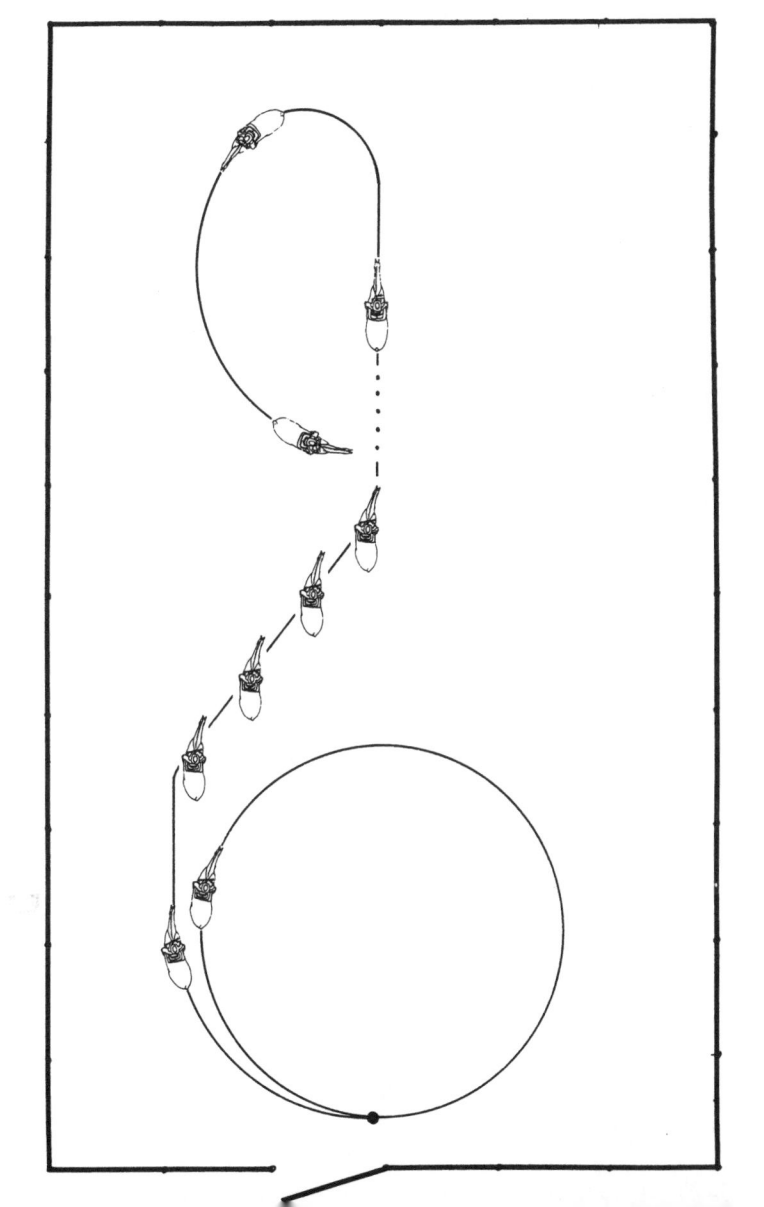

The rider's harshly driving seat, loose leg, and pulling on the reins have created a hollow-backed canter with hindquarters trailing. This horse and rider must perfect a collected canter (lope) before even thinking about attempting this half-pass exercise.

For contrast see drawings in Exercises #12, #29, #79, and #80.

NOTE

When a horse is *fully straight* after the half pass, he is prepared and balanced for a flying change.

★

Remember as you practice this exercise and all others that it is the QUALITY of the work that is most important. It is a much greater accomplishment to do simple things well than it is to stumble through advanced maneuvers in poor form and with erratic rhythm. Keep your mind in the middle and a leg on each side.

★

Suggested Reading

Dunning, Al. 1983. *Reining*. Colorado Springs, CO: Western Horseman.

German National Equestrian Federation. 1986. *Advanced Techniques of Riding*. Gaithersburg, MD: Half Halt Press.

German National Equestrian Federation. 1985. *Principles of Riding*. NY: Arco.

Haas, Jessie. 1994. *Safe Horse, Safe Rider: A Young Rider's Guide to Care and Enjoyment*. Pownal, VT: Storey Publishing.

Hill, Cherry. 1995. *Your Pony, Your Horse: A Kid's Guide to Care and Enjoyment*. Pownal, VT: Storey Publishing.

Hill, Cherry. 1993. *Making Not Breaking: The First Year Under Saddle*. Ossining, NY: Breakthrough.

Hill, Cherry. 1991. *Becoming An Effective Rider*. Pownal, VT: Storey Communications, Inc., Garden Way Publishing.

Hill, Cherry. 1997. *Horse Health Care: A Step-by-Step Photographic Guide*. Pownal, VT: Storey Communications, Inc.

Hill, Cherry. 1990. *Horsekeeping on a Small Acreage: Facilities, Design and Management*. Pownal, VT: Storey Communications, Inc., Garden Way Publishing.

Hill, Cherry. 1988. *The Formative Years, Raising and Training the Horse from Birth to Two Years*. Ossining, NY: Breakthrough.

Hill, Cherry. 1988. *From the Center of the Ring: An Inside View of Horse Competitions*. Pownal, VT: Storey Communications, Inc., Garden Way Publishing.

Hill, Cherry, and Richard Klimesh. 1994. *Maximum Hoof Power: How to Improve Your Horse's Performance through Proper Hoof Management*. New York, NY: Macmillan.

Loomis, Bob. 1991. *Reining*. Lomita, CA: EquiMedia Corp.

Swift, Sally. 1985. *Centered Riding*. New York: St. Martin's.

Hill, Cherry. 1997. *Horse Handling & Grooming: A Step-by-Step Photographic Guide*. Pownal, VT: Storey Communications, Inc.